TRUST IN THE FORCE!!

VWEEN

岸本斉史

Science Fiction movies are on the rise again...Right now they rank at the top of the box office in revenue, so I was thinking to myself, "Wow, everyone must really like Sci Fi..." and then I realized I'm one of those people too!

—*Masashi Kishimoto, 2002*

Author/artist Masashi Kishimoto was born in 1974 in rural Okayama Prefecture, Japan. After spending time in art college, he won the Hop Step Award for new manga artists with his manga **Karakuri** (Mechanism). Kishimoto decided to base his next story on traditional Japanese culture. His first version of **Naruto**, drawn in 1997, was a one-shot story about fox spirits; his final version, which debuted in **Weekly Shonen Jump** in 1999, quickly became the most popular ninja manga in Japan.

NARUTO VOL. 13
SHONEN JUMP Manga Edition

This graphic novel contains material that was originally published in English in **SHONEN JUMP** #48–50. Artwork in the magazine may have been slightly altered from that presented here.

STORY AND ART BY MASASHI KISHIMOTO

Translation & English Adaptation/Mari Morimoto
Touch-up Art & Lettering/Inori Fukuda Trant
Additional Touch-up/Josh Simpson
Design/Sean Lee
Editor/Joel Enos

VP, Production/Alvin Lu
VP, Sales & Product Marketing/Gonzalo Ferreyra
VP, Creative/Linda Espinosa
Publisher/Hyoe Narita

Printed in the U.S.A.

Published by VIZ Media, LLC
P.O. Box 77010
San Francisco, CA 94107

10 9 8 7 6 5 4 3
First printing, March 2007
Third printing, February 2010

www.viz.com

THE WORLD'S MOST POPULAR MANGA

www.shonenjump.com

SHONEN JUMP MANGA

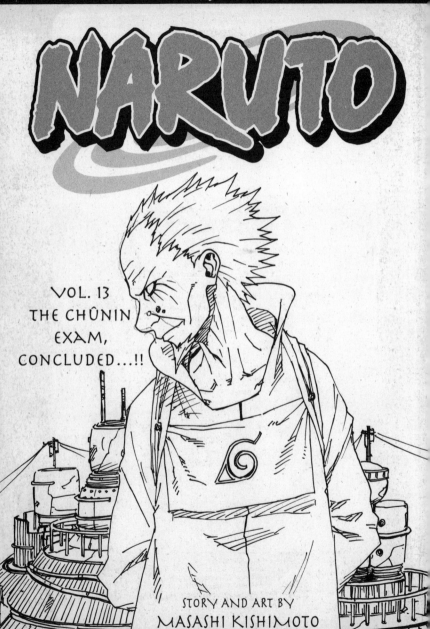

NARUTO

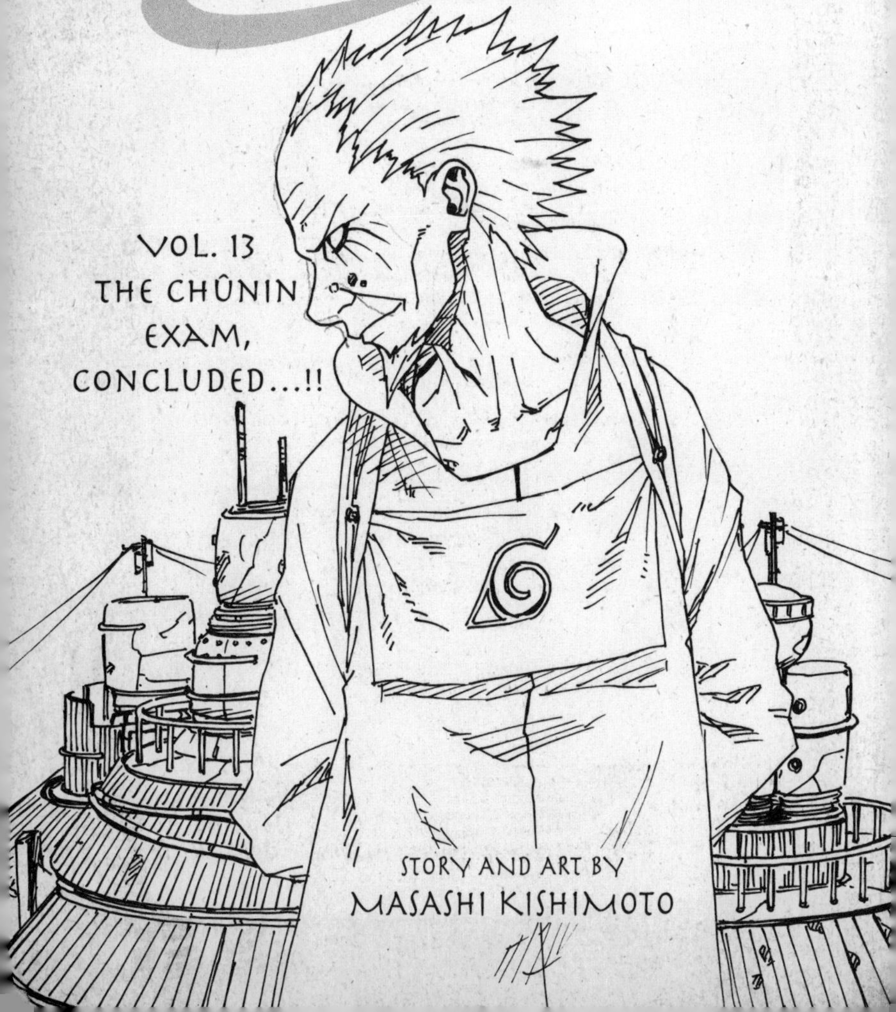

VOL. 13
THE CHÛNIN EXAM, CONCLUDED...!!

STORY AND ART BY
MASASHI KISHIMOTO

SAKURA サクラ

Smart and studious, Sakura is the brightest of Naruto's classmates, but she's constantly distracted by her crush on Sasuke. Her goal: to win Sasuke's heart!

NARUTO ナルト

When Naruto was born, a destructive fox spirit was imprisoned inside his body. Spurned by the older villagers, he's grown into an attention-seeking trouble-maker. His goal: to become the village's next *Hokage*.

SASUKE サスケ

The top student in Naruto's class, Sasuke comes from the prestigious Uchiha clan. His goal: to get revenge on a mysterious person who wronged him in the past.

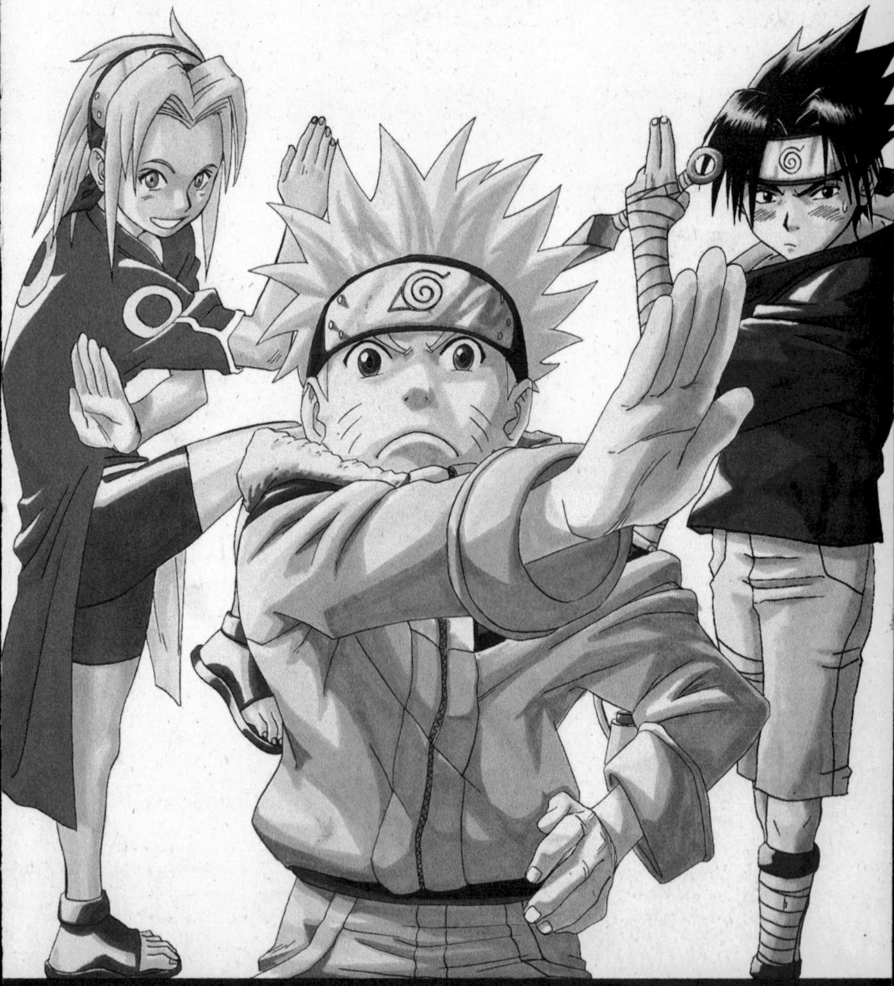

Kazekage 風影
The shadowy leader of
Sunagakure (the Village Hidden
in the Sand) within the Land
of Wind.

Gaara 我愛羅
Mysterious, bloodthirsty
Gaara may be the scariest
ninja competing in the
Chûnin Exams.

Rock Lee ロック・リー
First, Lee seemed weak, only
able to perform physical taijutsu.
But he's got powerful tricks and
unrivaled super speed.

Might Guy マイト・ガイ
The flamboyant Master Guy is
Lee's idol…and Kakashi's rival!

Hokage 火影
The leader of Konohagakure. He
was retired, but stepped back
into the position when the
fourth Hokage was killed by the
nine-tailed fox spirit.

Kakashi カカシ
Although he doesn't have an
especially warm personality,
Kakashi is protective of his
students.

THE STORY SO FAR...

Twelve years ago, a destructive nine-tailed fox spirit attacked the ninja village of Konohagakure. The
Hokage, or village champion, defeated the fox by sealing its soul into the body of a baby boy. Now that
boy, Uzumaki Naruto, has grown up to become a ninja-in-training, learning the art of *ninjutsu* with his
teammates Sakura and Sasuke.

During the Second Chûnin Exam, in the Forest of Death, Naruto and the others were attacked
by the mysterious shinobi Orochimaru, who left a curse mark on Sasuke and vanished…

Now it's the Chûnin Exam finals! But Sasuke is missing! To prevent Sasuke from losing to Gaara
by forfeit, the next two scheduled matches were moved up. Things went downhill from there:
Kankuro withdrew from his match against Shino to reserve his secret moves for the coming
coup. Shikamaru almost beat Temari, but called it quits at the last minute. But now, at last, it's the
fight you've all been waiting for…!

NARUTO

VOL. 13
THE CHÛNIN
EXAM, CONCLUDED...!!

CONTENTS

Number 109: Tree Leaves, Dancing...!!

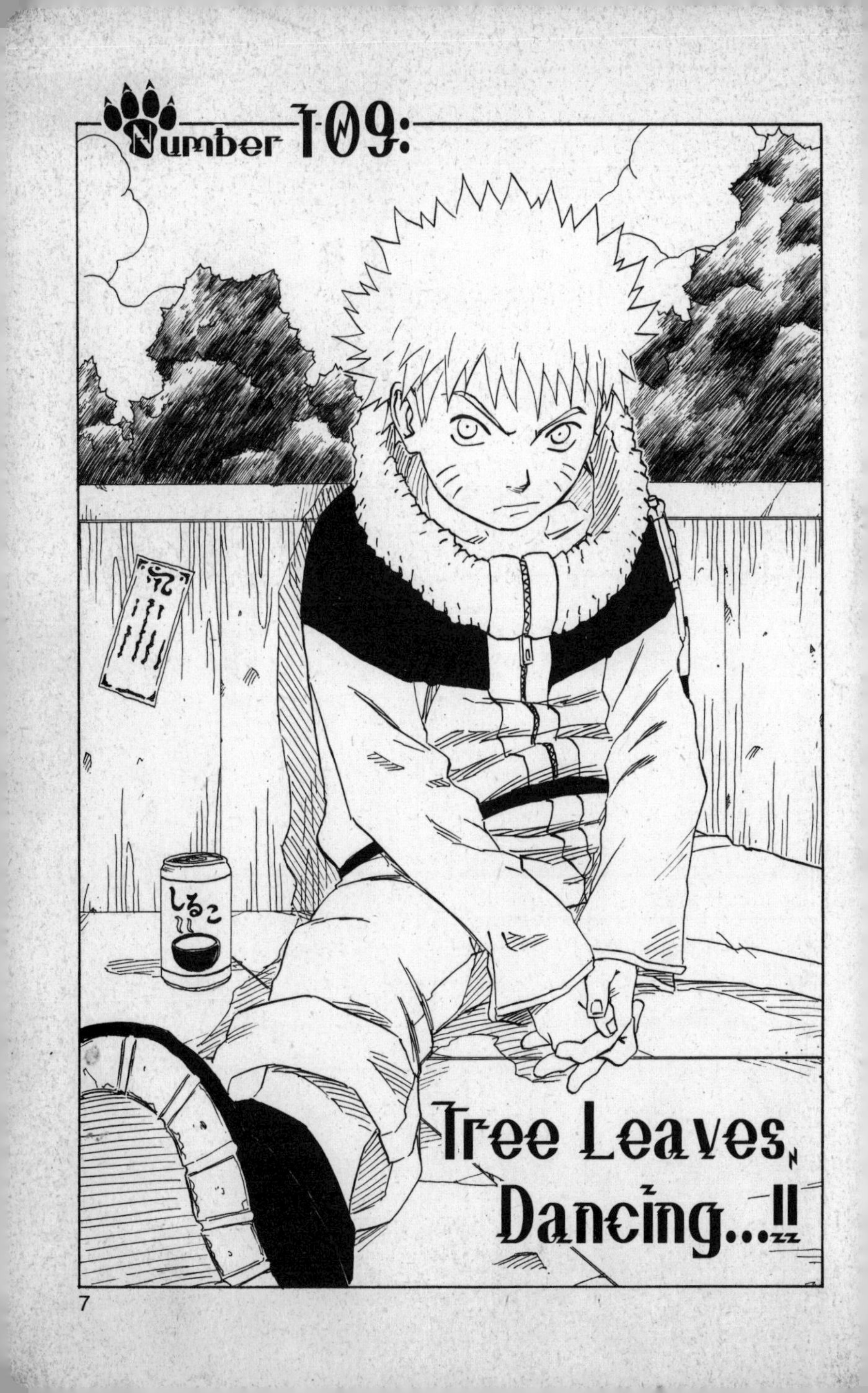
しるこ

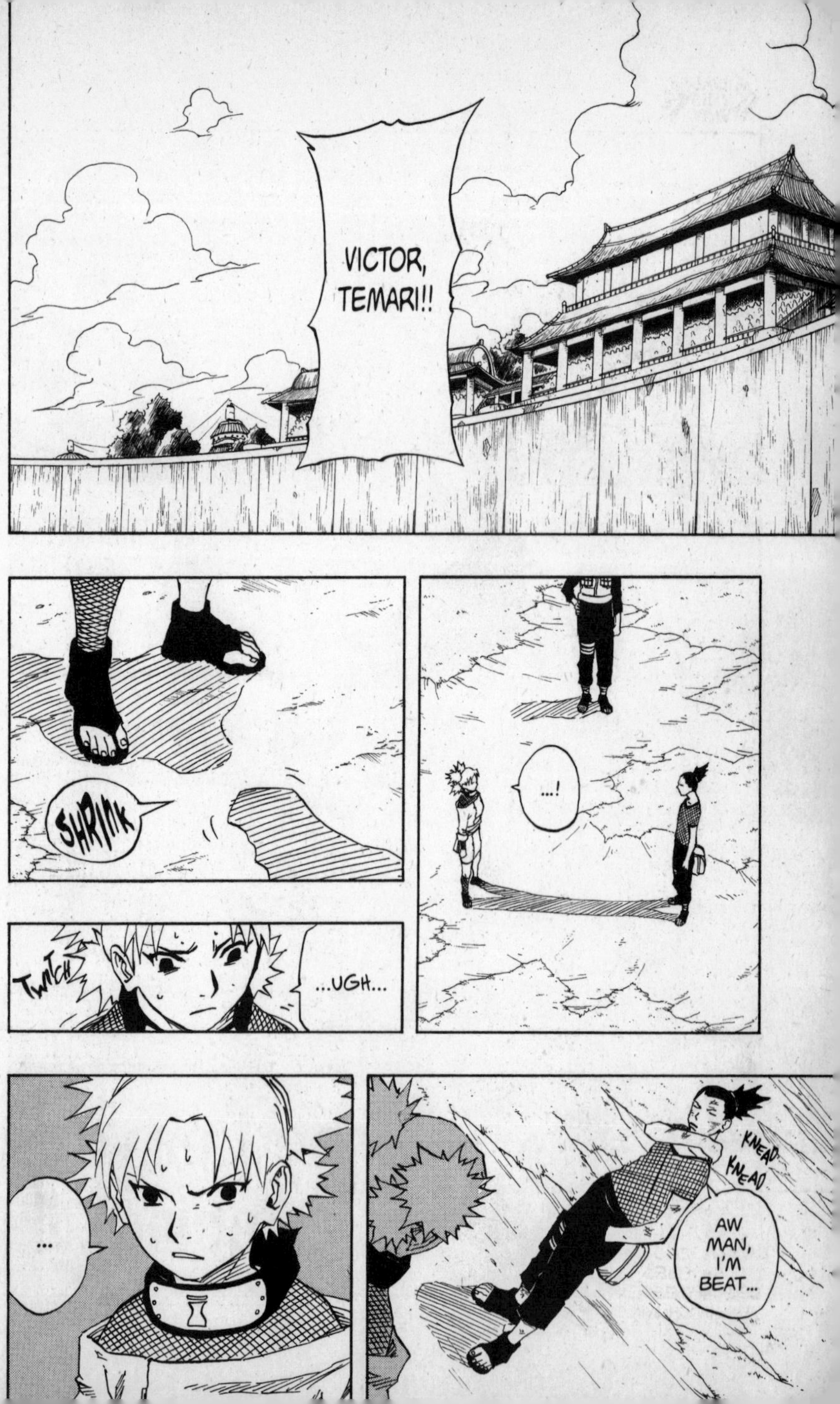
VICTOR, TEMARI!!
...!
SHRINK
TWITCH
...UGH...
KNEAD
KNEAD
AW MAN, I'M BEAT...
...

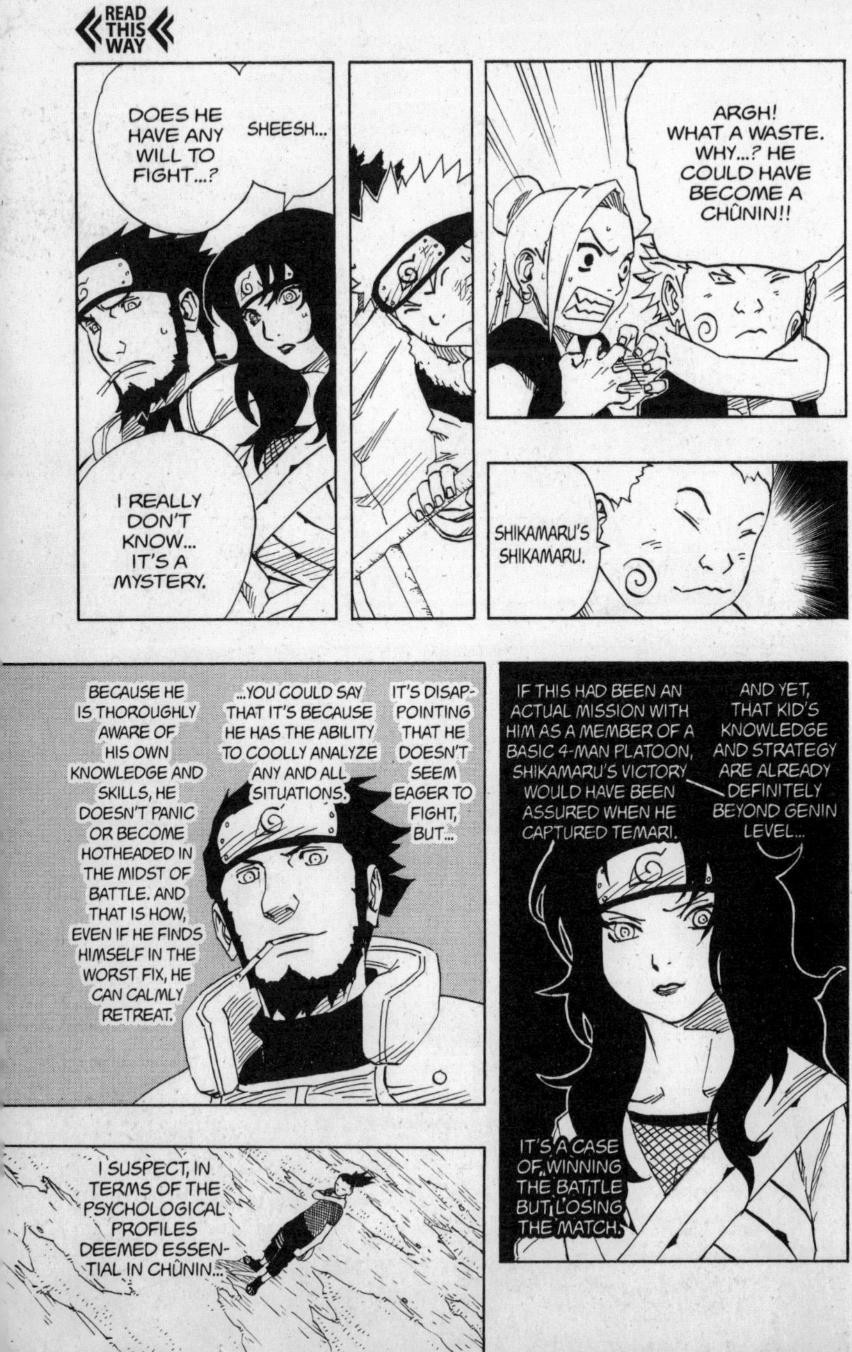
READ THIS WAY
ARGH! WHAT A WASTE. WHY...? HE COULD HAVE BECOME A CHÛNIN!!
SHIKAMARU'S SHIKAMARU.
SHEESH...
DOES HE HAVE ANY WILL TO FIGHT...?
I REALLY DON'T KNOW... IT'S A MYSTERY.
AND YET, THAT KID'S KNOWLEDGE AND STRATEGY ARE ALREADY DEFINITELY BEYOND GENIN LEVEL...
IF THIS HAD BEEN AN ACTUAL MISSION WITH HIM AS A MEMBER OF A BASIC 4-MAN PLATOON, SHIKAMARU'S VICTORY WOULD HAVE BEEN ASSURED WHEN HE CAPTURED TEMARI.
IT'S A CASE OF WINNING THE BATTLE BUT LOSING THE MATCH.
IT'S DISAP-POINTING THAT HE DOESN'T SEEM EAGER TO FIGHT, BUT...
...YOU COULD SAY THAT IT'S BECAUSE HE HAS THE ABILITY TO COOLLY ANALYZE ANY AND ALL SITUATIONS.
BECAUSE HE IS THOROUGHLY AWARE OF HIS OWN KNOWLEDGE AND SKILLS, HE DOESN'T PANIC OR BECOME HOTHEADED IN THE MIDST OF BATTLE. AND THAT IS HOW, EVEN IF HE FINDS HIMSELF IN THE WORST FIX, HE CAN CALMLY RETREAT.
I SUSPECT, IN TERMS OF THE PSYCHOLOGICAL PROFILES DEEMED ESSEN-TIAL IN CHÛNIN...

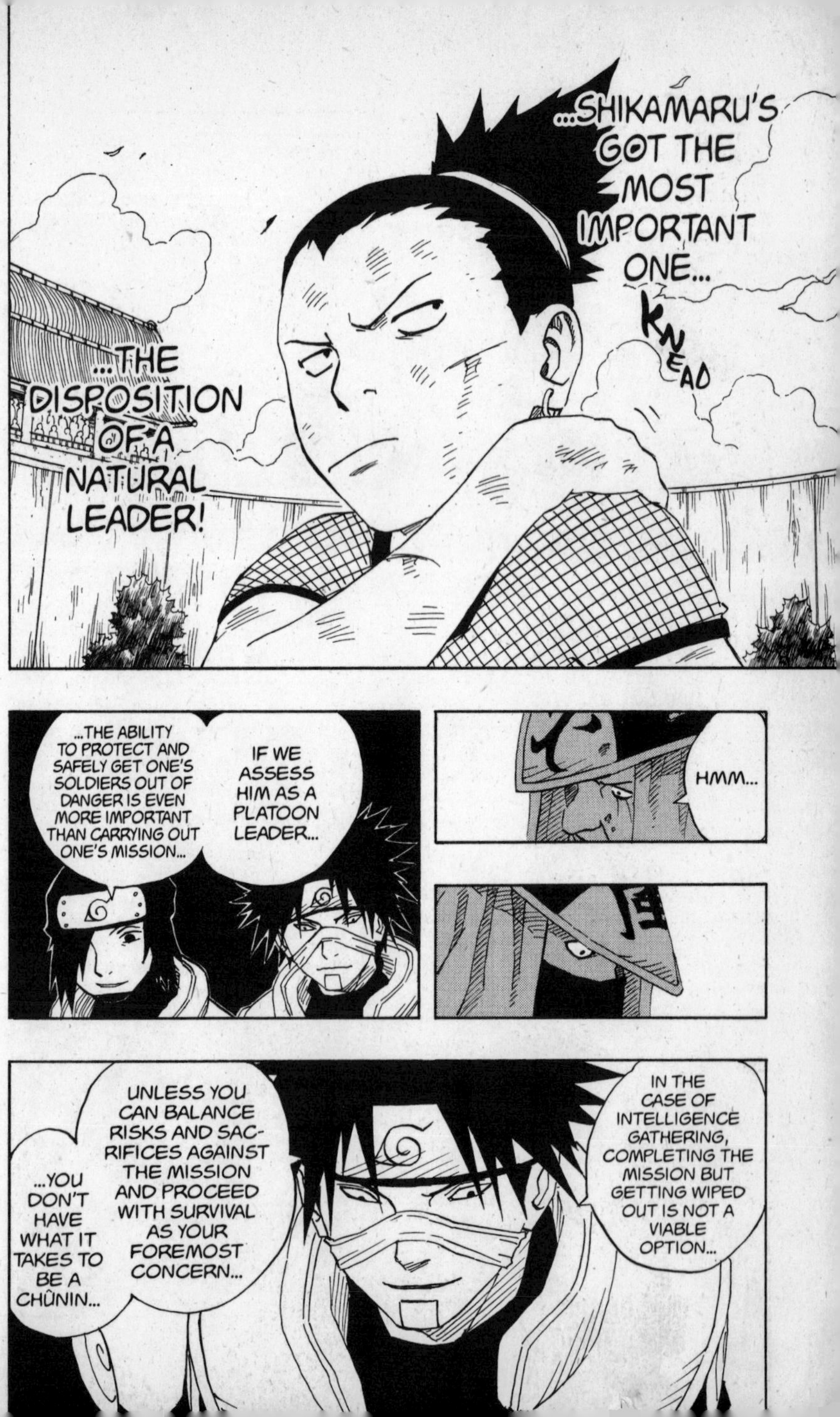
...SHIKAMARU'S GOT THE MOST IMPORTANT ONE...
KNEAD
...THE DISPOSITION OF A NATURAL LEADER!
HMM...
IF WE ASSESS HIM AS A PLATOON LEADER...
...THE ABILITY TO PROTECT AND SAFELY GET ONE'S SOLDIERS OUT OF DANGER IS EVEN MORE IMPORTANT THAN CARRYING OUT ONE'S MISSION...
IN THE CASE OF INTELLIGENCE GATHERING, COMPLETING THE MISSION BUT GETTING WIPED OUT IS NOT A VIABLE OPTION...
UNLESS YOU CAN BALANCE RISKS AND SAC-RIFICES AGAINST THE MISSION AND PROCEED WITH SURVIVAL AS YOUR FOREMOST CONCERN...
...YOU DON'T HAVE WHAT IT TAKES TO BE A CHŪNIN...

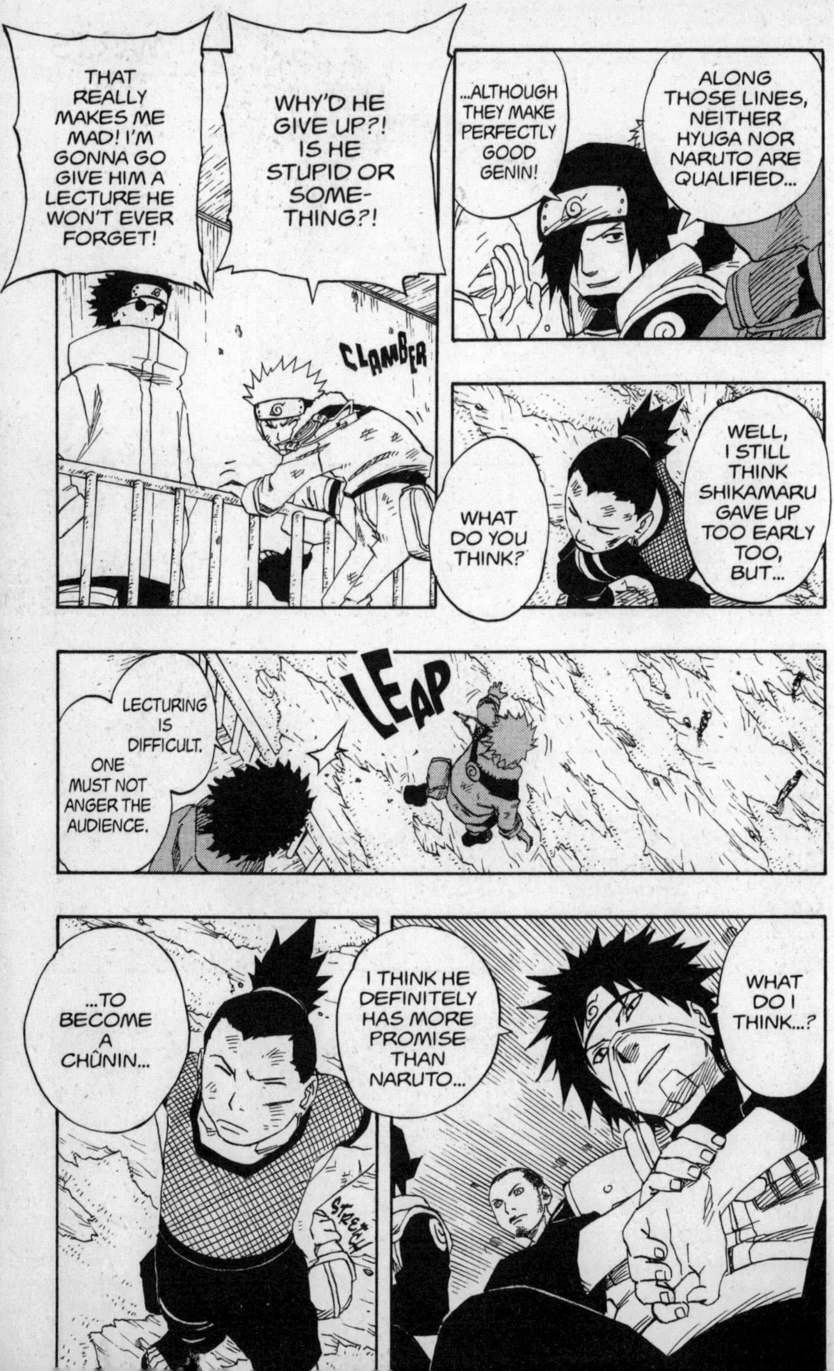
ALONG THOSE LINES, NEITHER HYUGA NOR NARUTO ARE QUALIFIED...
...ALTHOUGH THEY MAKE PERFECTLY GOOD GENIN!
WELL, I STILL THINK SHIKAMARU GAVE UP TOO EARLY TOO, BUT...
WHAT DO YOU THINK?
WHY'D HE GIVE UP?! IS HE STUPID OR SOME-THING?!
THAT REALLY MAKES ME MAD! I'M GONNA GO GIVE HIM A LECTURE HE WON'T EVER FORGET!
CLAMBER
LEAP
LECTURING IS DIFFICULT.
ONE MUST NOT ANGER THE AUDIENCE.
WHAT DO I THINK...?
I THINK HE DEFINITELY HAS MORE PROMISE THAN NARUTO...
...TO BECOME A CHÛNIN...
STRETCH

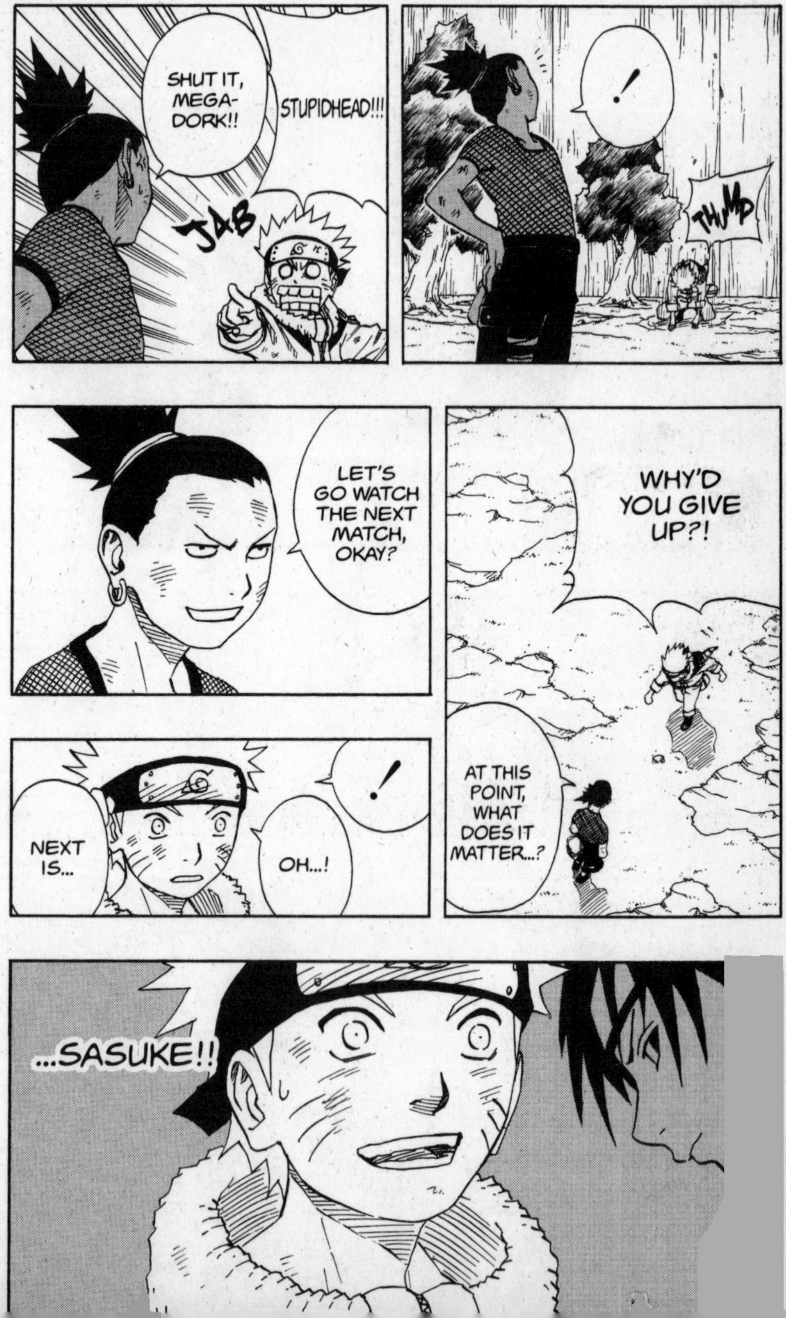
!
THUMP
SHUT IT, MEGA-DORK!!
STUPIDHEAD!!!
JAB
WHY'D YOU GIVE UP?!
AT THIS POINT, WHAT DOES IT MATTER...?
LET'S GO WATCH THE NEXT MATCH, OKAY?
!
OH...!
NEXT IS...
...SASUKE!!

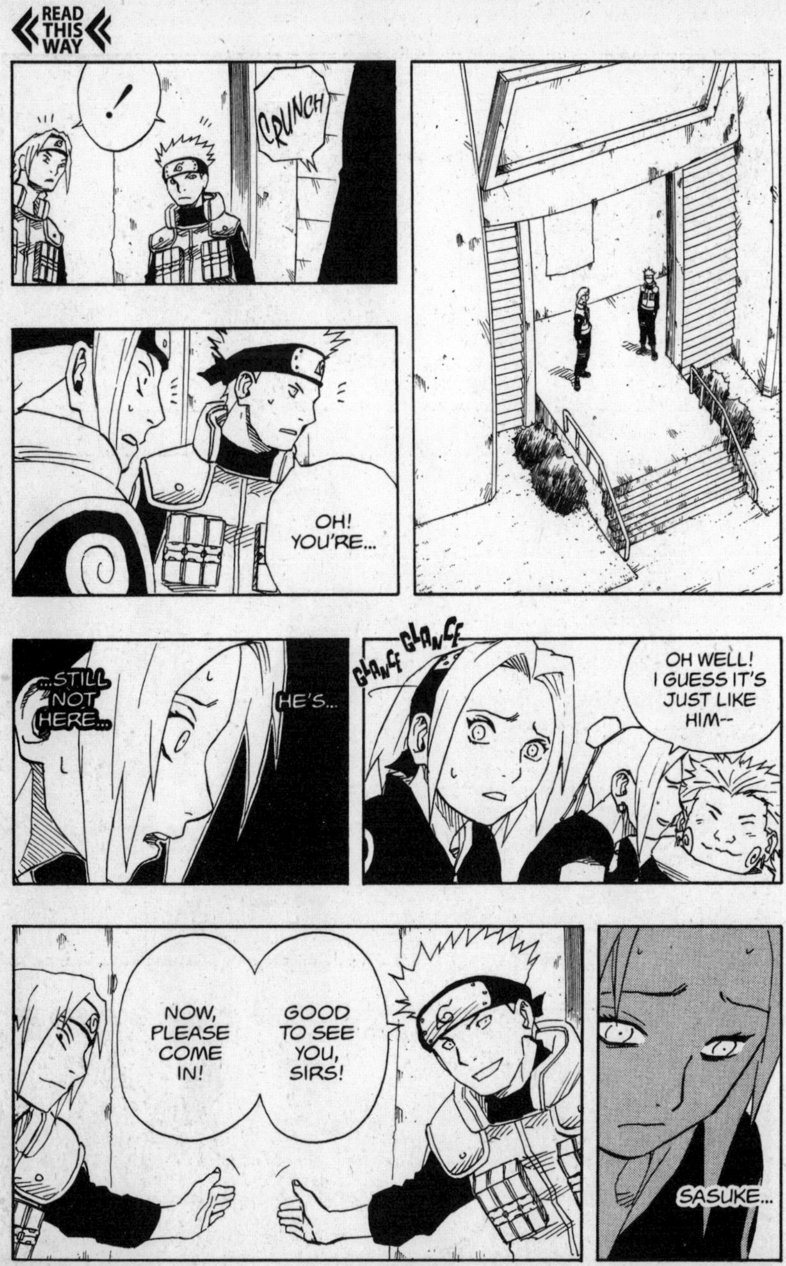
READ THIS WAY
!
CRUNCH
OH! YOU'RE...
GLANCE GLANCE
OH WELL! I GUESS IT'S JUST LIKE HIM--
HE'S...
...STILL NOT HERE...
SASUKE...
GOOD TO SEE YOU, SIRS!
NOW, PLEASE COME IN!

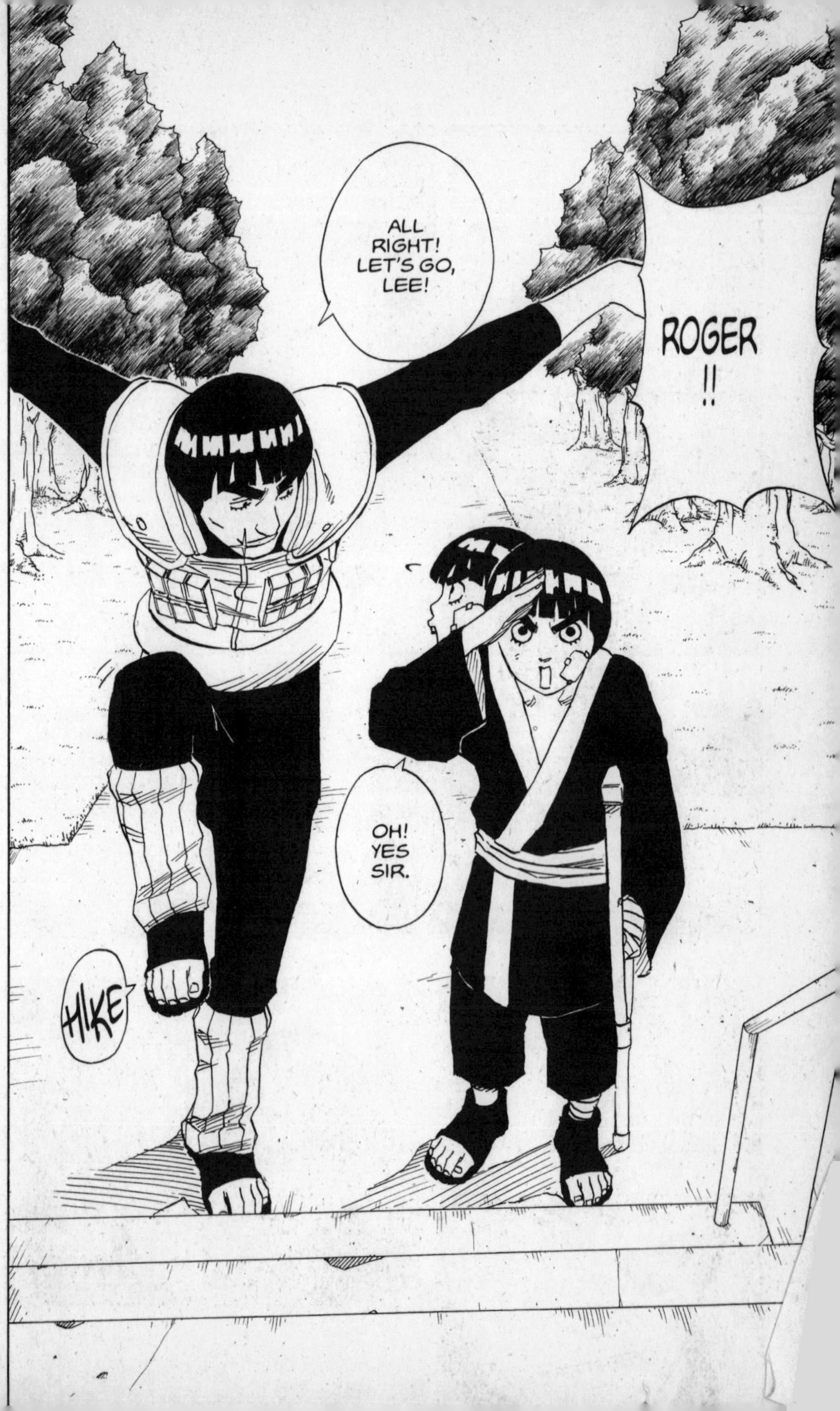
ALL RIGHT! LET'S GO, LEE!
ROGER!!
OH! YES SIR.
HIKE

READ THIS WAY

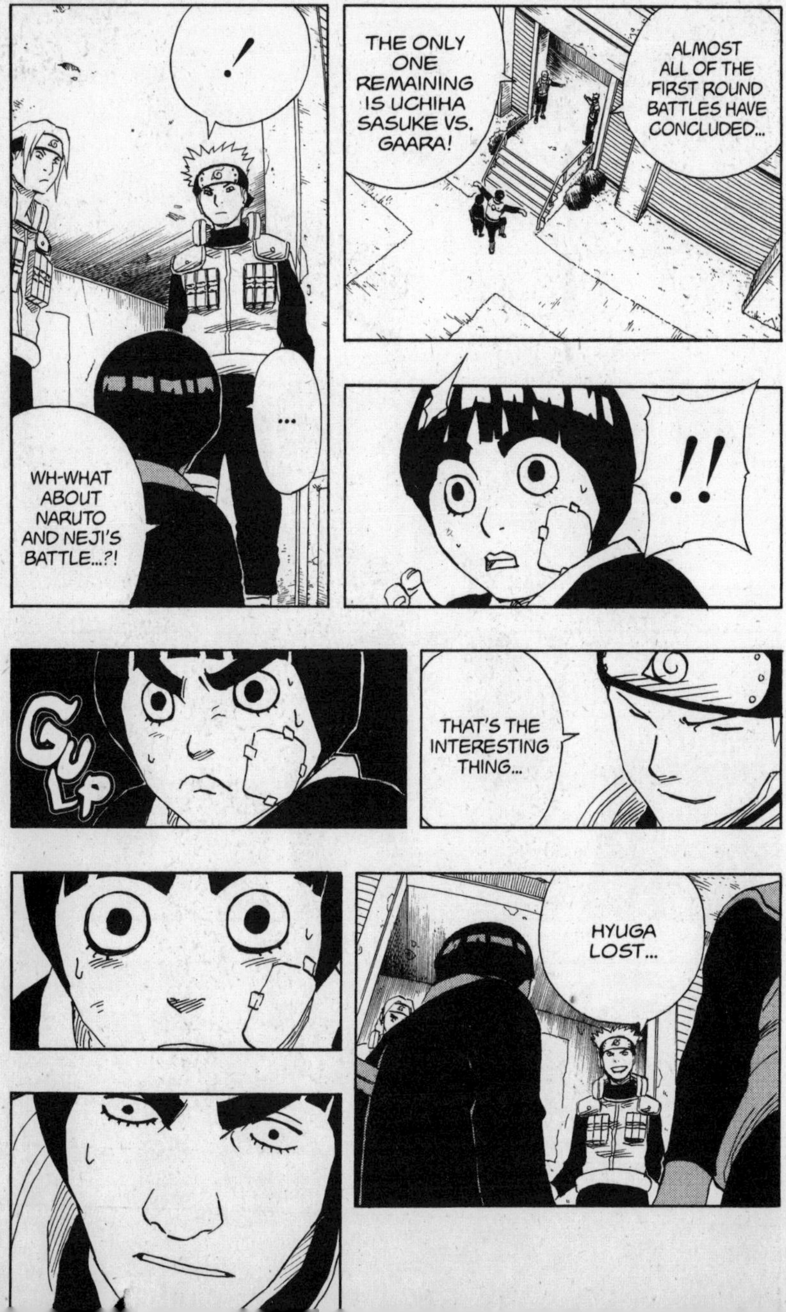
ALMOST ALL OF THE FIRST ROUND BATTLES HAVE CONCLUDED...
THE ONLY ONE REMAINING IS UCHIHA SASUKE VS. GAARA!
!!
!
...
WH-WHAT ABOUT NARUTO AND NEJI'S BATTLE...?!
THAT'S THE INTERESTING THING...
GULP
HYUGA LOST...

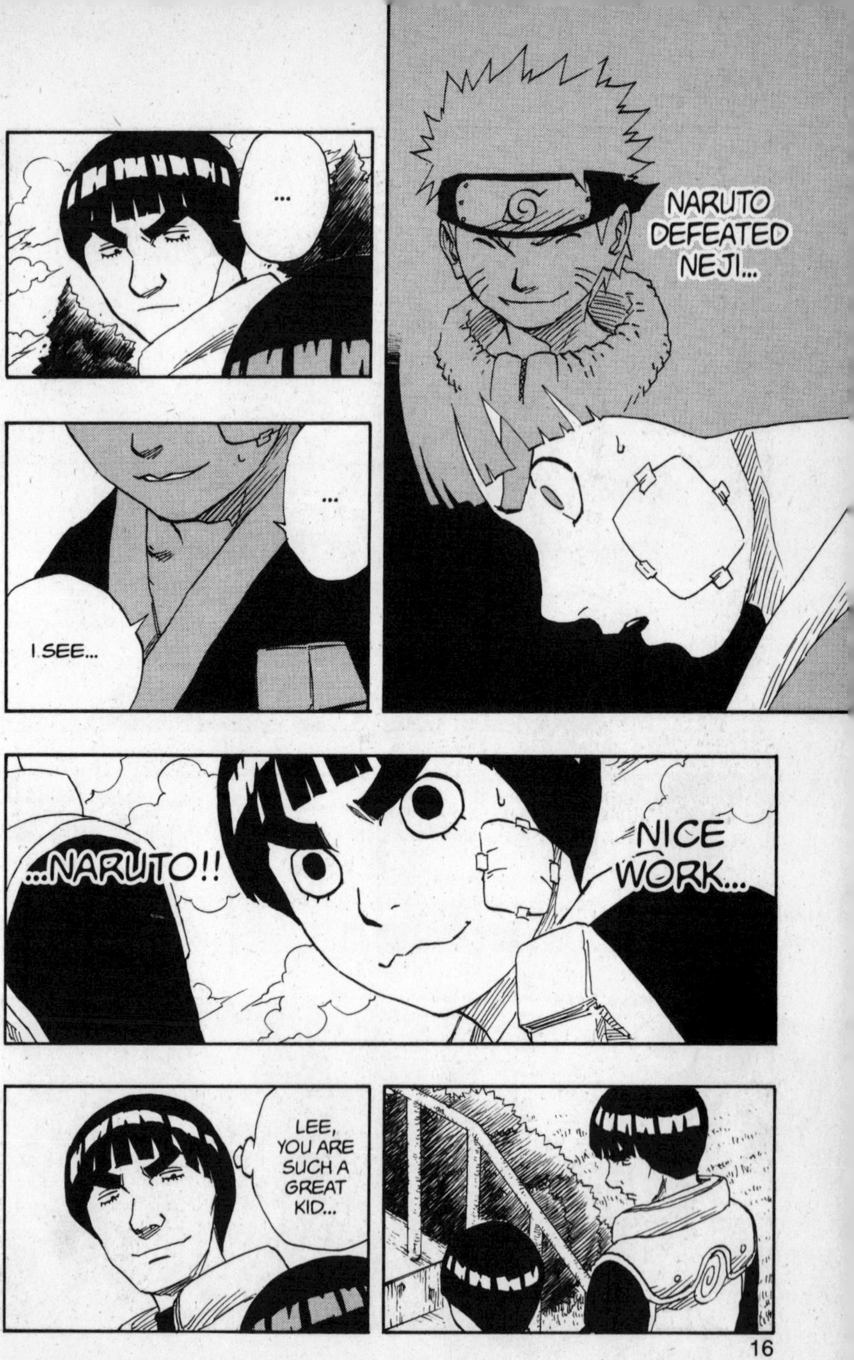
NARUTO DEFEATED NEJI...
...
...
I SEE...
NICE WORK...
...NARUTO!!
LEE, YOU ARE SUCH A GREAT KID...

READ THIS WAY

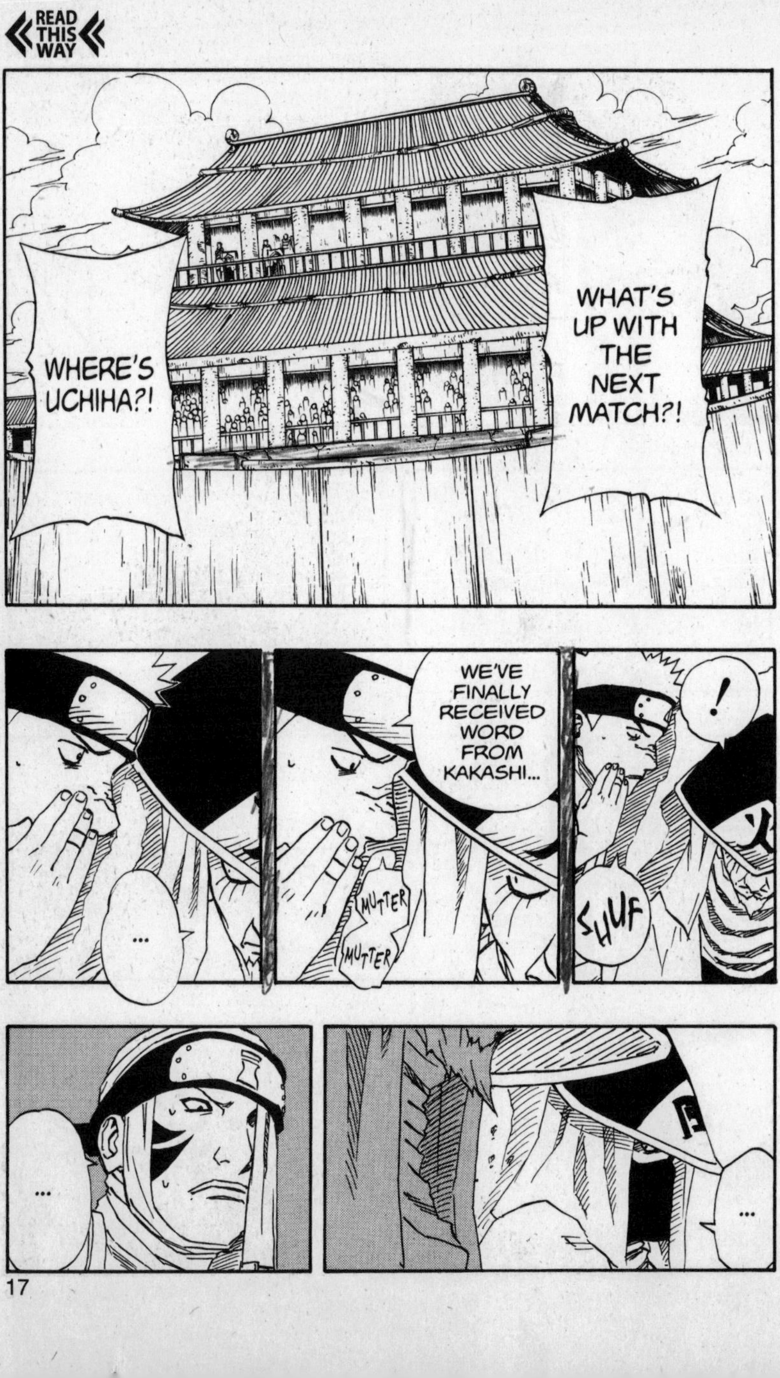

WHAT'S UP WITH THE NEXT MATCH?!
WHERE'S UCHIHA?!
!
SHUF
WE'VE FINALLY RECEIVED WORD FROM KAKASHI...
MUTTER
MUTTER
...
...
...

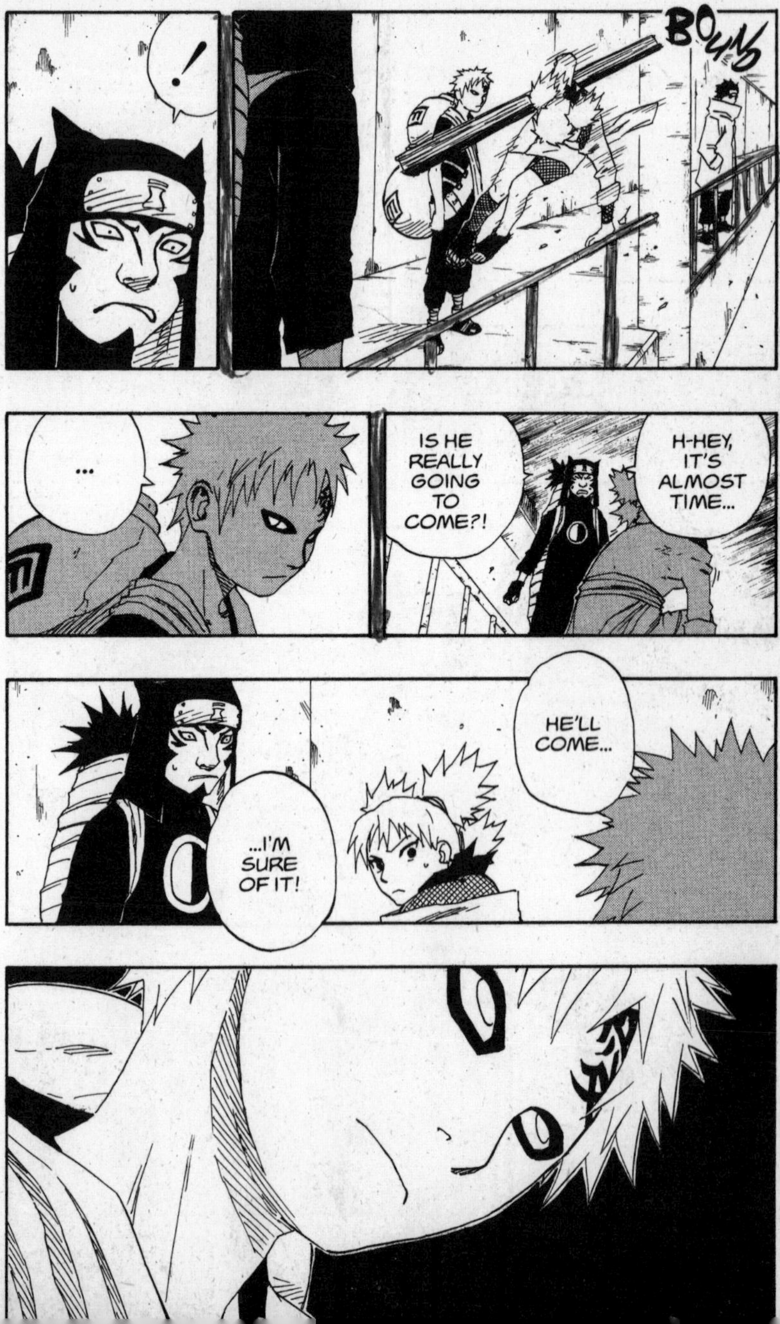
BOWNG
!
H-HEY, IT'S ALMOST TIME...
IS HE REALLY GOING TO COME?!
...
HE'LL COME...
...I'M SURE OF IT!

READ THIS WAY

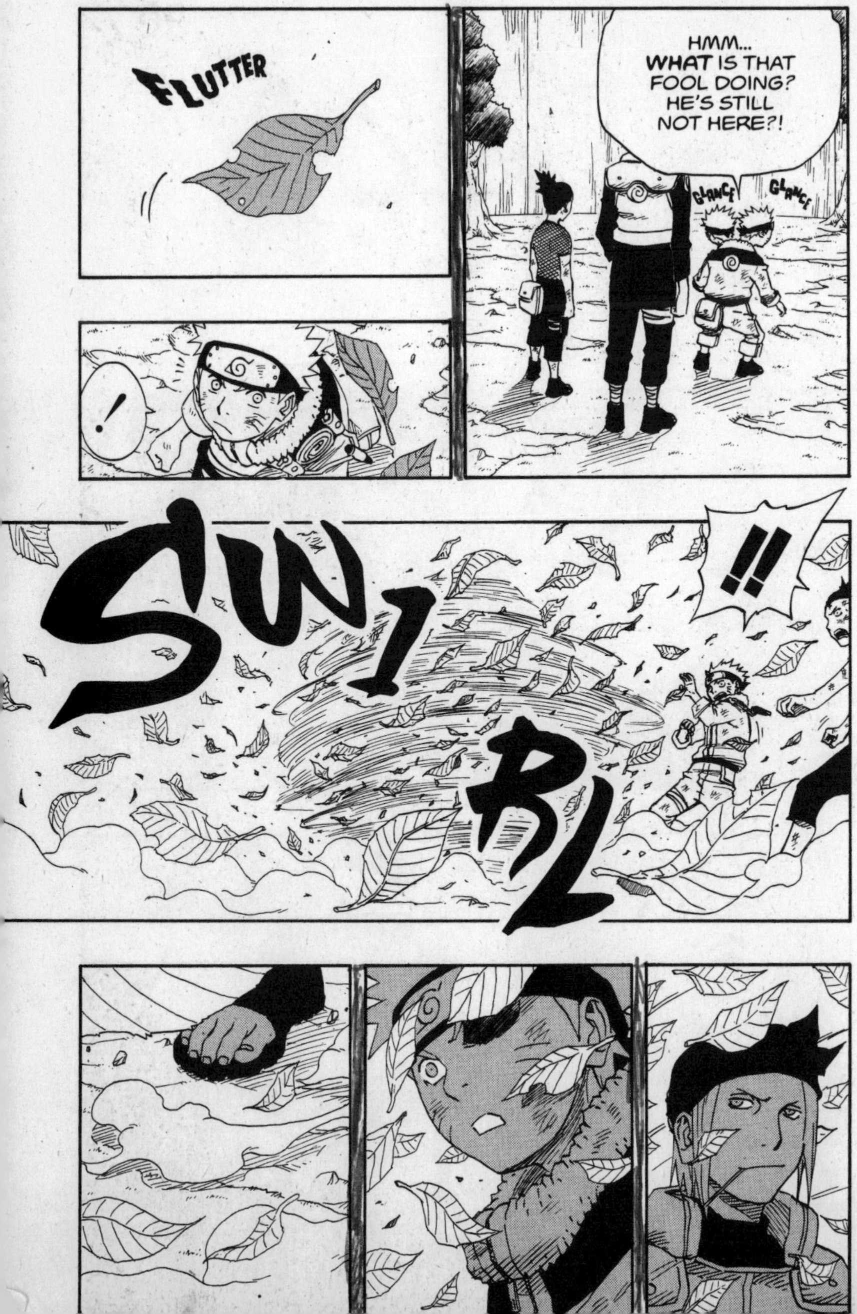
HMM... WHAT IS THAT FOOL DOING? HE'S STILL NOT HERE?!
GLANCE
GLANCE
FLUTTER
!
SWIRL
!!

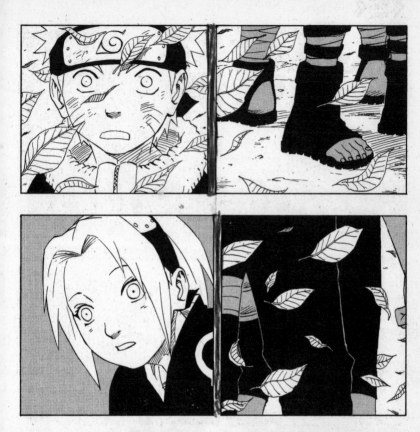

READ THIS WAY

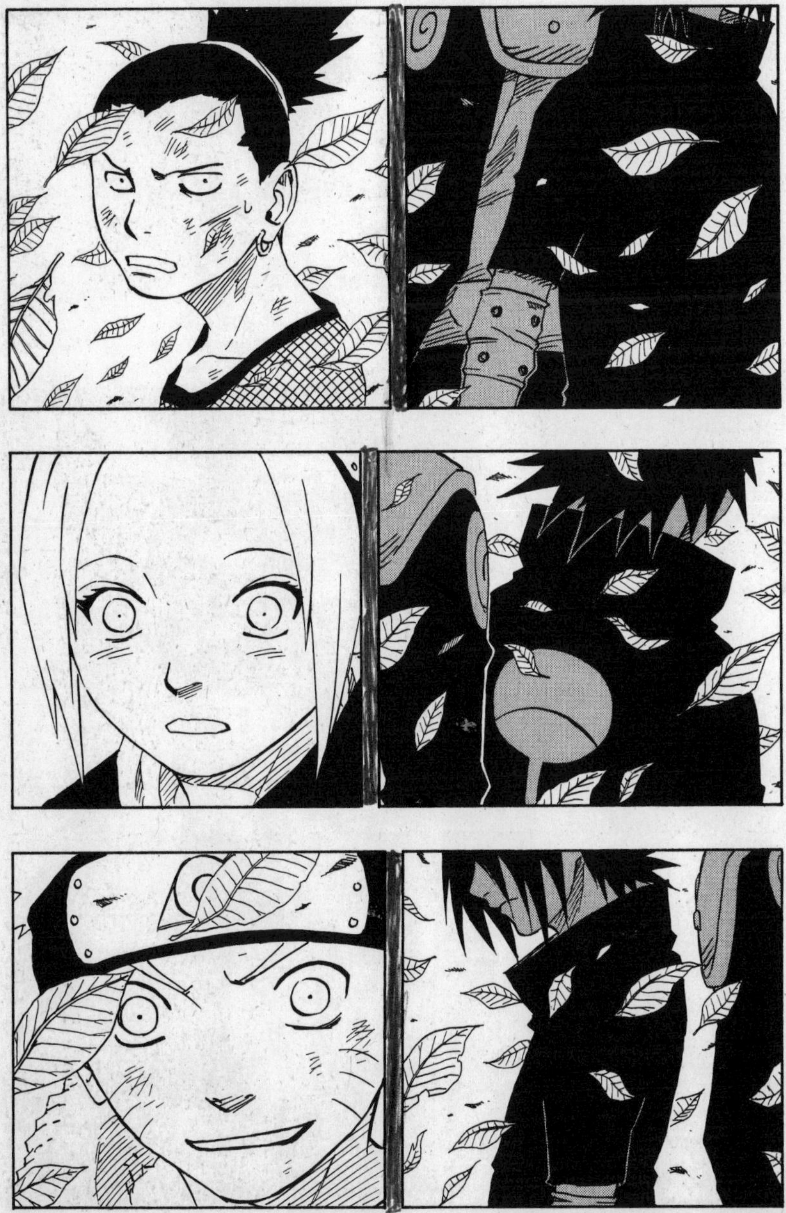

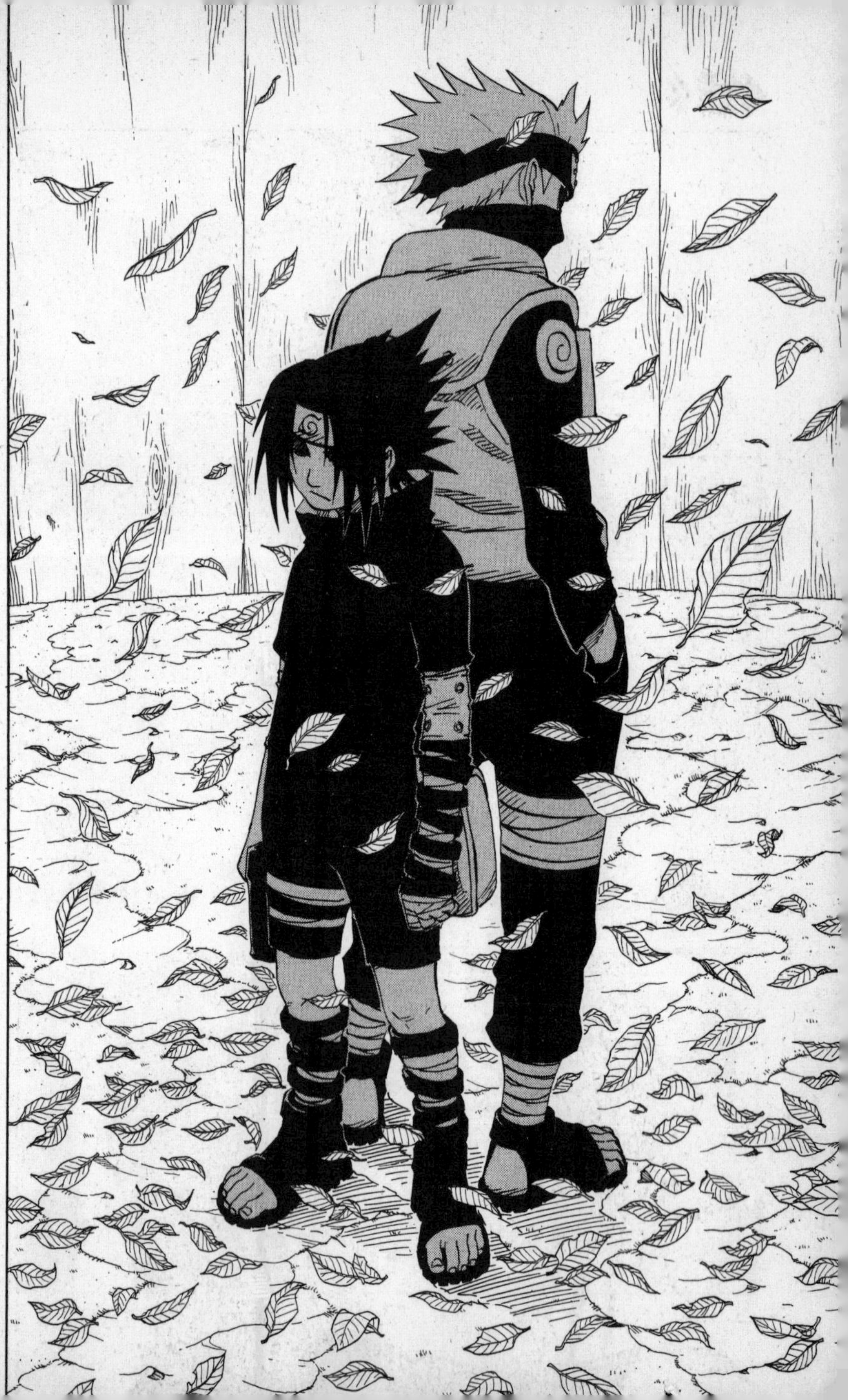

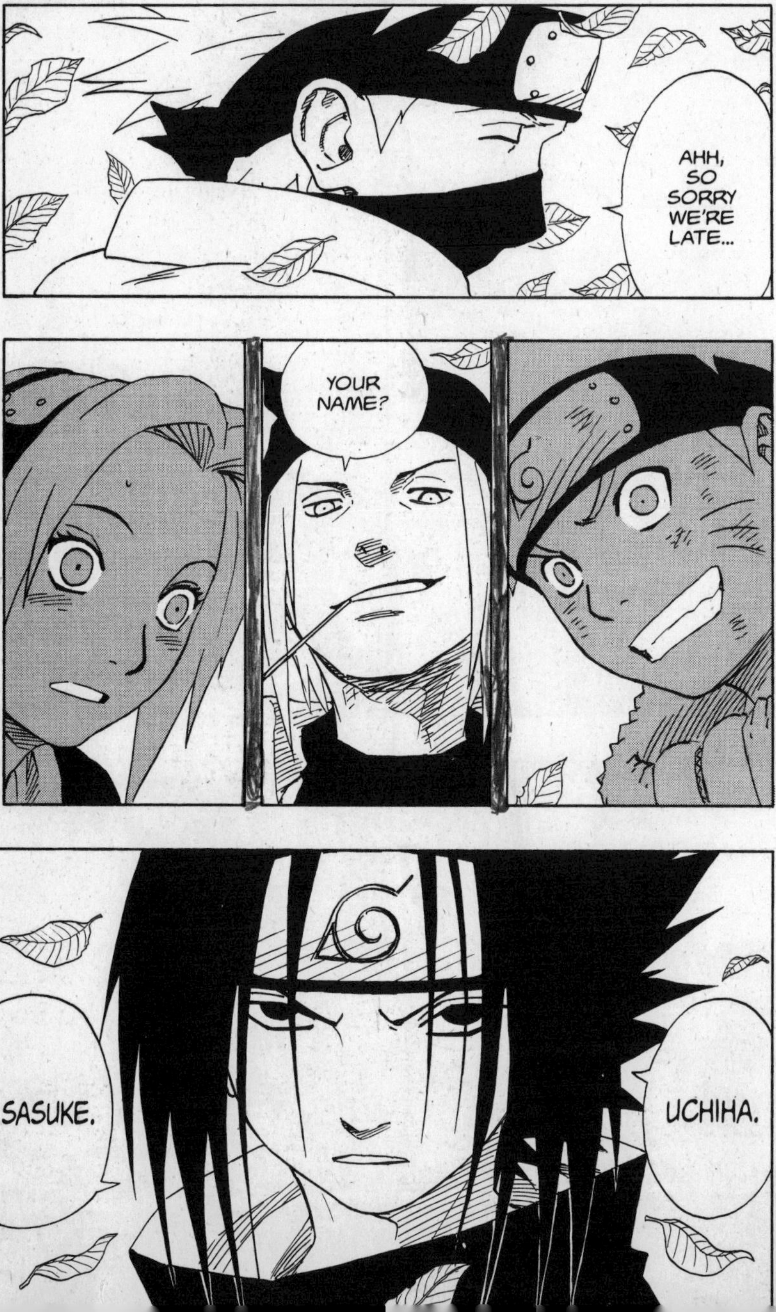
READ THIS WAY
AHH, SO SORRY WE'RE LATE...
YOUR NAME?
UCHIHA.
SASUKE.

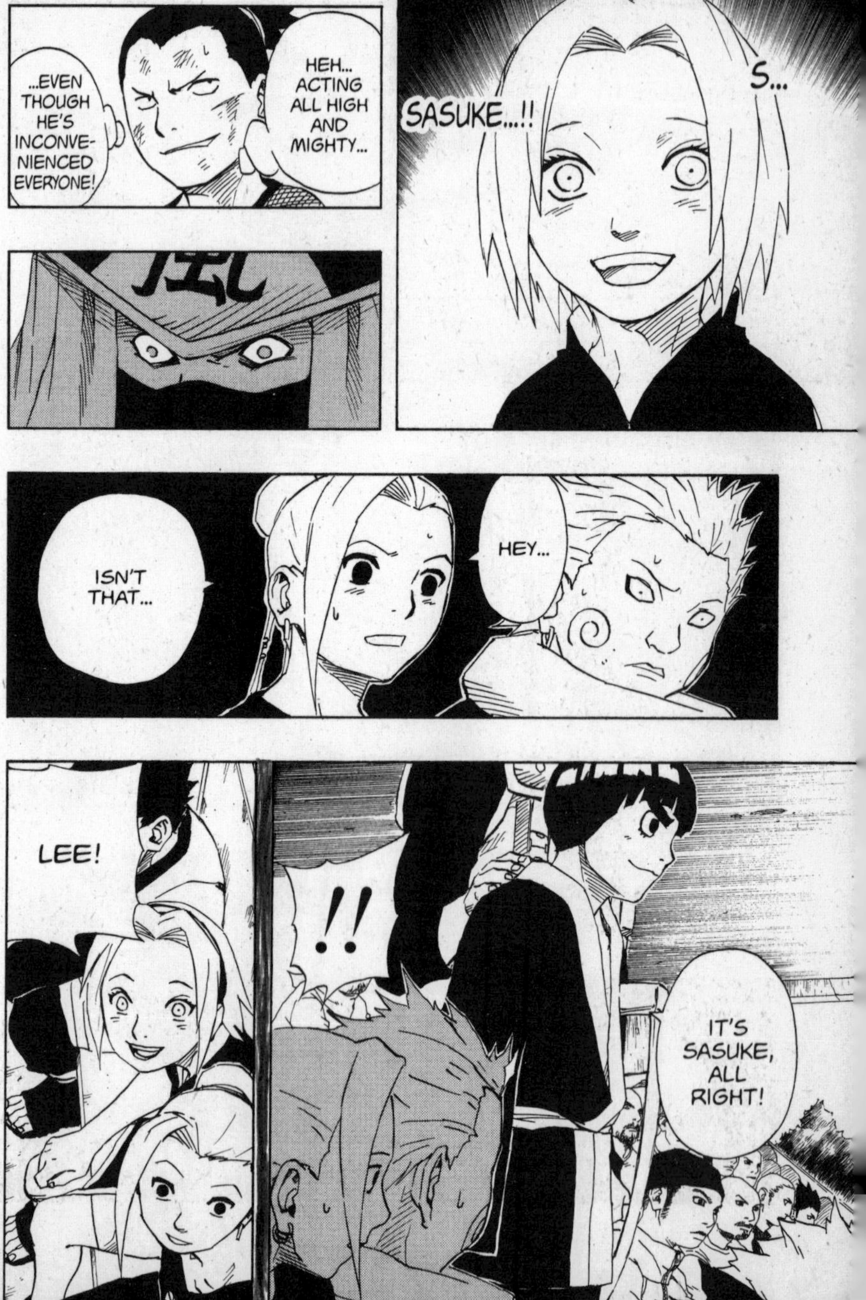
S...
SASUKE...!!
HEH... ACTING ALL HIGH AND MIGHTY...
...EVEN THOUGH HE'S INCONVE-NIENCED EVERYONE!
HEY...
ISN'T THAT...
IT'S SASUKE, ALL RIGHT!
!!
LEE!

READ THIS WAY

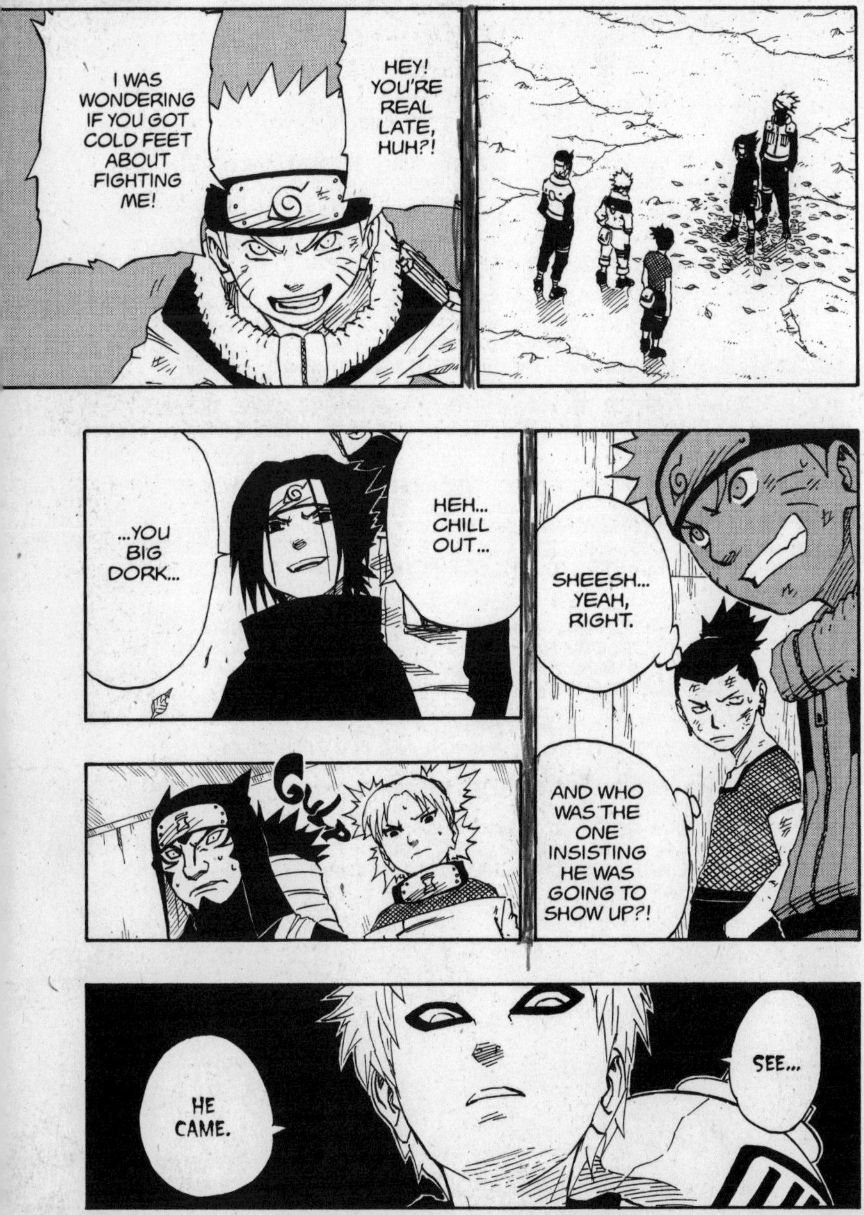
HEY! YOU'RE REAL LATE, HUH?!
I WAS WONDERING IF YOU GOT COLD FEET ABOUT FIGHTING ME!
SHEESH... YEAH, RIGHT.
AND WHO WAS THE ONE INSISTING HE WAS GOING TO SHOW UP?!
HEH... CHILL OUT...
...YOU BIG DORK...
GULP
SEE...
HE CAME.

THE WORLD OF KISHIMOTO MASASHI
MY PERSONAL HISTORY, PART 16

IN HIGH SCHOOL I WAS DRAWING MANGA ALL THE TIME, AND EVEN
THOUGH I WAS IN THE PROGRESSIVE TRACK, MY HOMEROOM
TEACHER TOLD ME I WOULDN'T GET INTO ANY COLLEGE BASED ON
MY GRADES IN THE STANDARD SUBJECTS. "..." "...HEH..." "SO WHAT!!" I
DIDN'T PANIC! I'D ALREADY THOUGHT IT OUT AND PLANNED AHEAD
FOR THAT! AND WHAT WAS IT THAT I HAD IN MIND...?

SINCE I WAS IN ELEMENTARY SCHOOL, FOR SOME UNKNOWN REASON,
MY GRADES IN ART HAVE ALWAYS BEEN EXCELLENT! ..."THAT'S RIGHT!
IF IT'S AN ART COLLEGE, I THINK I CAN GET IN!" THIS COMPLETELY
GROUNDLESS CONFIDENCE HAD SECRETLY ALLAYED MY FEARS!

(P.S. BECAUSE IT WAS A PROGRESSIVE TRACK, THERE WERE NO ART
CLASSES AT ALL!) MOST ART SCHOOLS ONLY TEST ART ON THEIR
APPLICATION EXAMS.

IN ANY CASE, TO BE HONEST, DESPITE THE FACT THAT I WAS CON-
STANTLY DRAWING IN HIGH SCHOOL, I WAS PAINFULLY AWARE THAT I
DIDN'T HAVE GOOD SKETCHING SKILLS. SO I SAID TO MYSELF, "I'LL
HONE MY SKETCHING ABILITY IN COLLEGE!" AND PRACTICED SKETCH-
ING THE SAMPLE PLASTER MODELS BEFORE HEADING OFF TO THE
ACTUAL EXAM!

WHILE DEEPLY REALIZING THAT HUMANS ARE CREATURES OF CONVE-
NIENCE WHO ONLY OFFER PRAYERS TO THE GODS WHEN FACED WITH
CRISES, I WAITED SEVERAL WEEKS FOR THE RESULTS!
A-AND THEN... THE GODS HADN'T YET ABANDONED ME...

I PASSED!!
"YES!! NOW I CAN DRAW MANGA ALL I WANT!! YEAH!!"

SO AMIDST HIGH STRESS, I WENT OFF TO ART SCHOOL!

AND THEN, BRIEFLY REFLECTING ON MY HIGH SCHOOL YEARS, I
WONDERED THUSLY: FOR THREE YEARS, I HAD DESPERATELY STRUG-
GLED THROUGH MATH, ENGLISH, GRAMMAR, CHEMISTRY, AND
HISTORY... TO WHAT END?

Number 110: At Long Last...!!

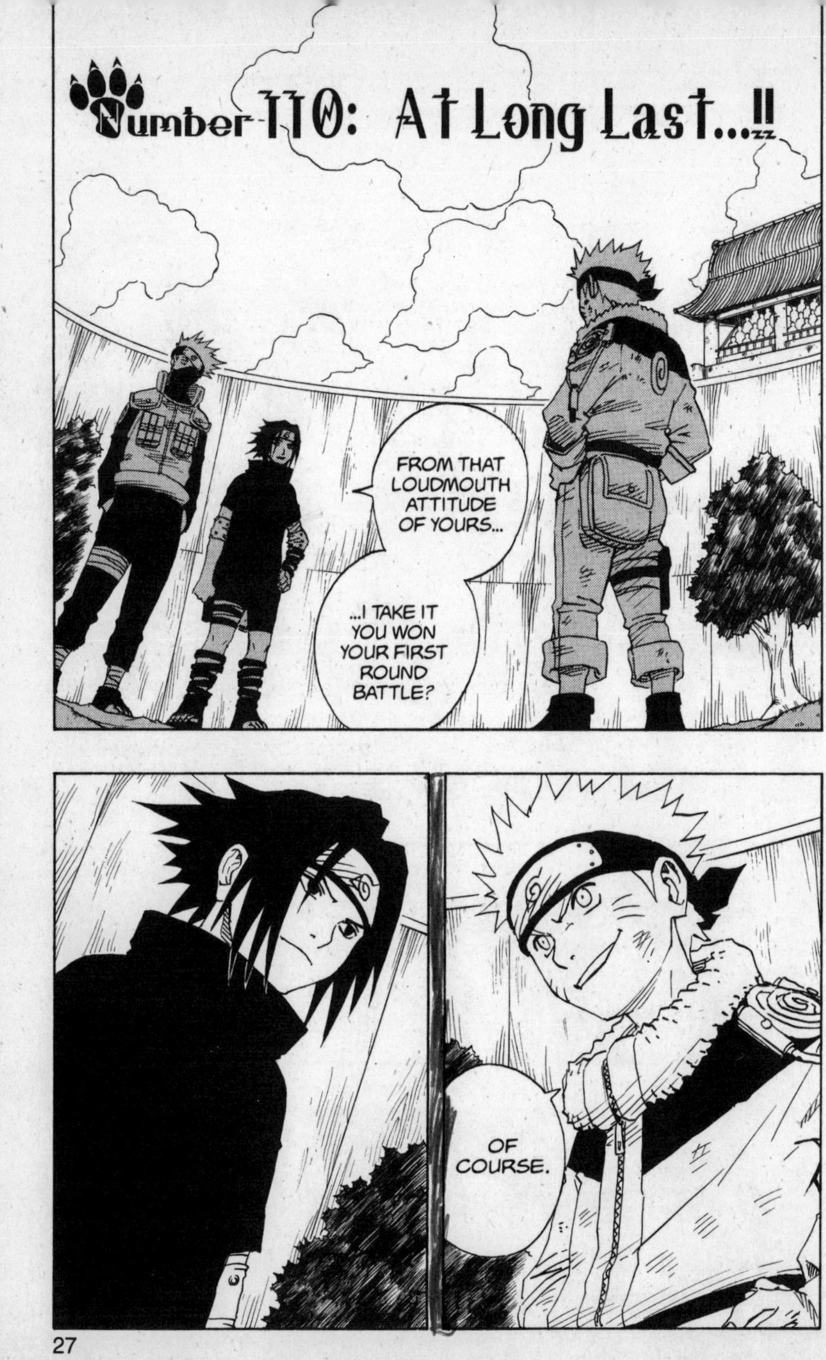
FROM THAT LOUDMOUTH ATTITUDE OF YOURS...
...I TAKE IT YOU WON YOUR FIRST ROUND BATTLE?
OF COURSE.

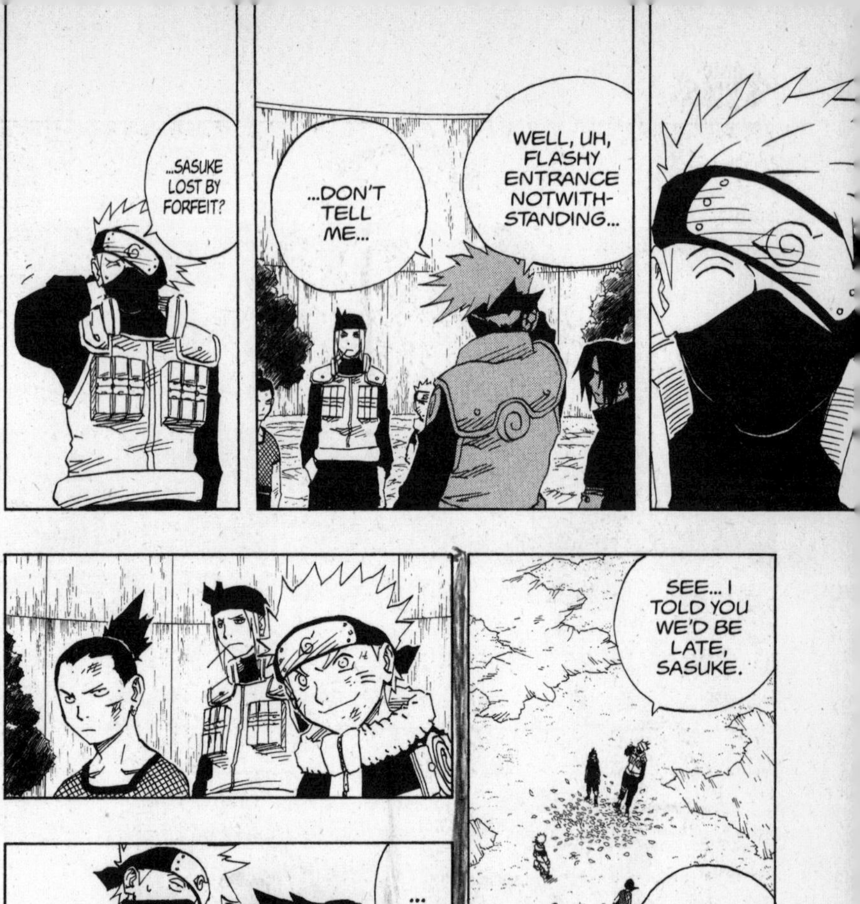
WELL, UH, FLASHY ENTRANCE NOTWITH- STANDING...
...DON'T TELL ME...
...SASUKE LOST BY FORFEIT?
SEE... I TOLD YOU WE'D BE LATE, SASUKE.
MAYBE YOUR TARDINESS IS CONTA- GIOUS?!
SHEESH!
...
SO... WHAT'S THE DEAL?
DON'T WORRY, YOU'RE SAFE!
SASUKE'S MATCH WAS POSTPONED.
HIS MATCH WASN'T FORFEITED.

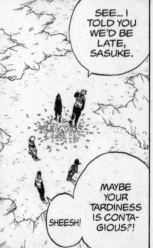

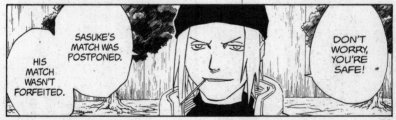

READ THIS WAY

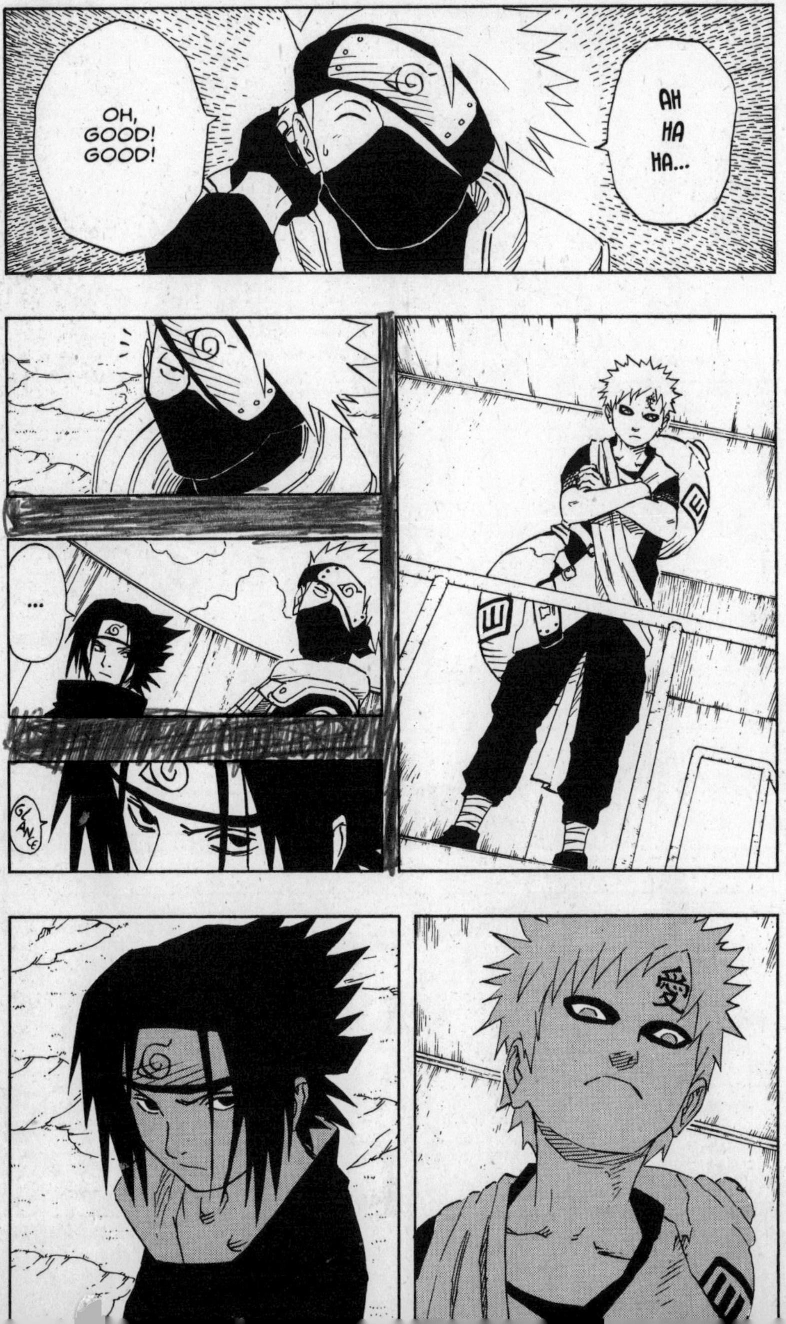
AH HA HA...
OH, GOOD! GOOD!
...
GLANCE

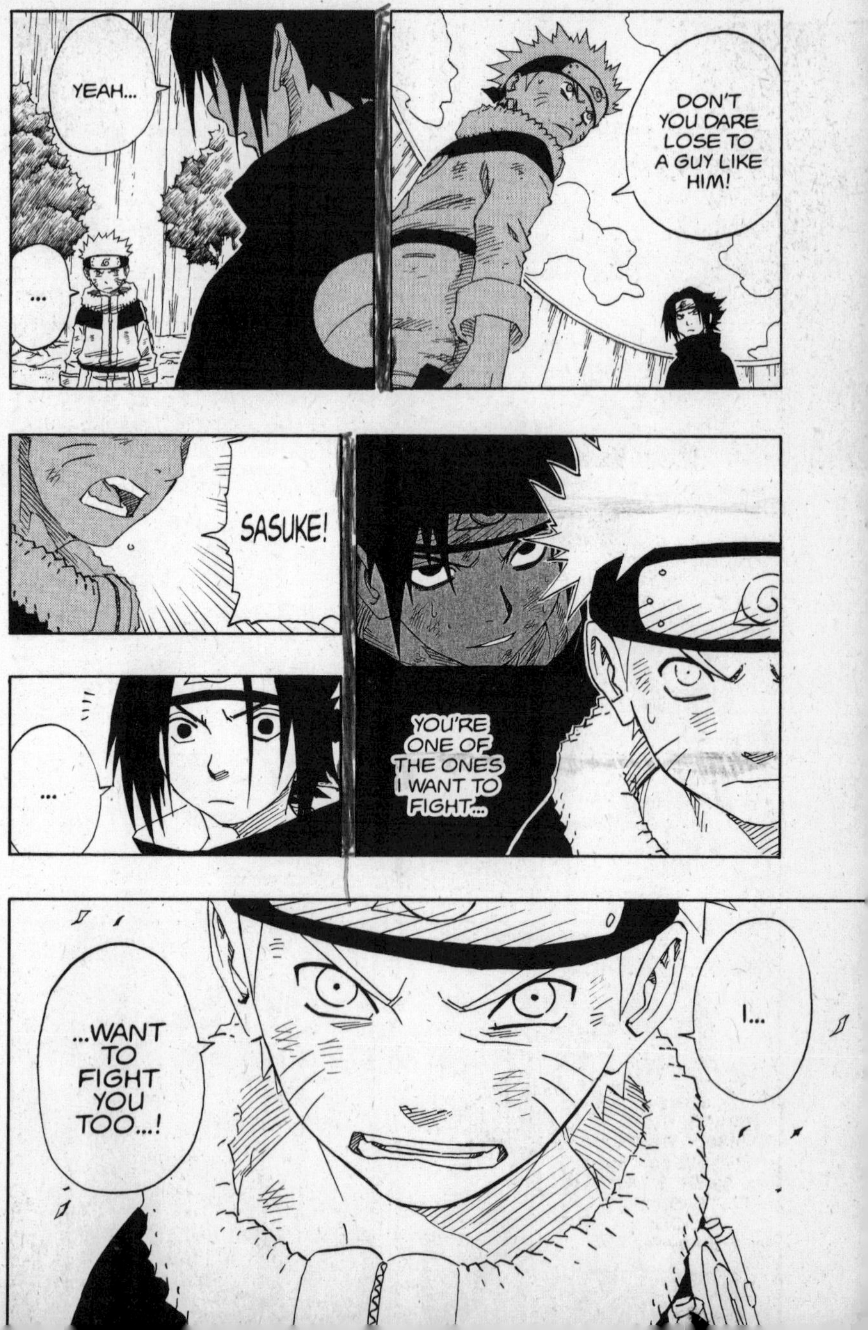
DON'T YOU DARE LOSE TO A GUY LIKE HIM!
YEAH...
...
YOU'RE ONE OF THE ONES I WANT TO FIGHT...
SASUKE!
...
I...
...WANT TO FIGHT YOU TOO...!

READ THIS WAY

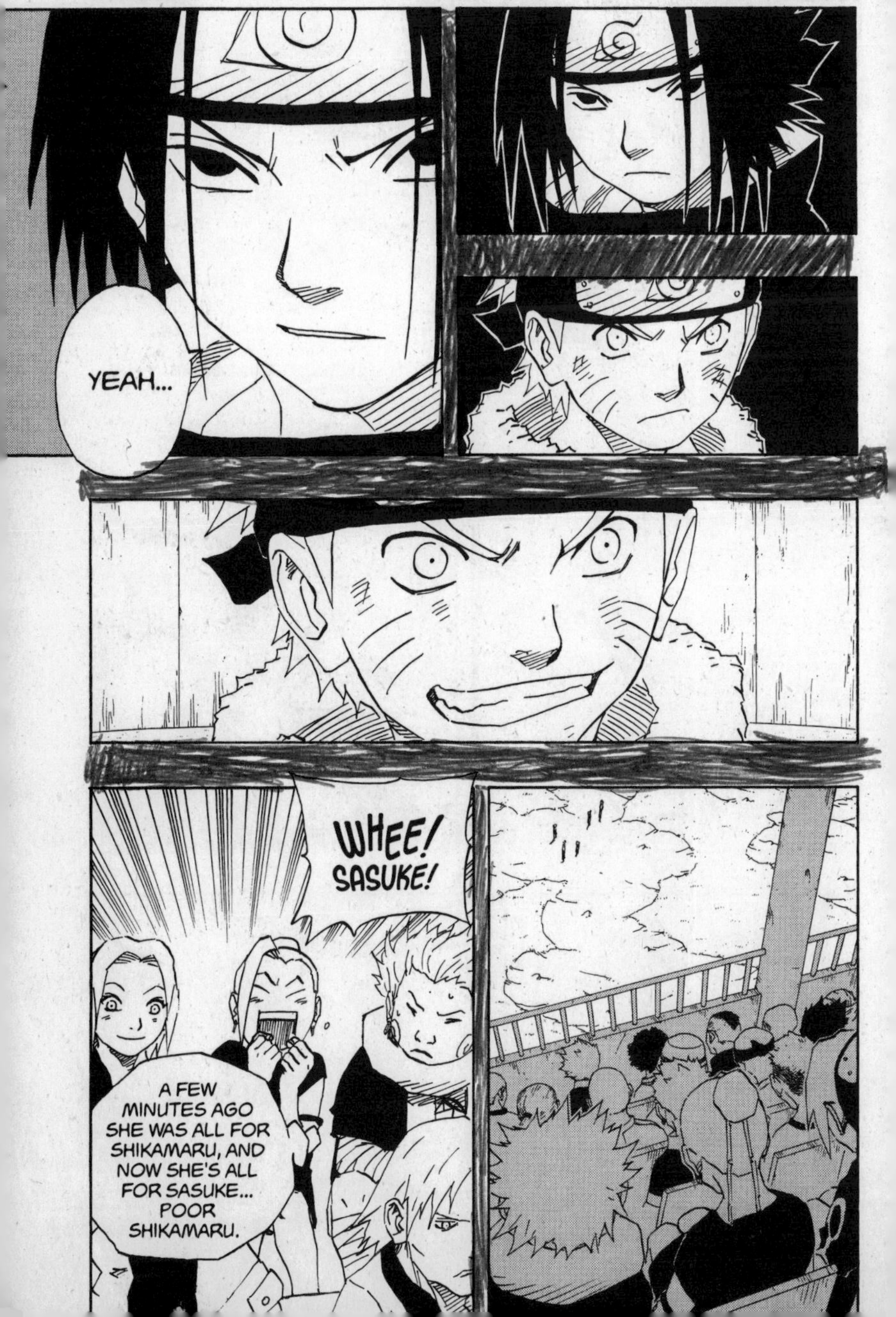
YEAH...
WHEE! SASUKE!
A FEW MINUTES AGO SHE WAS ALL FOR SHIKAMARU, AND NOW SHE'S ALL FOR SASUKE... POOR SHIKAMARU.

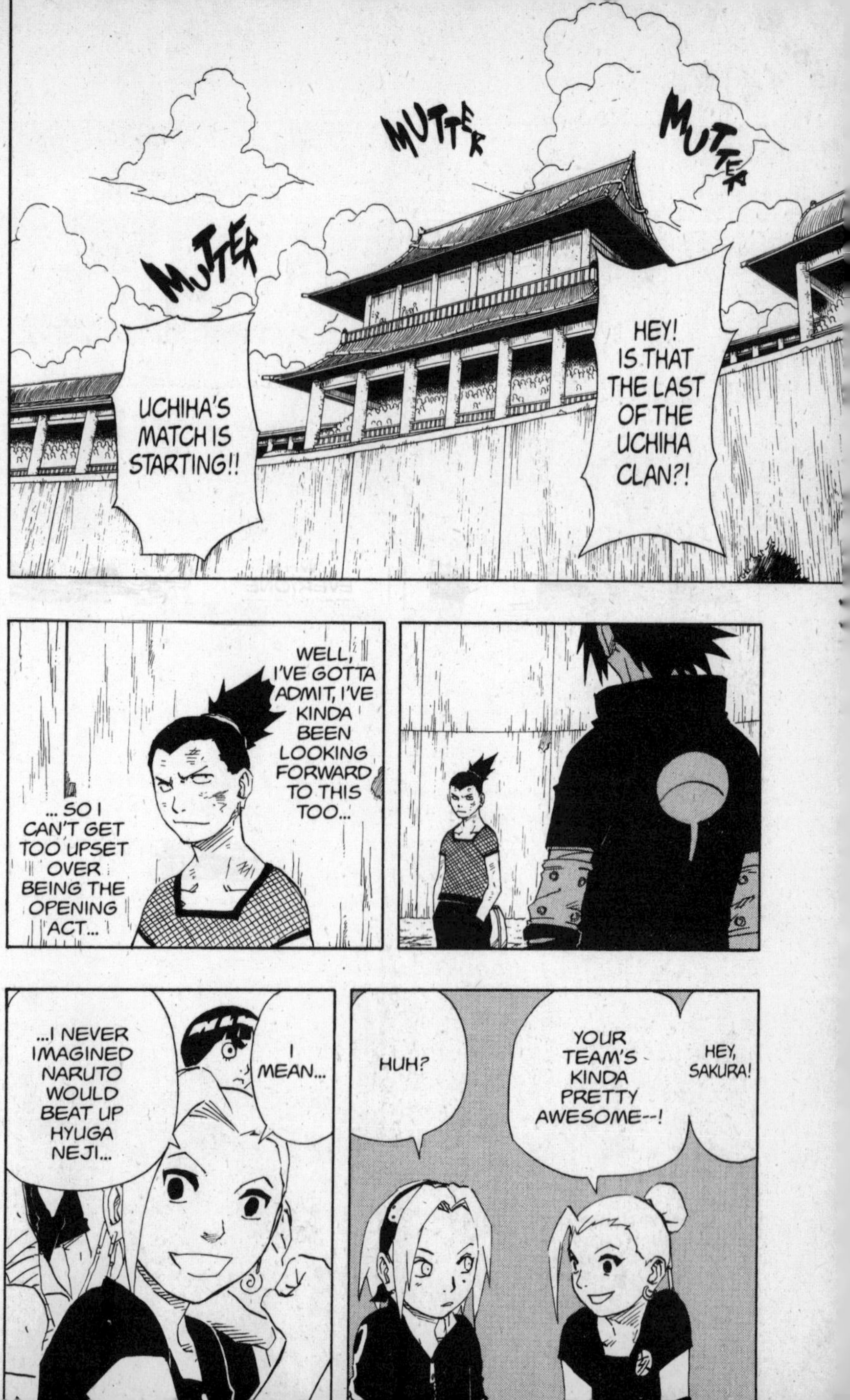
MUTTER
MUTTER
HEY! IS THAT THE LAST OF THE UCHIHA CLAN?!
MUTTER
UCHIHA'S MATCH IS STARTING!!
WELL, I'VE GOTTA ADMIT, I'VE KINDA BEEN LOOKING FORWARD TO THIS TOO...
... SO I CAN'T GET TOO UPSET OVER BEING THE OPENING ACT...
HEY, SAKURA!
YOUR TEAM'S KINDA PRETTY AWESOME--!
HUH?
I MEAN...
...I NEVER IMAGINED NARUTO WOULD BEAT UP HYUGA NEJI...

READ THIS WAY

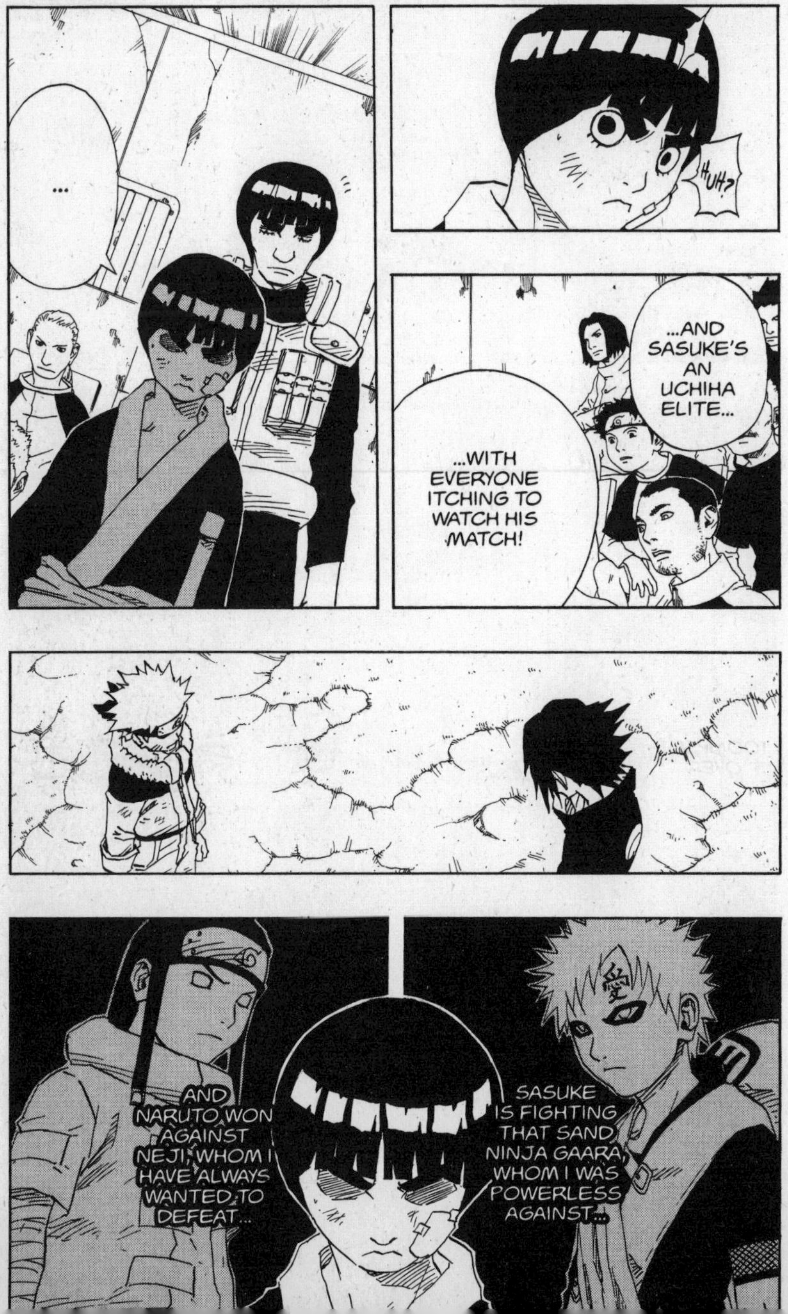
HUH?
...AND SASUKE'S AN UCHIHA ELITE...
...WITH EVERYONE ITCHING TO WATCH HIS MATCH!
...
SASUKE IS FIGHTING THAT SAND NINJA GAARA, WHOM I WAS POWERLESS AGAINST...
AND NARUTO WON AGAINST NEJI, WHOM I HAVE ALWAYS WANTED TO DEFEAT...

WHY...

SEEP

...

DRIP

WHY AM I SO...

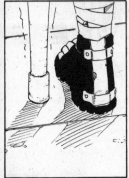

RATTLE

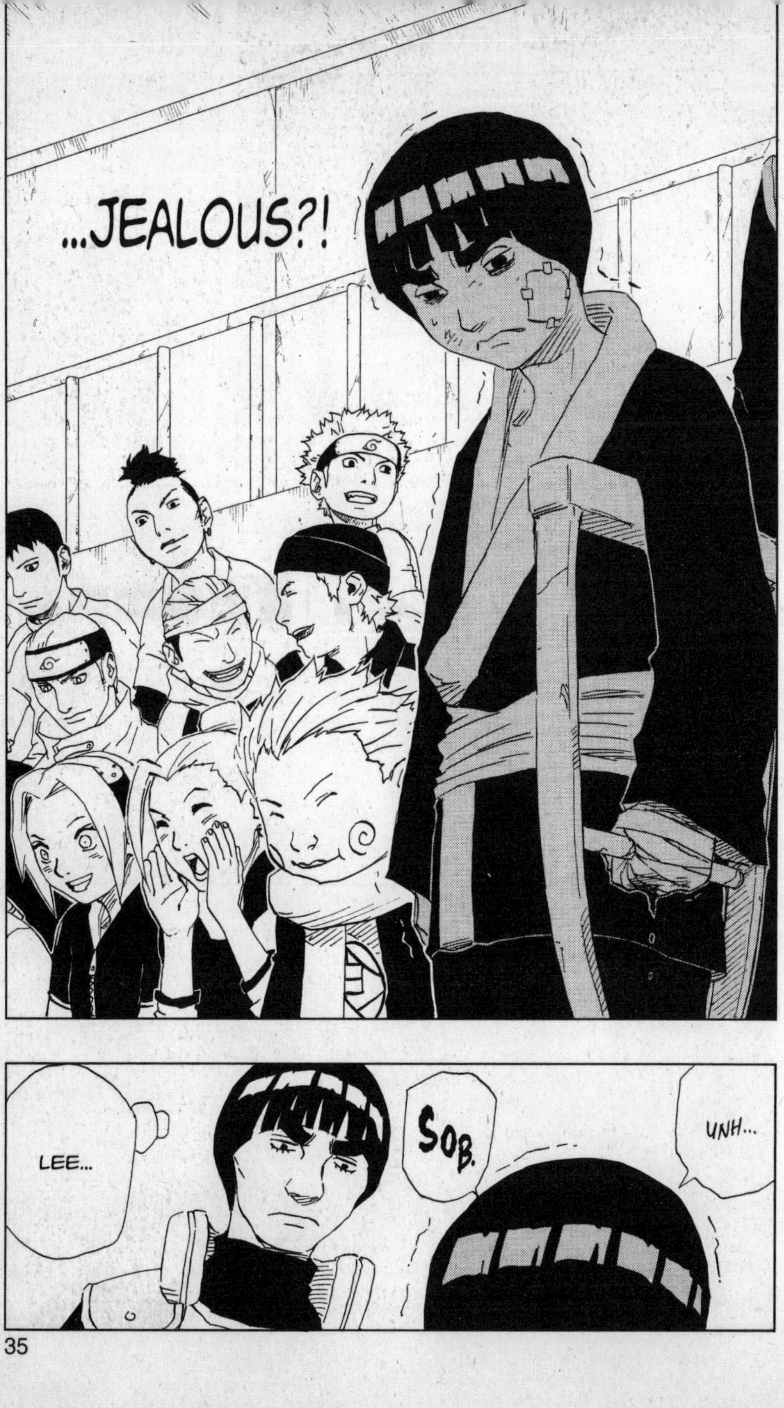
...JEALOUS?!
UNH...
SOB.
LEE...

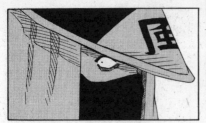

...

HEH HEH, AT LONG LAST...

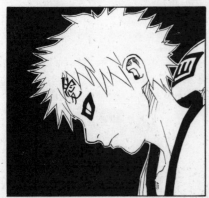

READ THIS WAY

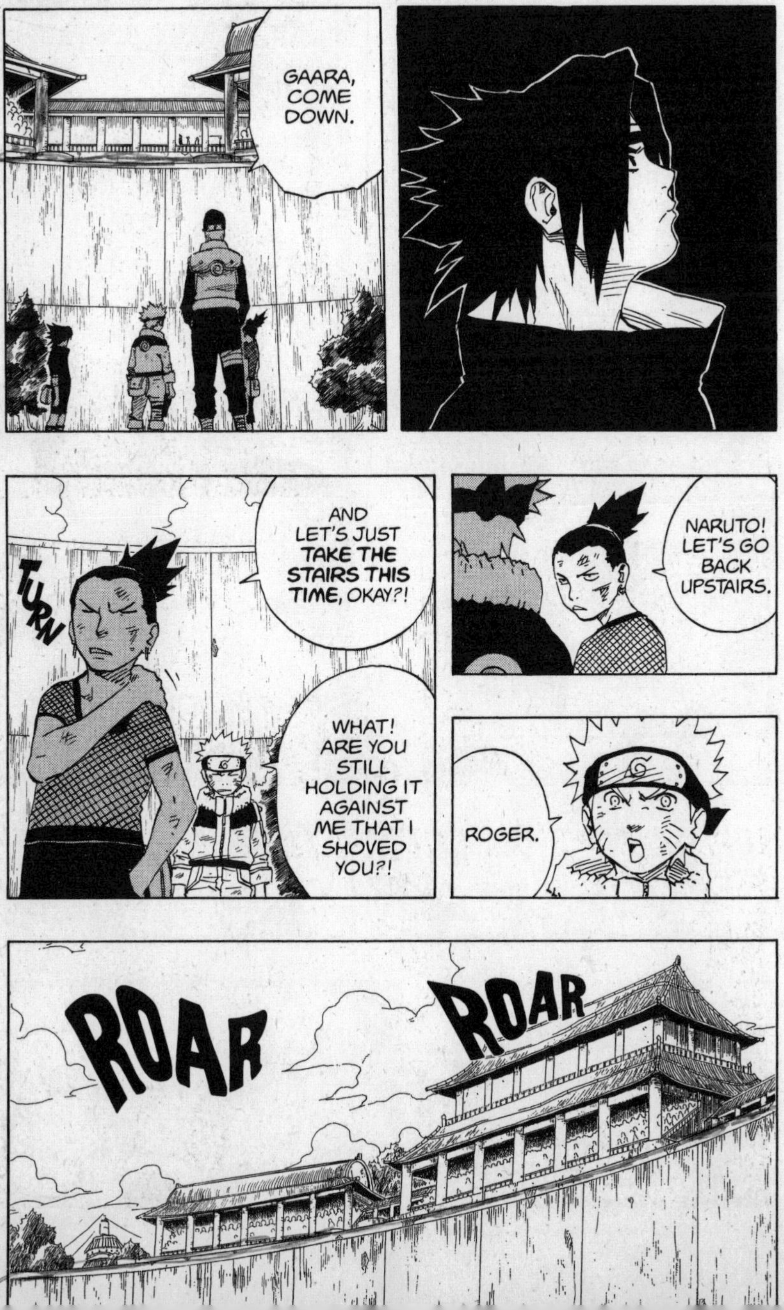
GAARA, COME DOWN.
NARUTO! LET'S GO BACK UPSTAIRS.
ROGER.
AND LET'S JUST TAKE THE STAIRS THIS TIME, OKAY?!
TURN
WHAT! ARE YOU STILL HOLDING IT AGAINST ME THAT I SHOVED YOU?!
ROAR
ROAR

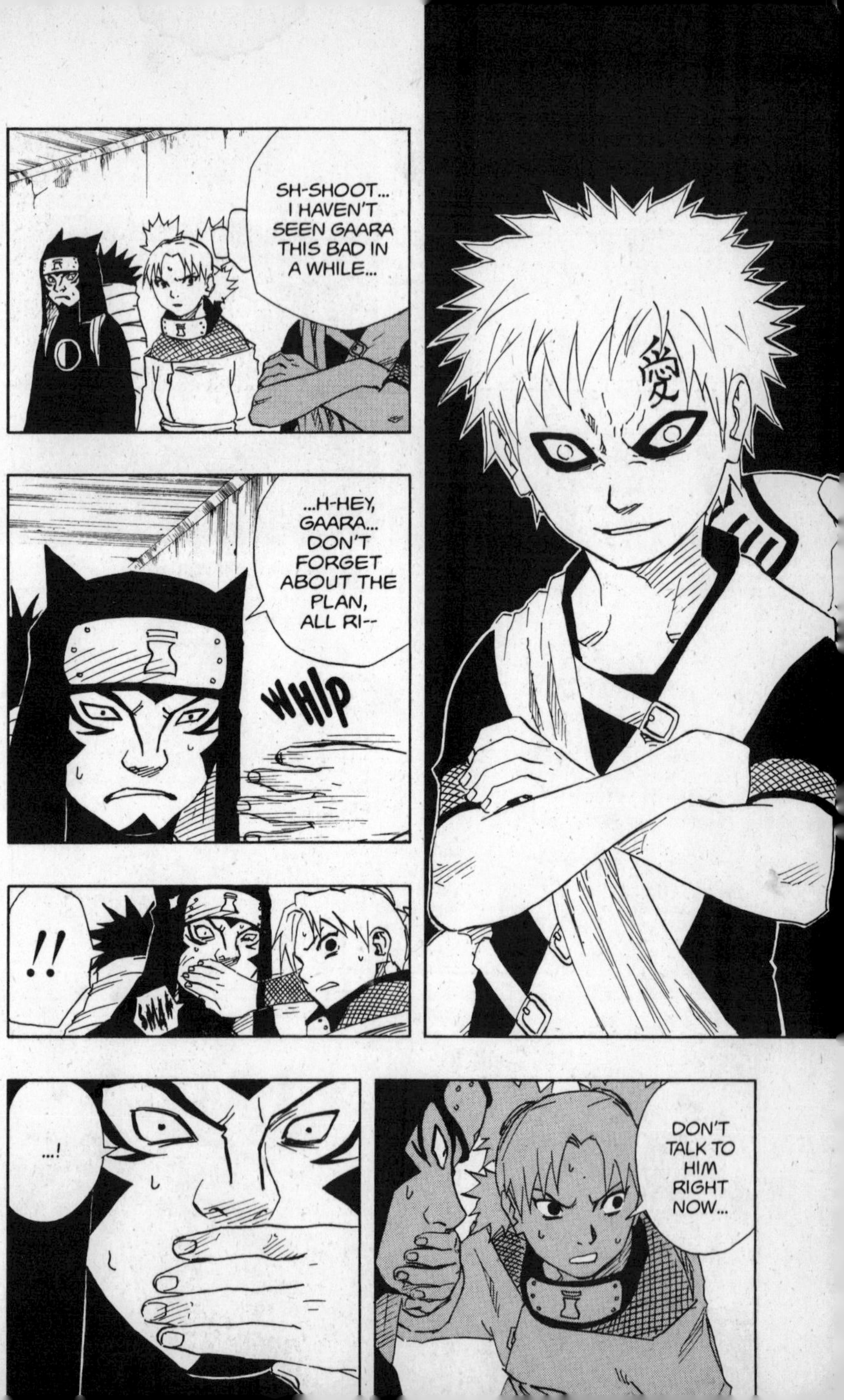
SH-SHOOT... I HAVEN'T SEEN GAARA THIS BAD IN A WHILE...
...H-HEY, GAARA... DON'T FORGET ABOUT THE PLAN, ALL RI--
WHIP
!!
DON'T TALK TO HIM RIGHT NOW...
...!

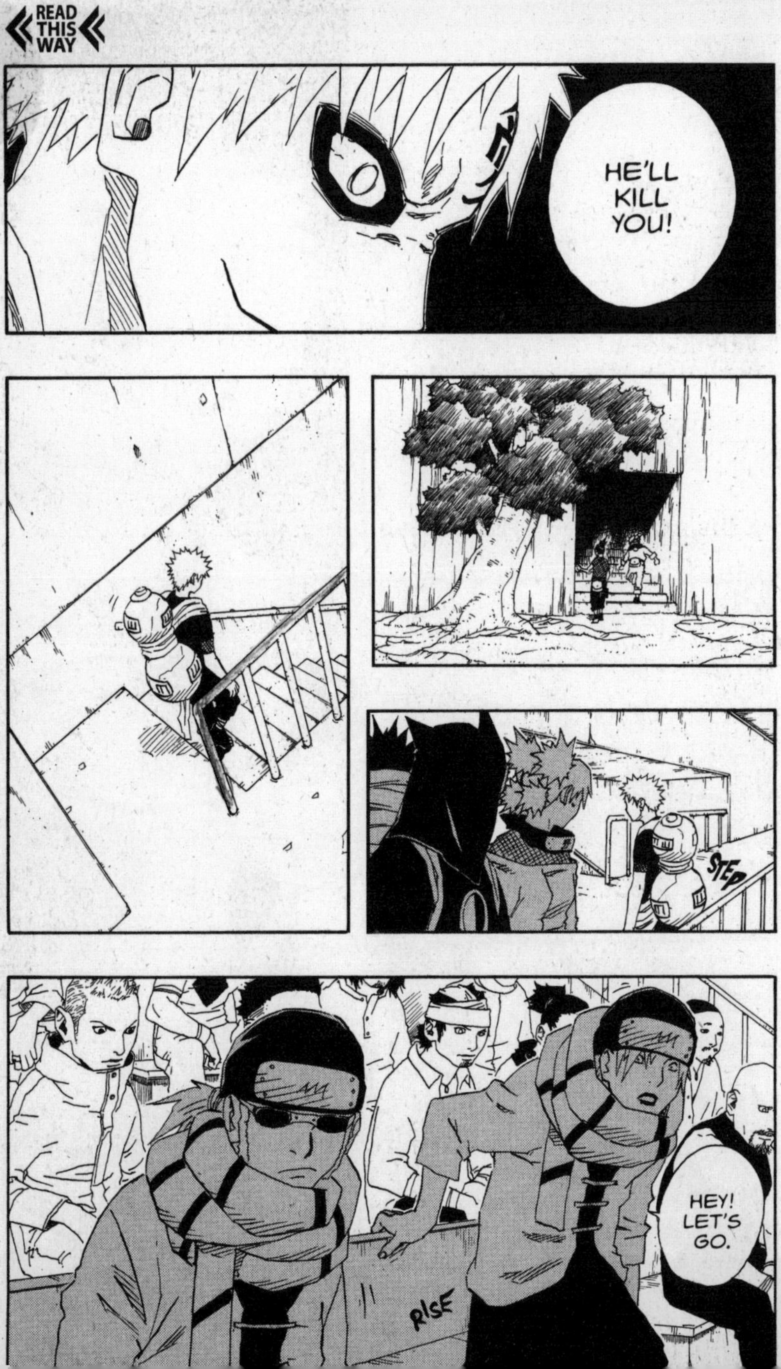
READ THIS WAY
HE'LL KILL YOU!
STEP
HEY! LET'S GO.
RISE

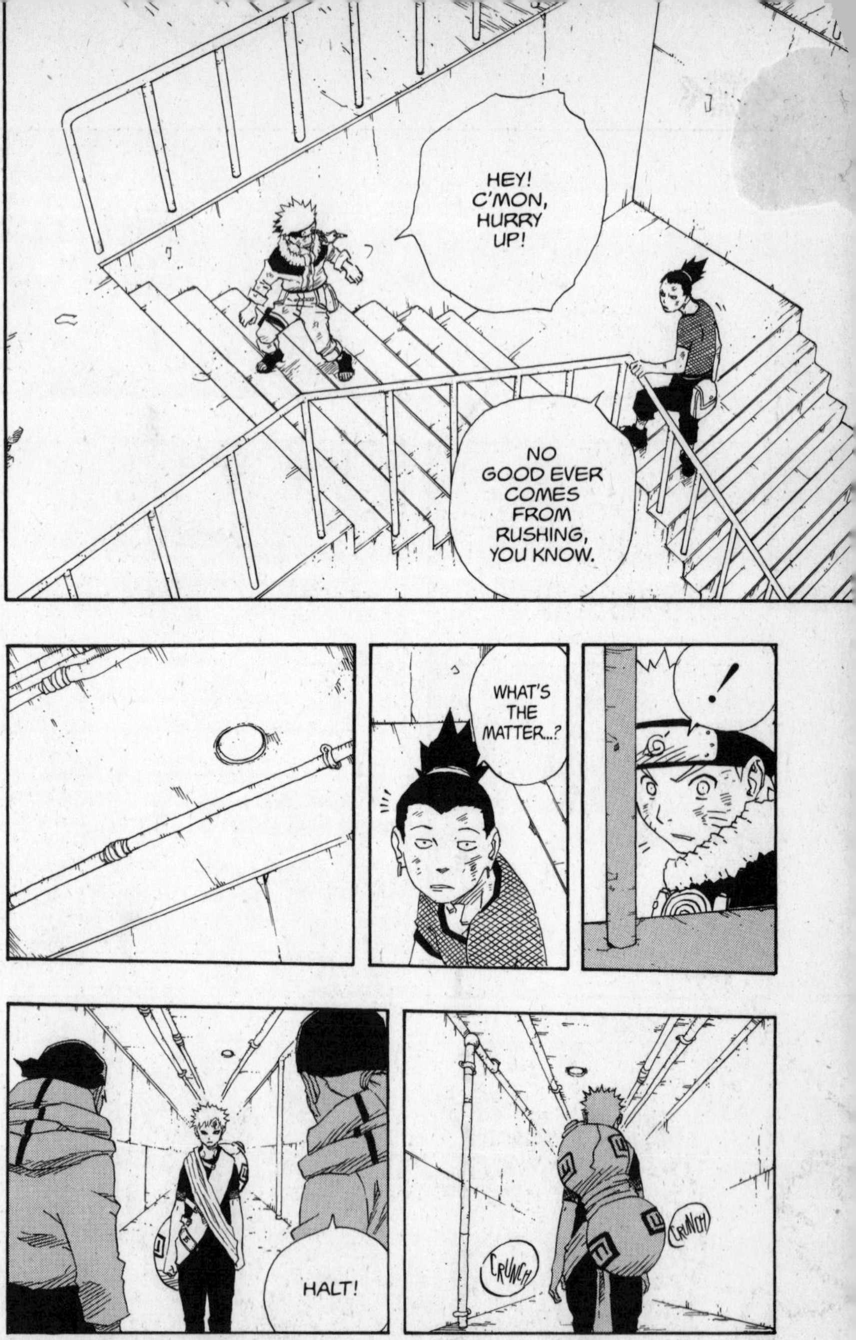
HEY! C'MON, HURRY UP!
NO GOOD EVER COMES FROM RUSHING, YOU KNOW.
!
WHAT'S THE MATTER...?
CRUNCH
CRUNCH
HALT!

READ THIS WAY

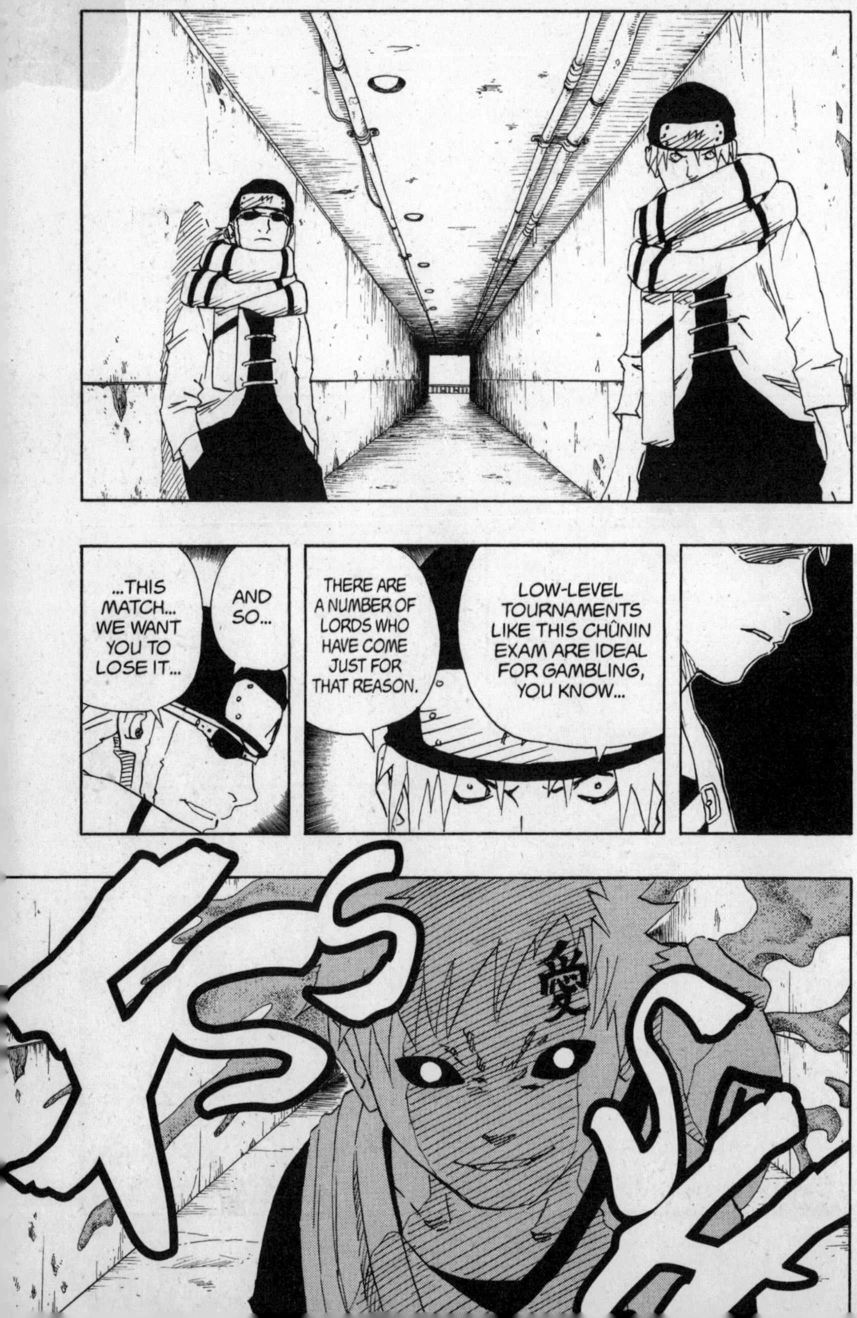
LOW-LEVEL TOURNAMENTS LIKE THIS CHÛNIN EXAM ARE IDEAL FOR GAMBLING, YOU KNOW...
THERE ARE A NUMBER OF LORDS WHO HAVE COME JUST FOR THAT REASON.
AND SO...
...THIS MATCH... WE WANT YOU TO LOSE IT...

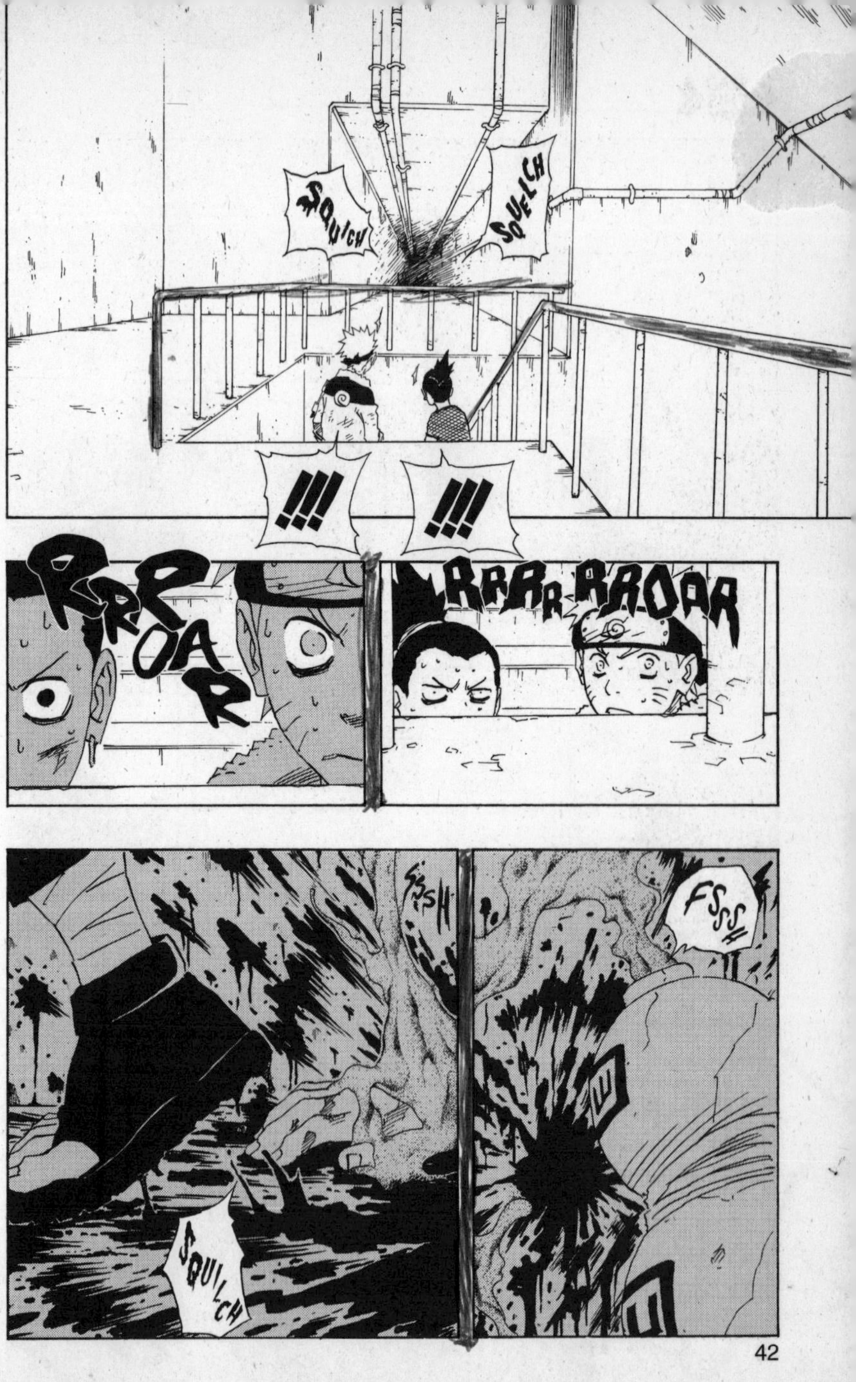
SQUELCH
SQUICH
!!!
!!!
RRRR-RROAR
RRROAR
FSSS
SSSH
SQUILCH

READ THIS WAY

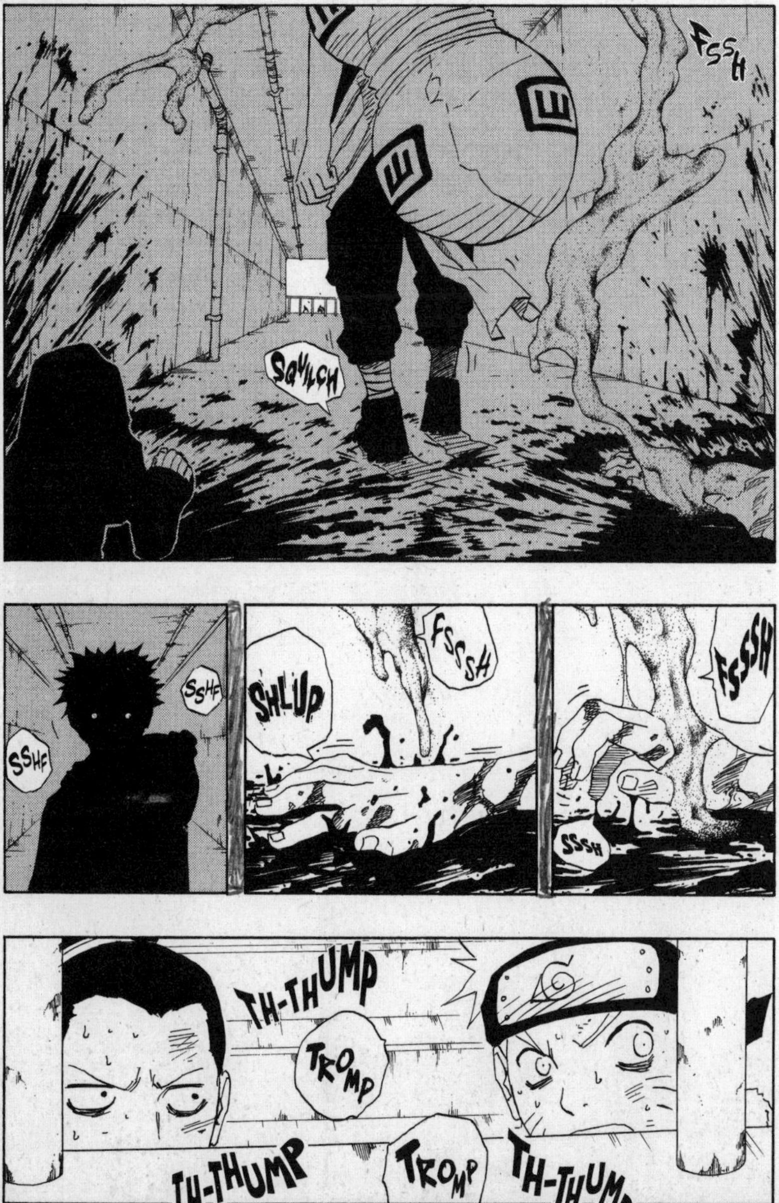
FSSH
SQUILCH
FSSSH
SSSH
FSSSH
SHLUP
SSHF
SSHF
TH-THUMP
TROMP
TH-THUMP
TROMP
TH-THUMP

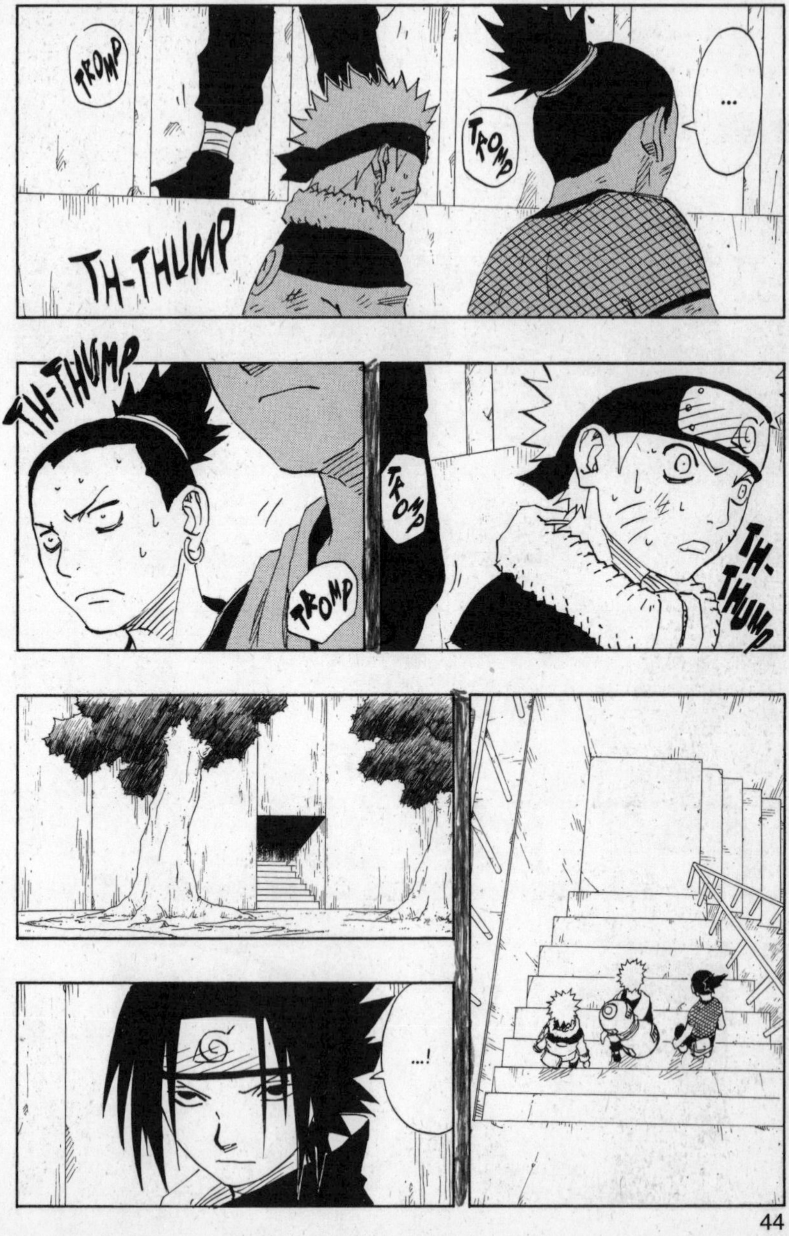
...
TROMP
TROMP
TH-THUMP
TROMP
TH-THUMP
TROMP
TROMP
TH-THUMP
...!

READ THIS WAY

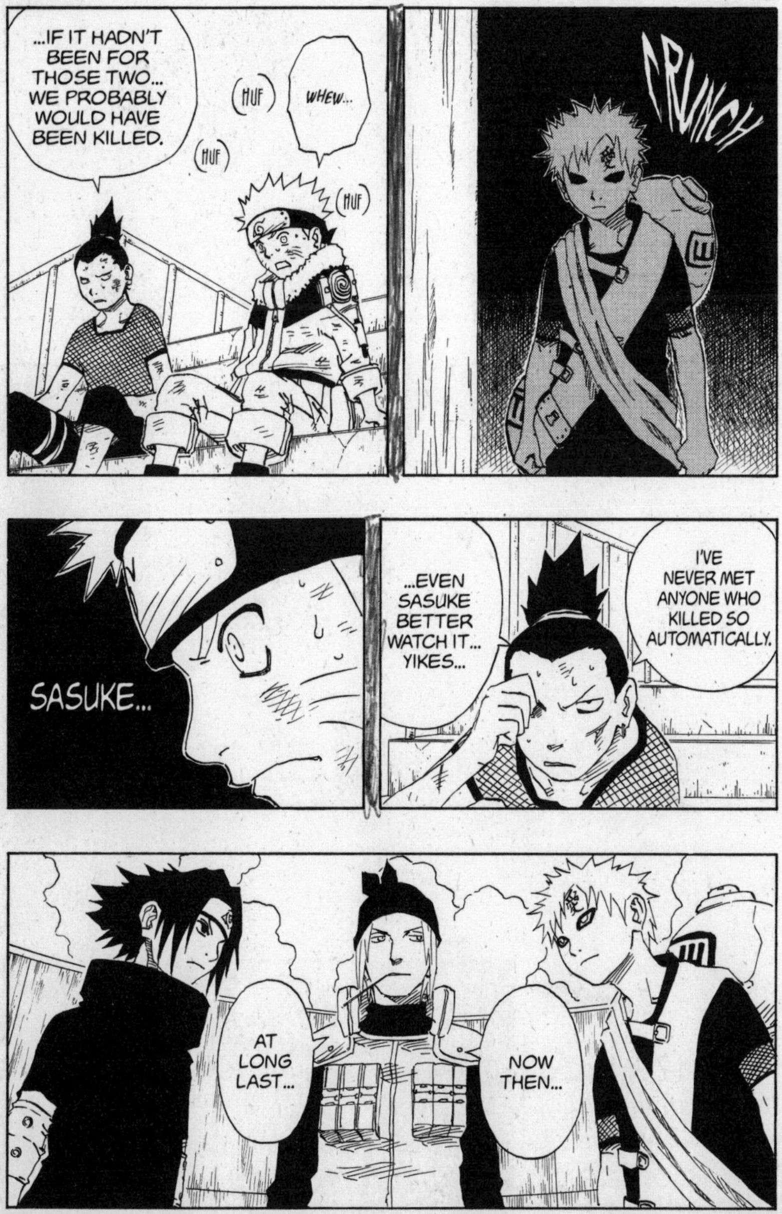
CRUNCH
WHEW...
HUF
HUF
...IF IT HADN'T BEEN FOR THOSE TWO... WE PROBABLY WOULD HAVE BEEN KILLED.
HUF
I'VE NEVER MET ANYONE WHO KILLED SO AUTOMATICALLY.
...EVEN SASUKE BETTER WATCH IT... YIKES...
SASUKE...
NOW THEN...
AT LONG LAST...

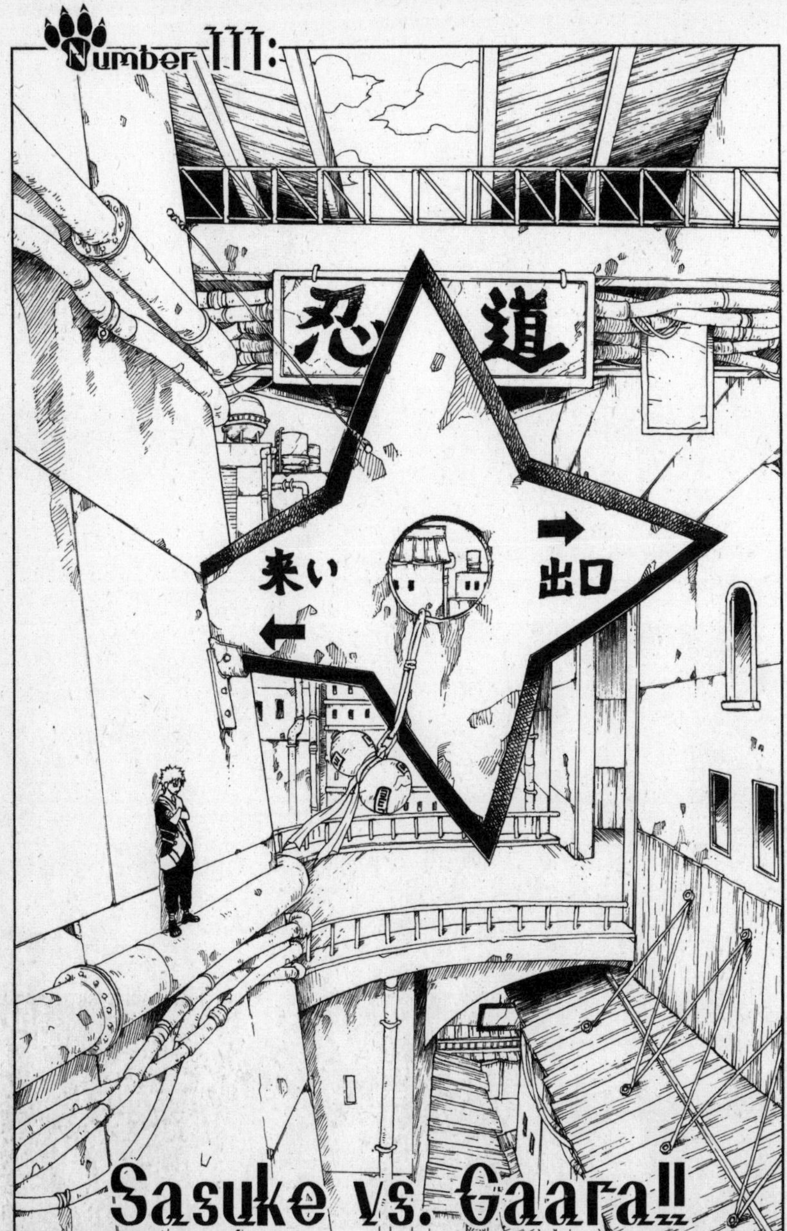
Number 111:
忍道
→ 出口
来い ←
Sasuke vs. Gaara!!

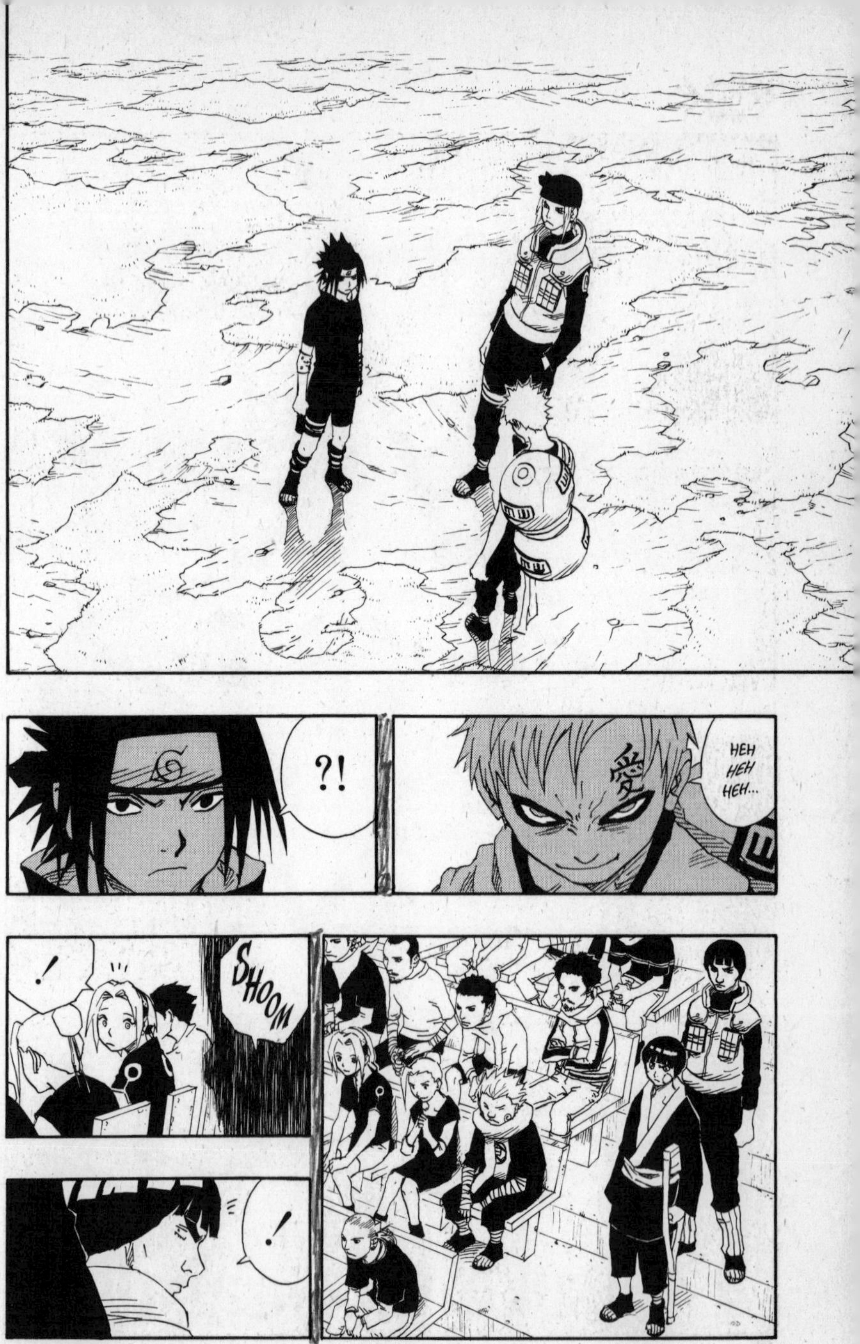
HEH HEH HEH...
?!
SHOOM
!
!

READ THIS WAY

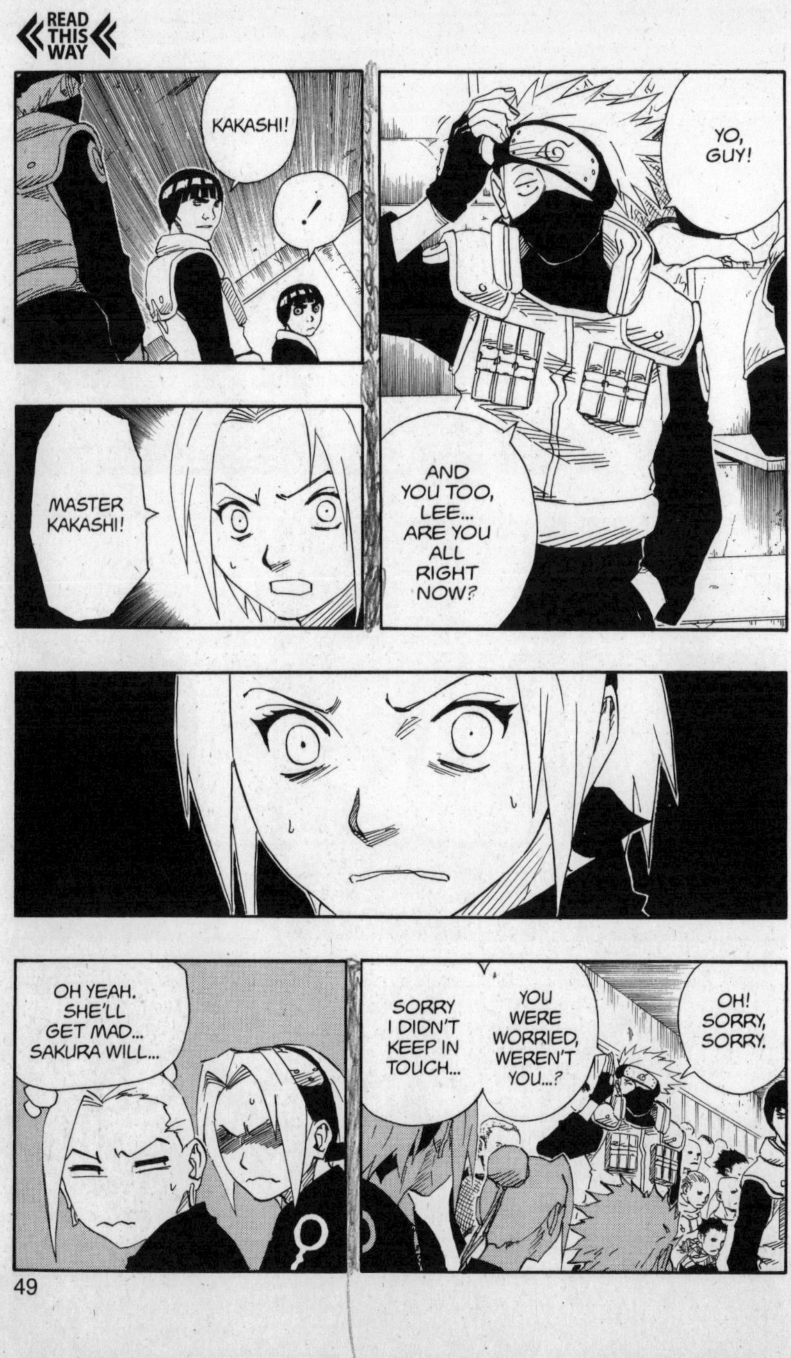
YO, GUY!
AND YOU TOO, LEE... ARE YOU ALL RIGHT NOW?
KAKASHI!
!
MASTER KAKASHI!
OH! SORRY, SORRY.
YOU WERE WORRIED, WEREN'T YOU...?
SORRY I DIDN'T KEEP IN TOUCH...
OH YEAH. SHE'LL GET MAD... SAKURA WILL...

! ...IT'S ALL RIGHT.

I CAN'T SEE IT VERY WELL FROM UP HERE...

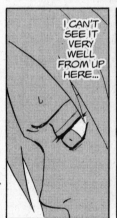

...!

...MASTER KAKASHI...

...

READ THIS WAY

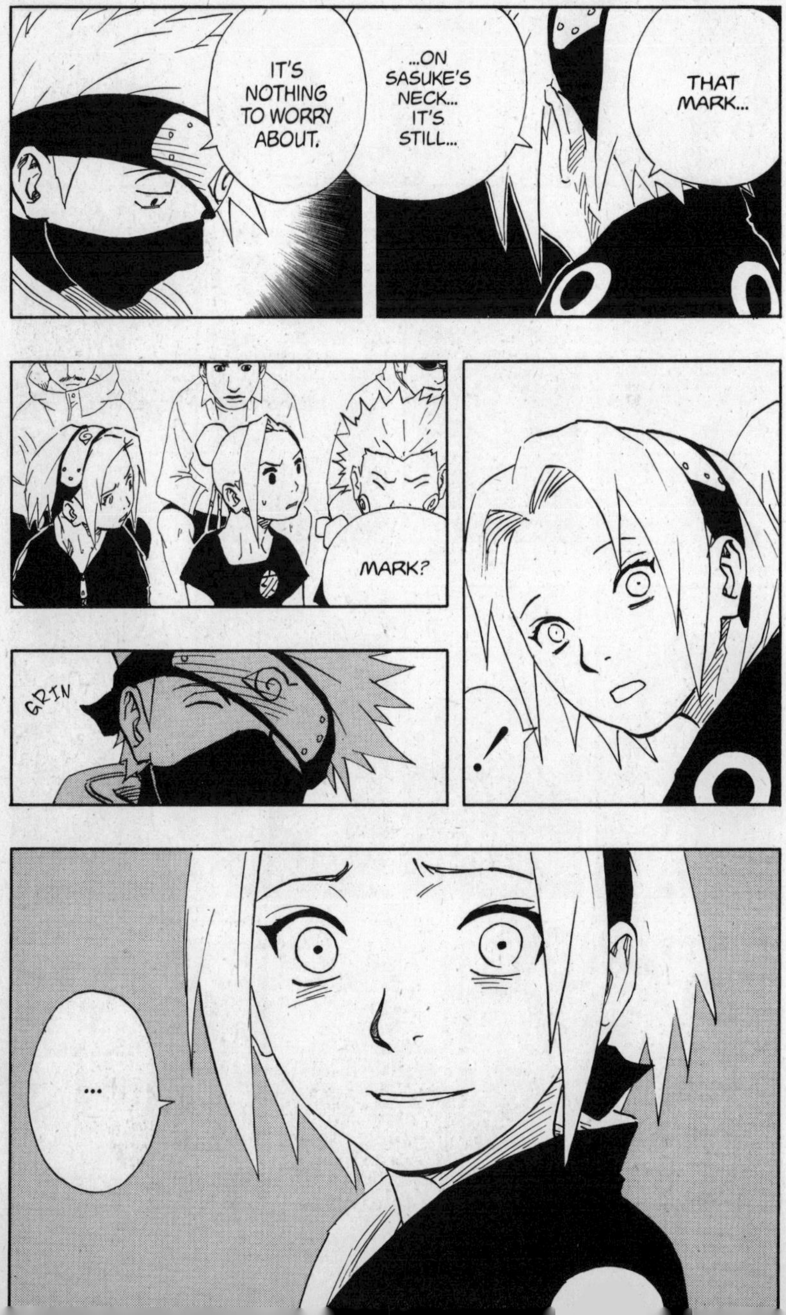
THAT MARK...
...ON SASUKE'S NECK... IT'S STILL...
IT'S NOTHING TO WORRY ABOUT.
!
MARK?
GRIN
...

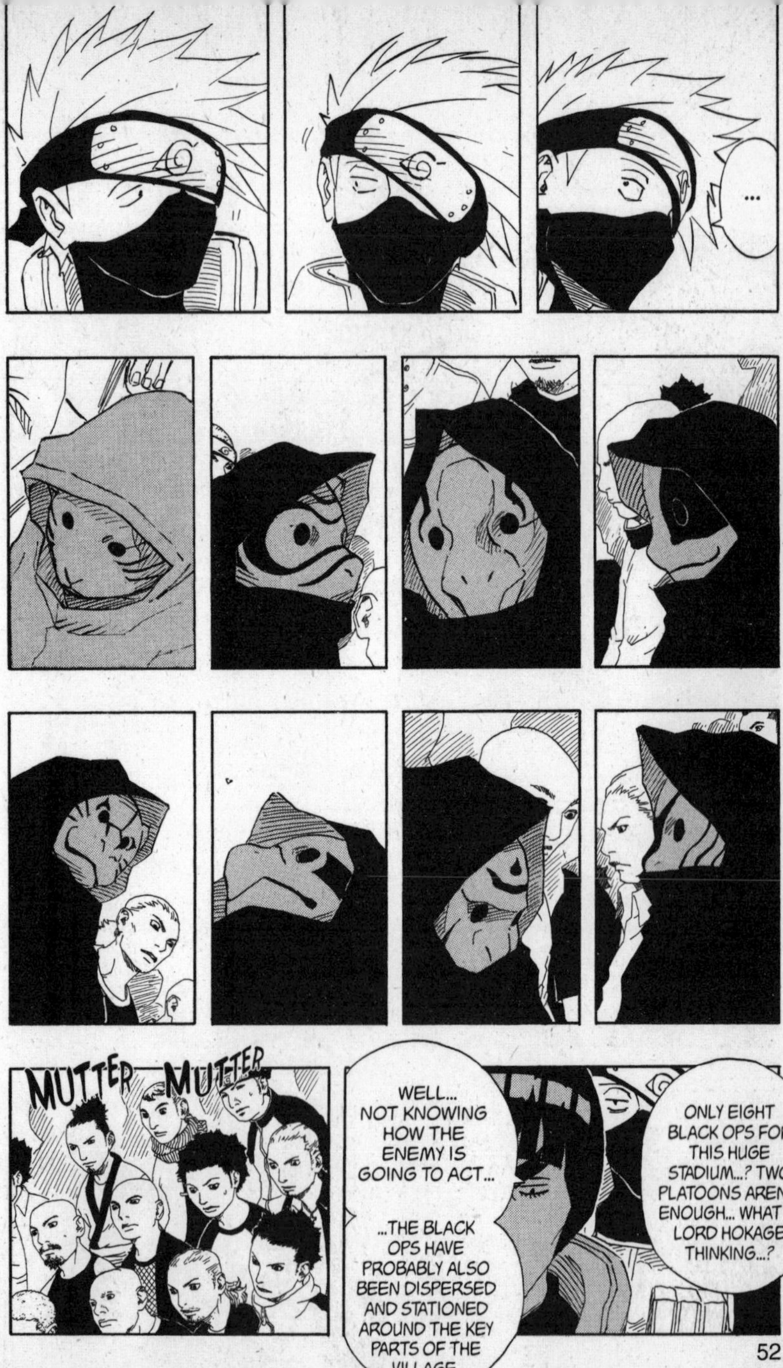
...
MUTTER MUTTER
WELL... NOT KNOWING HOW THE ENEMY IS GOING TO ACT...
...THE BLACK OPS HAVE PROBABLY ALSO BEEN DISPERSED AND STATIONED AROUND THE KEY PARTS OF THE VILLAGE.
ONLY EIGHT BLACK OPS FOR THIS HUGE STADIUM...? TWO PLATOONS AREN'T ENOUGH... WHAT IS LORD HOKAGE THINKING...?

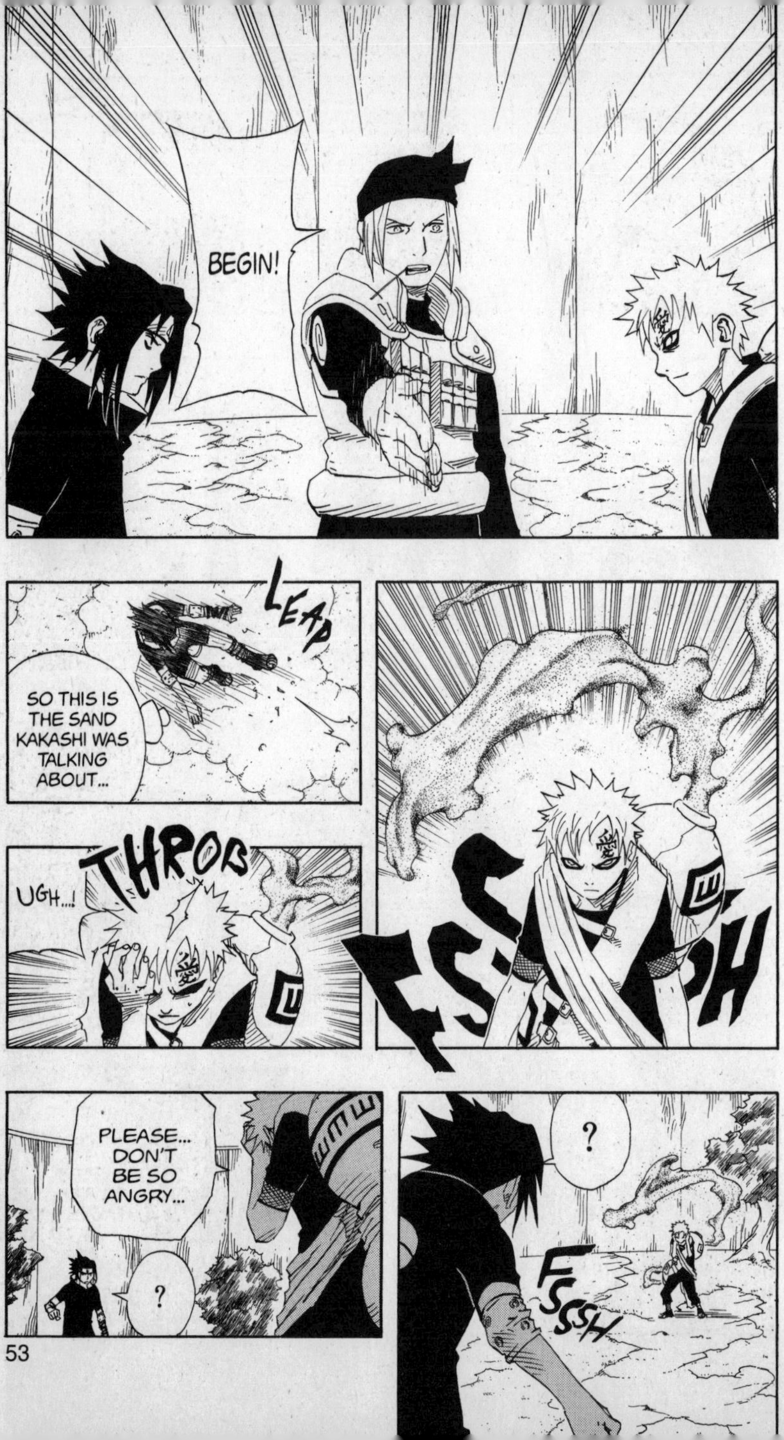
BEGIN!
LEAP
SO THIS IS THE SAND KAKASHI WAS TALKING ABOUT...
THROB
UGH...!
?
FSSSH
PLEASE... DON'T BE SO ANGRY...
?

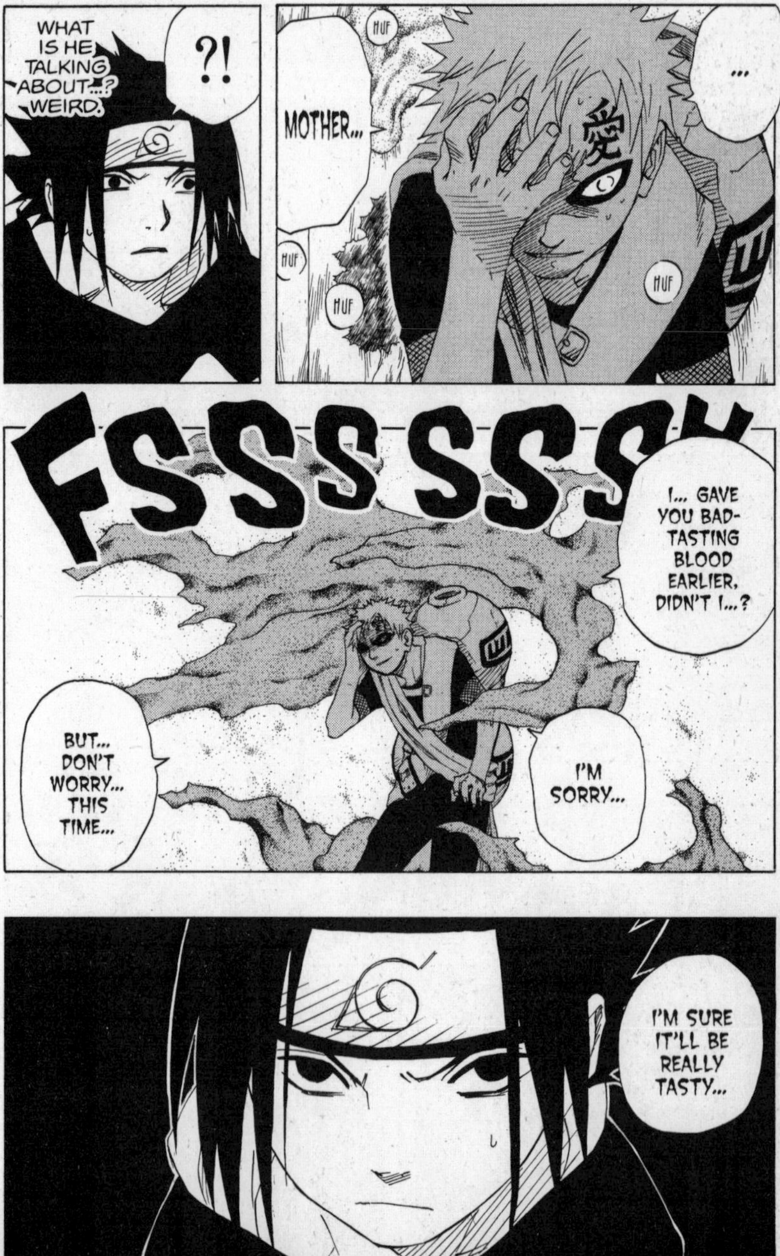
...
HUF
MOTHER...
HUF
HUF
HUF
?!
WHAT IS HE TALKING ABOUT...? WEIRD.
FSSSSS
I... GAVE YOU BAD-TASTING BLOOD EARLIER, DIDN'T I...?
I'M SORRY...
BUT... DON'T WORRY... THIS TIME...
I'M SURE IT'LL BE REALLY TASTY...

READ THIS WAY

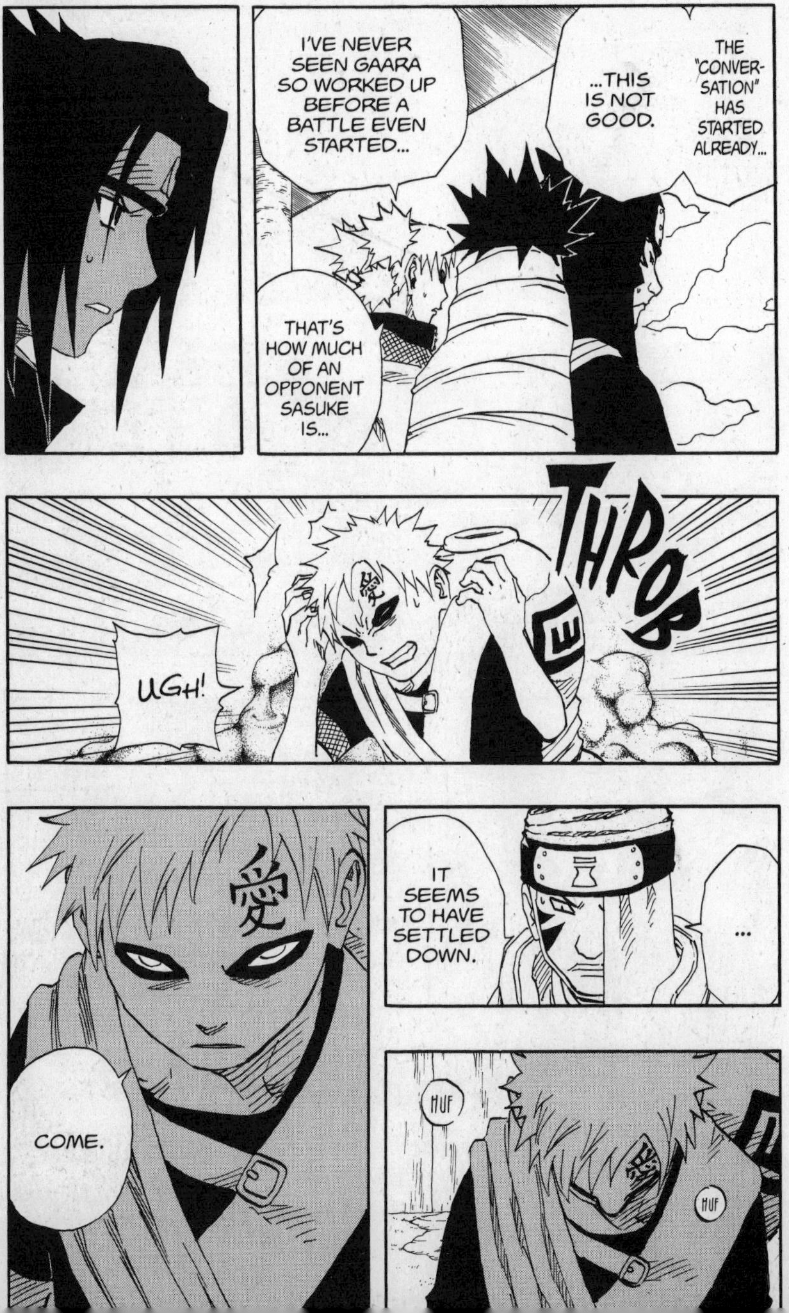
THE "CONVER-SATION" HAS STARTED ALREADY...
...THIS IS NOT GOOD.
I'VE NEVER SEEN GAARA SO WORKED UP BEFORE A BATTLE EVEN STARTED...
THAT'S HOW MUCH OF AN OPPONENT SASUKE IS...
THROB
UGH!
...
IT SEEMS TO HAVE SETTLED DOWN.
HUF
HUF
COME.

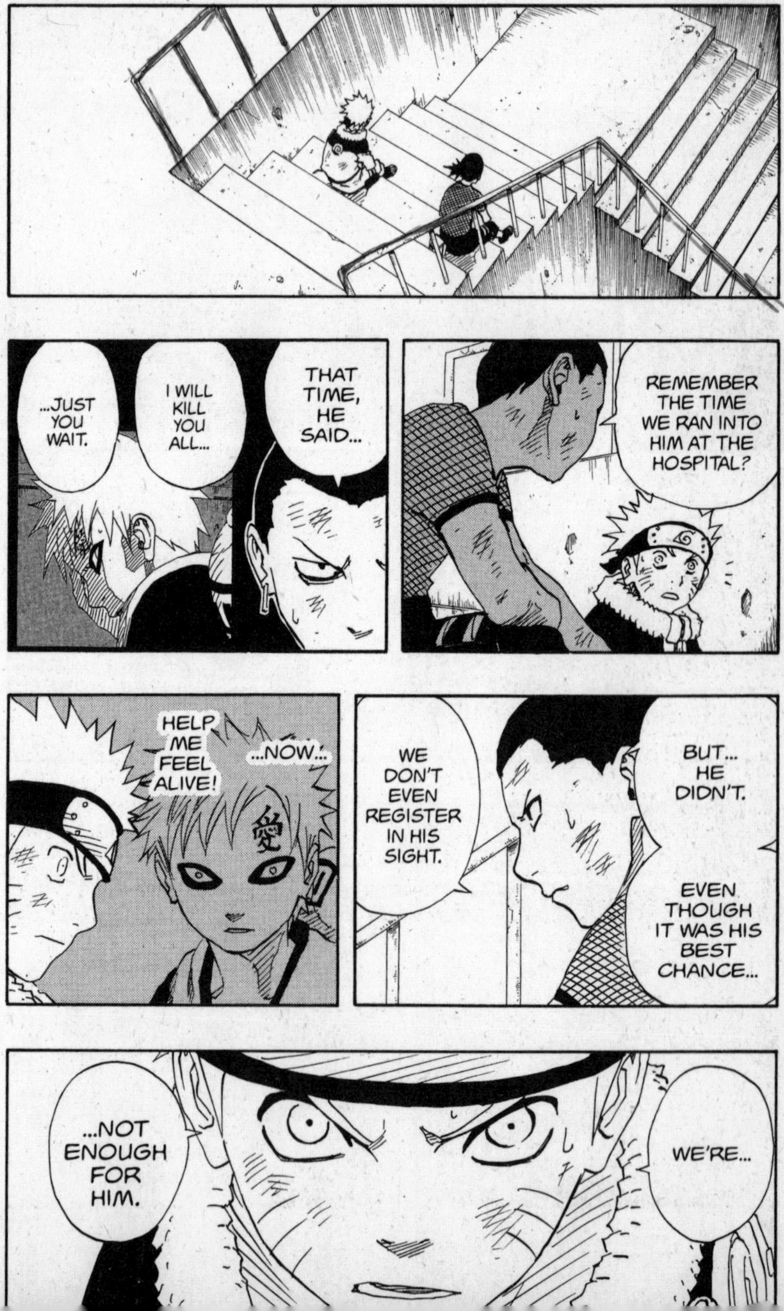
REMEMBER THE TIME WE RAN INTO HIM AT THE HOSPITAL?
THAT TIME, HE SAID...
I WILL KILL YOU ALL...
...JUST YOU WAIT.
BUT... HE DIDN'T.
EVEN THOUGH IT WAS HIS BEST CHANCE...
WE DON'T EVEN REGISTER IN HIS SIGHT.
...NOW...
HELP ME FEEL ALIVE!
WE'RE...
...NOT ENOUGH FOR HIM.

READ THIS WAY

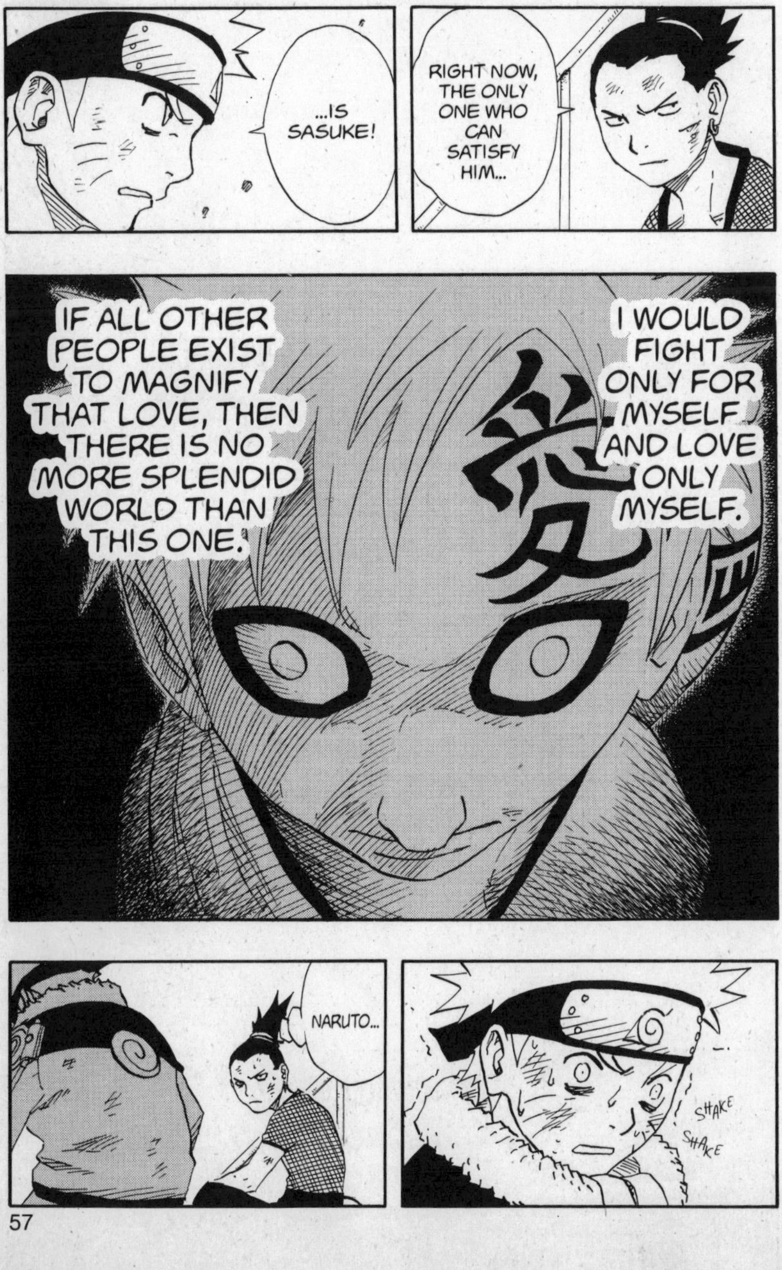

RIGHT NOW, THE ONLY ONE WHO CAN SATISFY HIM...
...IS SASUKE!
I WOULD FIGHT ONLY FOR MYSELF AND LOVE ONLY MYSELF.
IF ALL OTHER PEOPLE EXIST TO MAGNIFY THAT LOVE, THEN THERE IS NO MORE SPLENDID WORLD THAN THIS ONE.
SHAKE
SHAKE
NARUTO...

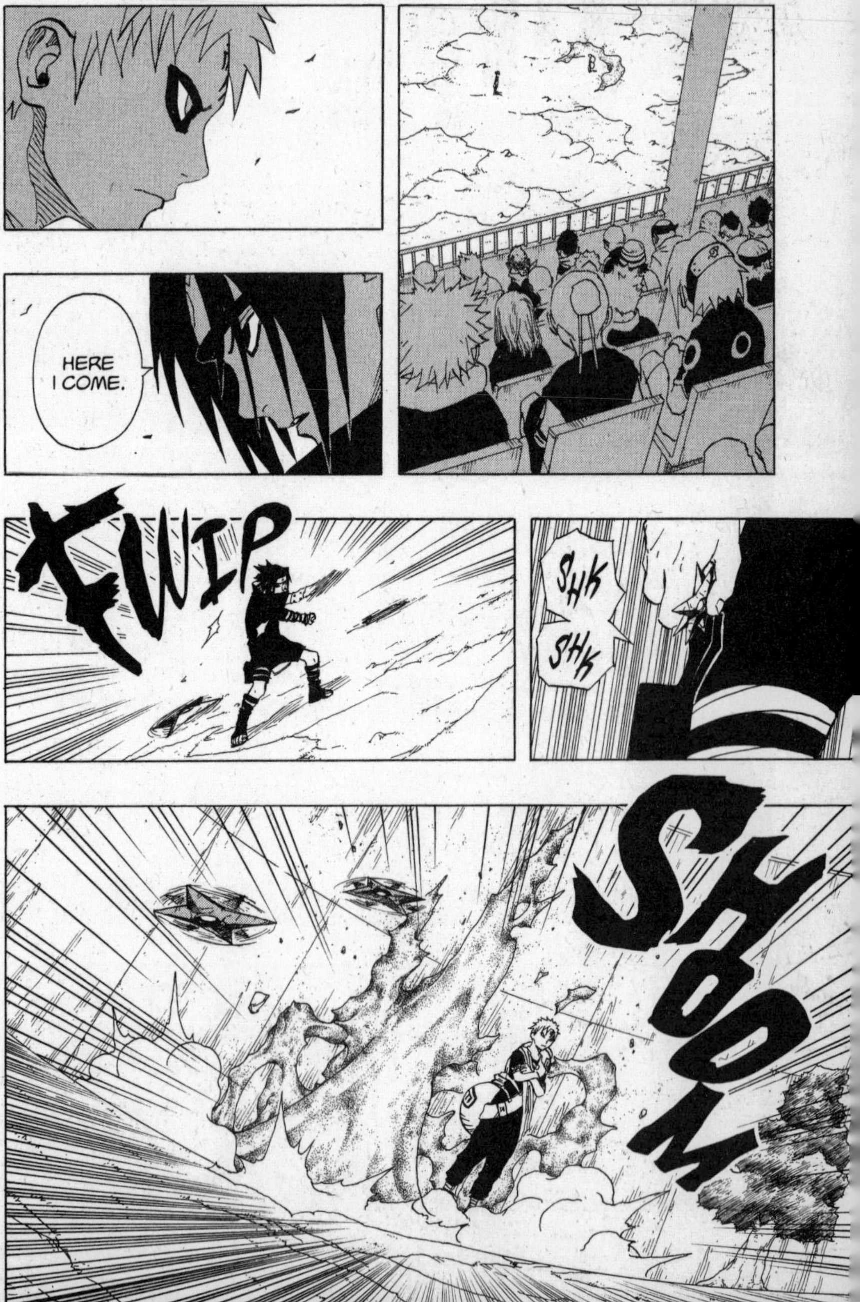
HERE I COME.
SHK
SHK
XWIP
SHOOM

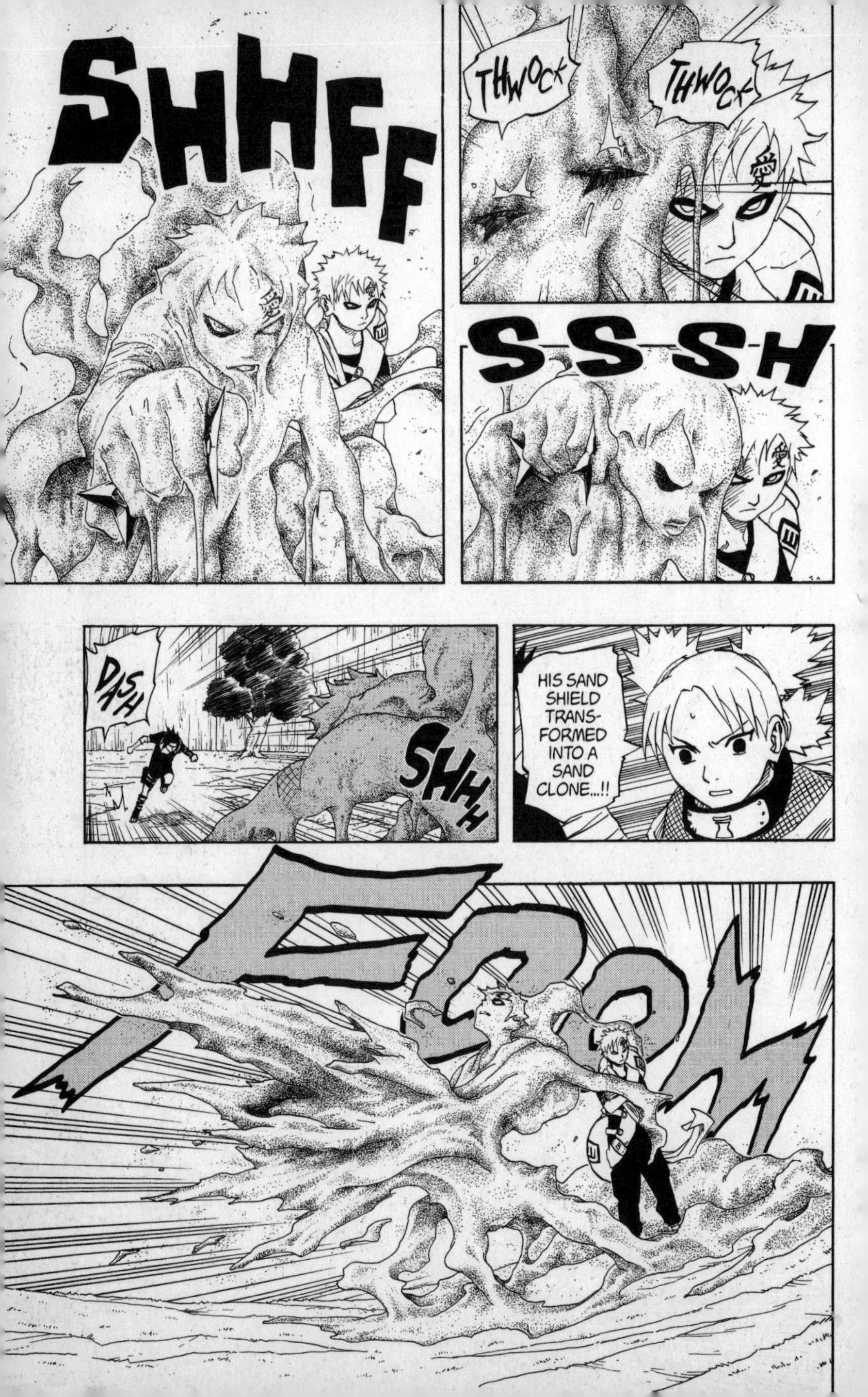
THWOCK
THWOCK
S-S-SH
SHHFF
HIS SAND SHIELD TRANSFORMED INTO A SAND CLONE...!!
DASH
SHHH

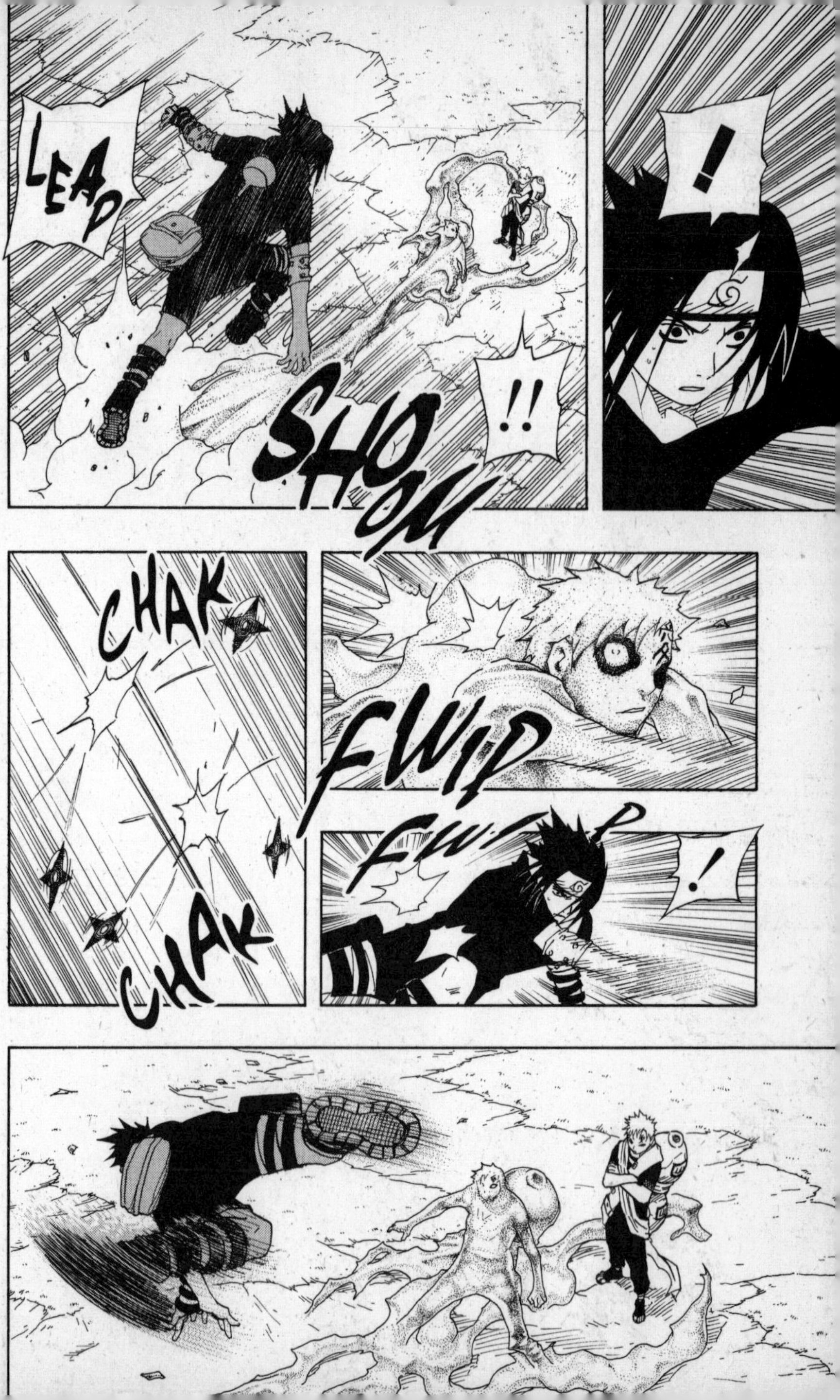
!
LEAP
!!
SHOOM
FWIP
FWUP
!
CHAK
CHAK

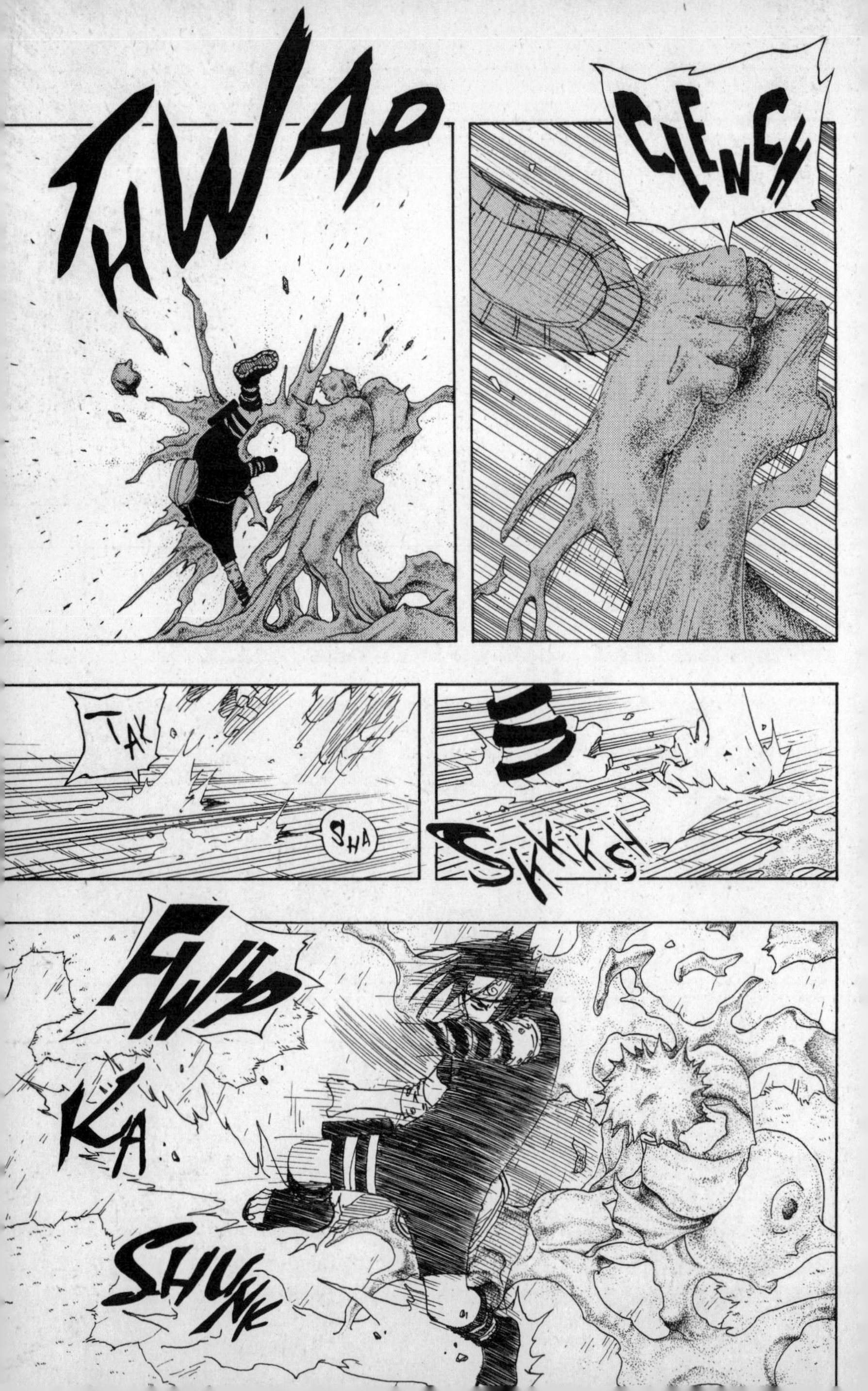

CLENCH
THWAP
SKKKSH
TAK
SHA
FWIP
KA
SHUNK

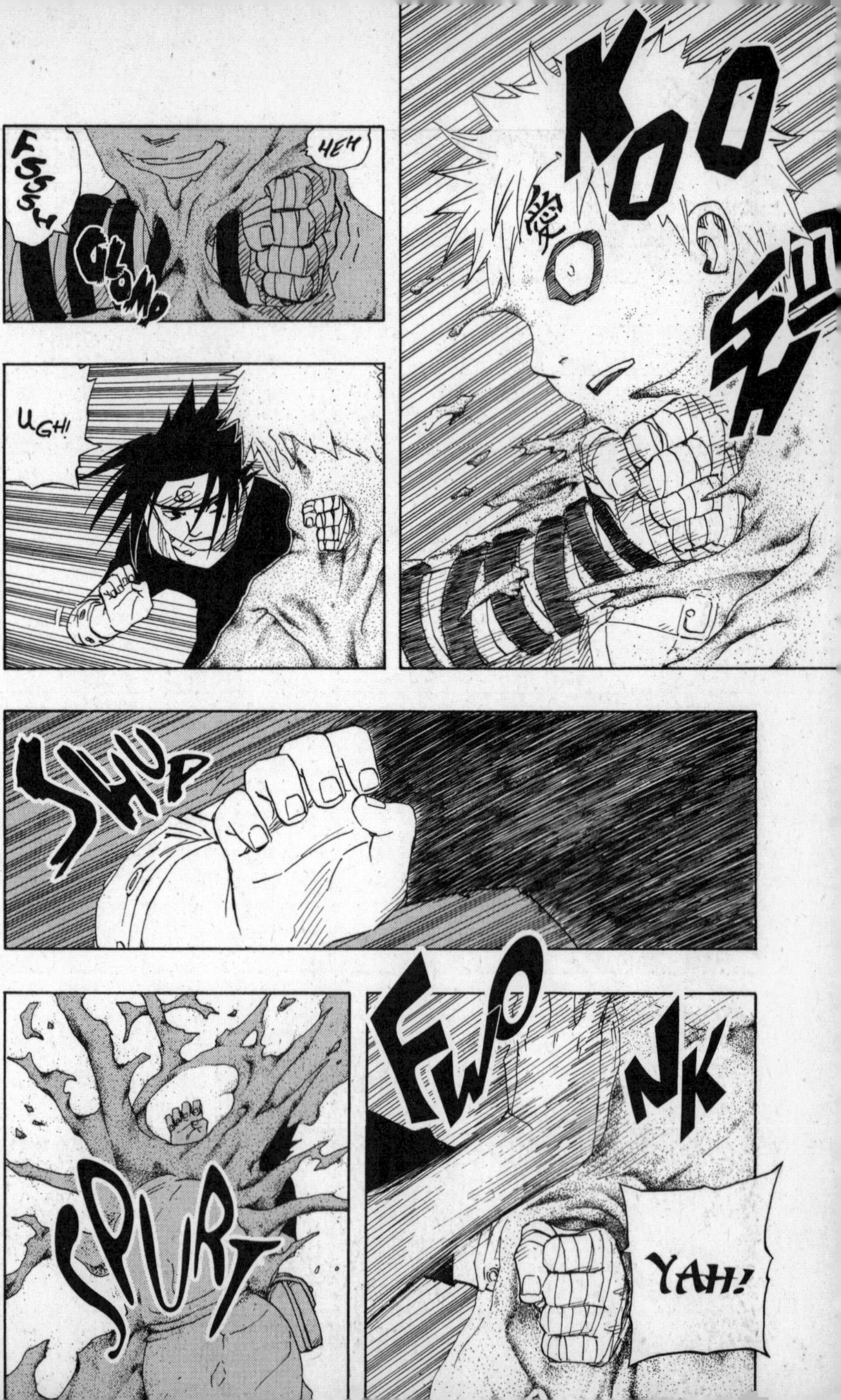
KOOSH
FSSSH
GLOMP
HEH
UGH!
SHUP
FWONK
YAH!
SPURT

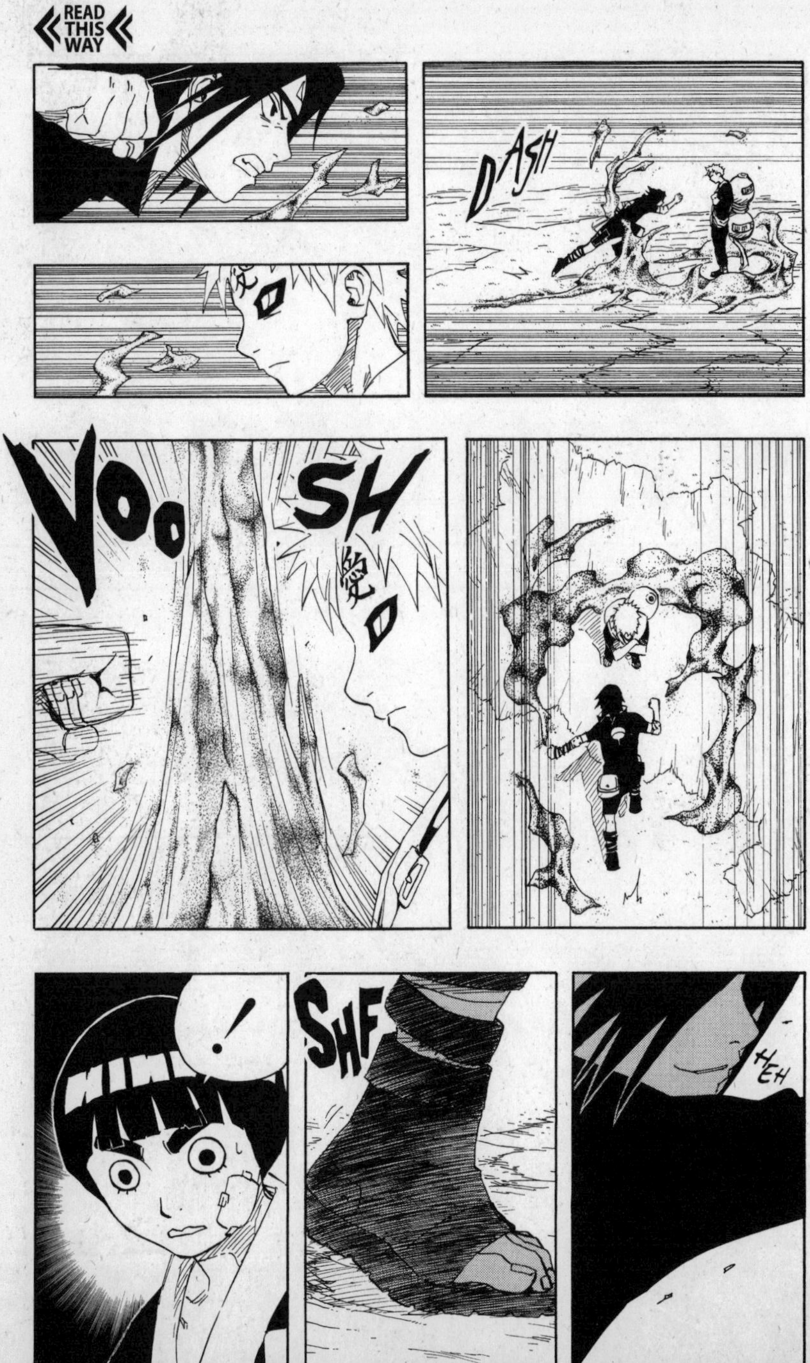
READ THIS WAY
DASH
VOOSH
!
SHF
HEH

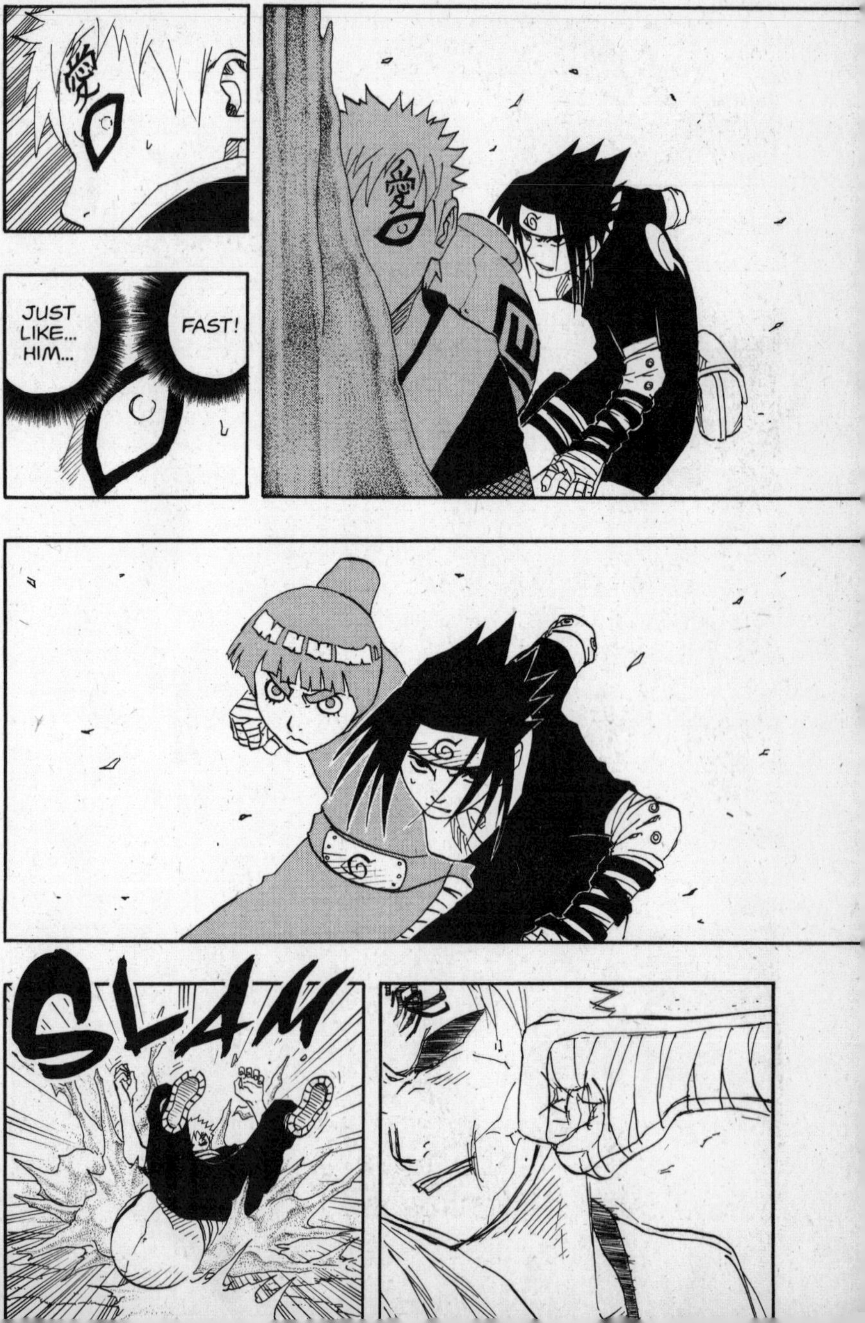
FAST!
JUST LIKE... HIM...
SLAM

READ THIS WAY

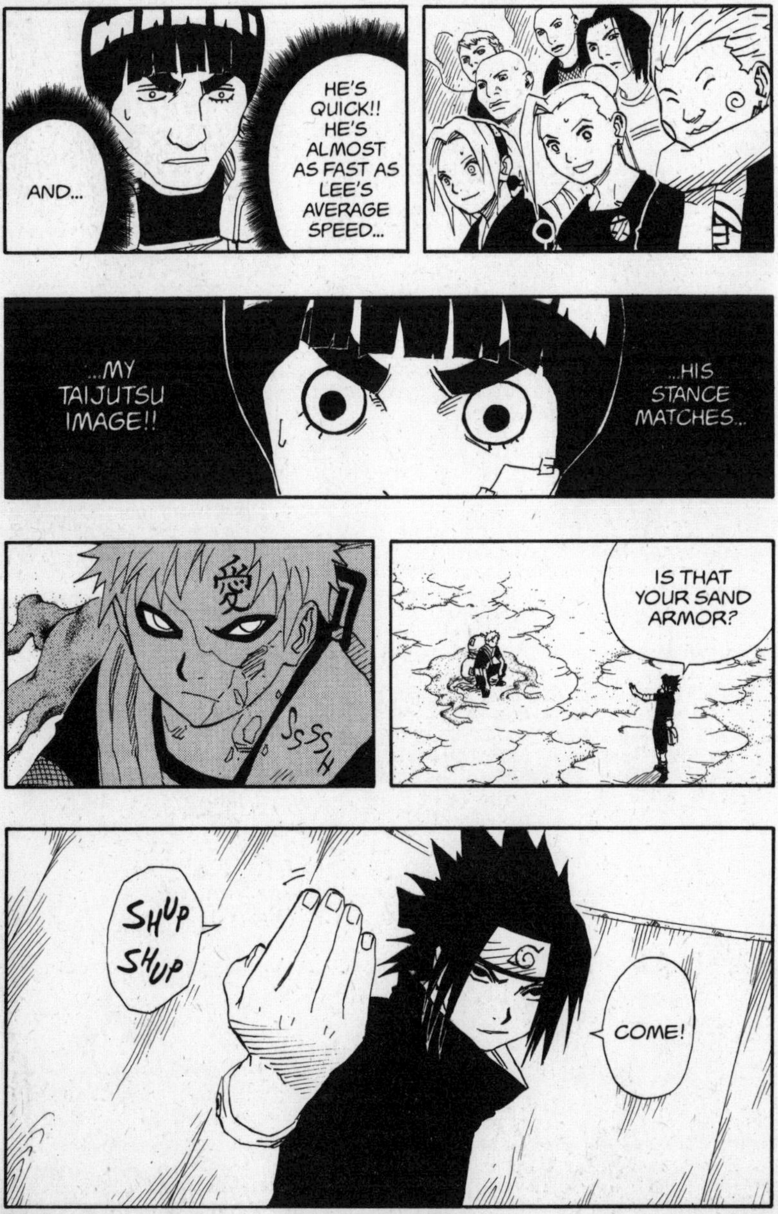
HE'S QUICK!! HE'S ALMOST AS FAST AS LEE'S AVERAGE SPEED...
AND...
...HIS STANCE MATCHES...
...MY TAIJUTSU IMAGE!!
IS THAT YOUR SAND ARMOR?
SS-SSH
COME!
SHUP SHUP

THE WORLD OF KISHIMOTO MASASHI
MY PERSONAL HISTORY, PART 17

HAVING BRILLIANTLY ACHIEVED COLLEGE STUDENT STATUS AND HAVING ALL OF MY CLASSES REVOLVE AROUND DRAWING MADE FOR A DREAMLIKE, HAPPY EXISTENCE FOR ME.

AND NOW THAT I WAS A FIRST-YEAR COLLEGE STUDENT, I WAS ABOUT TO TURN 19 YEARS OLD! I STARTED FURIOUSLY DRAWING MANGA, WITH *JUMP'S* HOP ☆ STEP AWARD AS MY GOAL. "I FEEL A SAMURAI MANGA COMING ON RIGHT NOW!" I THOUGHT, SO I STEADILY DREW A SAMURAI MANGA, BUT THEN, JUST AS I WAS ABOUT TO COMPLETE IT, AN UNBE-LIEVABLE THING HAPPENED...!!

YIKES! A DOUBLE PUNCH OF NEWCOMERS WHO WERE BOTH THINKING THE SAME THING AND HAD GOOD ART SENSE--I COULDN'T BELIEVE THERE WERE SO MANY!! AND IN THIS WORLD, THE EARLY BIRD REALLY DOES GET THE WORM...!

IN THE STAND-ALONE STORY SECTION OF *JUMP* APPEARED A MANGA BY *RUROUNI KENSHIN* AUTHOR WATSUKI NOBUHIRO-SENSEI! AT THE TIME, THE TITLE DID NOT YET HAVE "KENSHIN" IN IT, BUT IT STILL HAD A HUGE EFFECT ON ME. IN ADDITION, AROUND THE SAME TIME, SAMURA HIROAKI OF THE IMMORTAL SAMURAI *BLADE OF THE IMMORTAL* FAME ALSO WON THE GRAND PRIZE AND FOREVER CHANGED THE STANDARD FOR *AFTERNOON'S* RISING ARTISTS' CONTEST!! SAMURA'S ART AND STORY WERE WAY ABOVE THE LEVEL OF A NEWCOMER, ALMOST THAT OF A FULL PRO!

I RECEIVED THE BIGGEST SHOCK OF MY LIFE SINCE *AKIRA*!

WHEN I CAREFULLY REREAD MY OWN SAMURAI MANGA WITH THOSE TWO AMAZING WORKS IN FRONT OF ME, I FELT MY OWN PUNINESS MORE THAN I CARED TO... OF COURSE, I STILL ENTERED THAT SAMURAI MANGA INTO THE CONTEST, BUT IT DIDN'T EVEN MAKE A MARK... MY PATH TOWARDS BECOMING A MANGA-KA STILL STRETCHED FAR BEFORE ME, WROUGHT WITH PERIL!

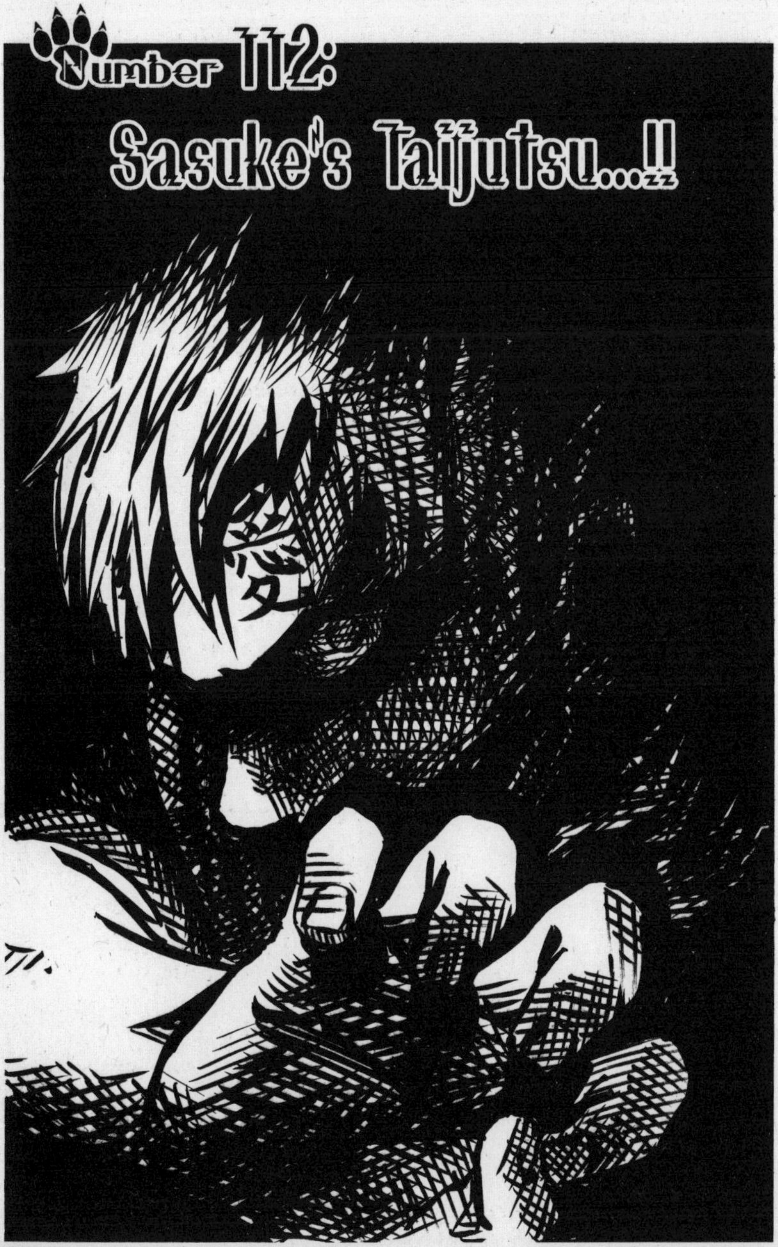
Number 112:
Sasuke's Taijutsu...!!

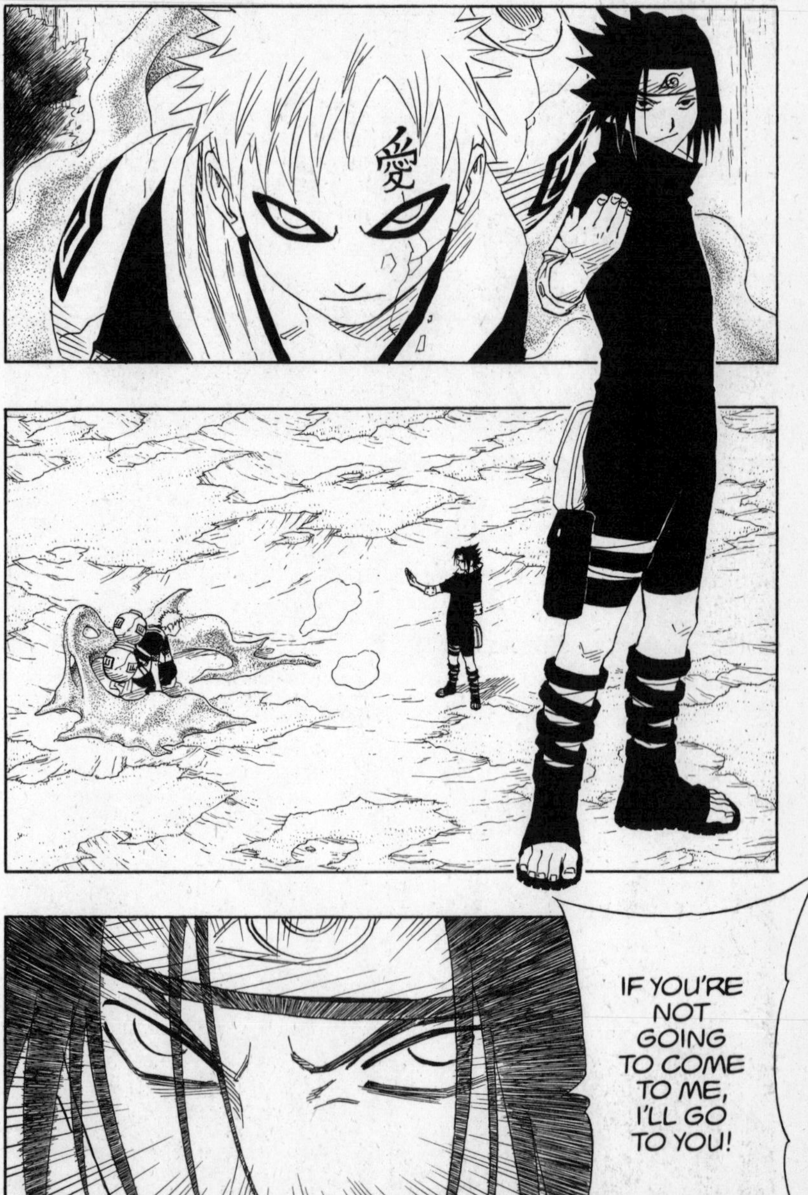
IF YOU'RE NOT GOING TO COME TO ME, I'LL GO TO YOU!

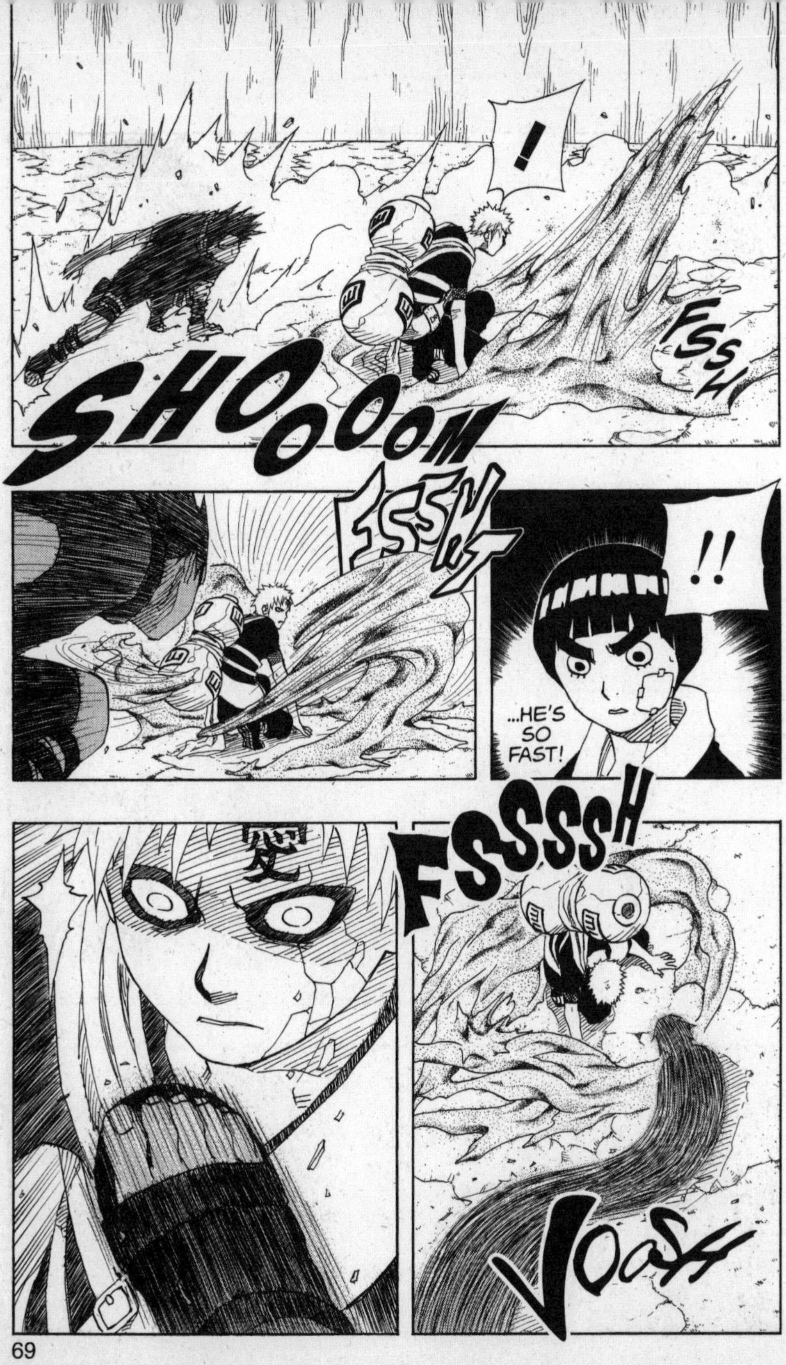
!
FSSH
SHOOOOOM
!!
...HE'S SO FAST!
FSSHT
FSSSSH
VOOSH

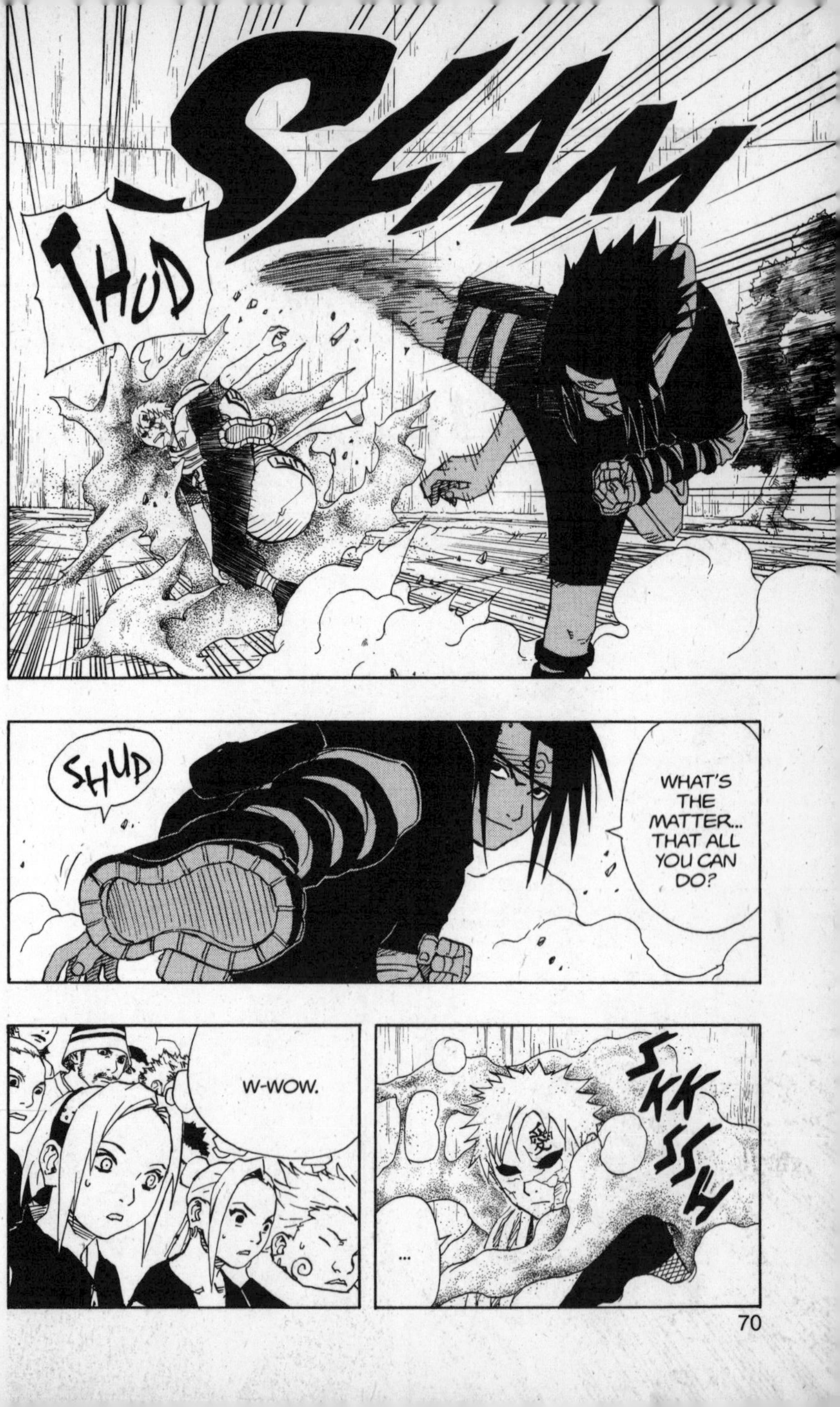
SLAM
THUD
WHAT'S THE MATTER... THAT ALL YOU CAN DO?
SHUD
SKKSSH
...
W-WOW.

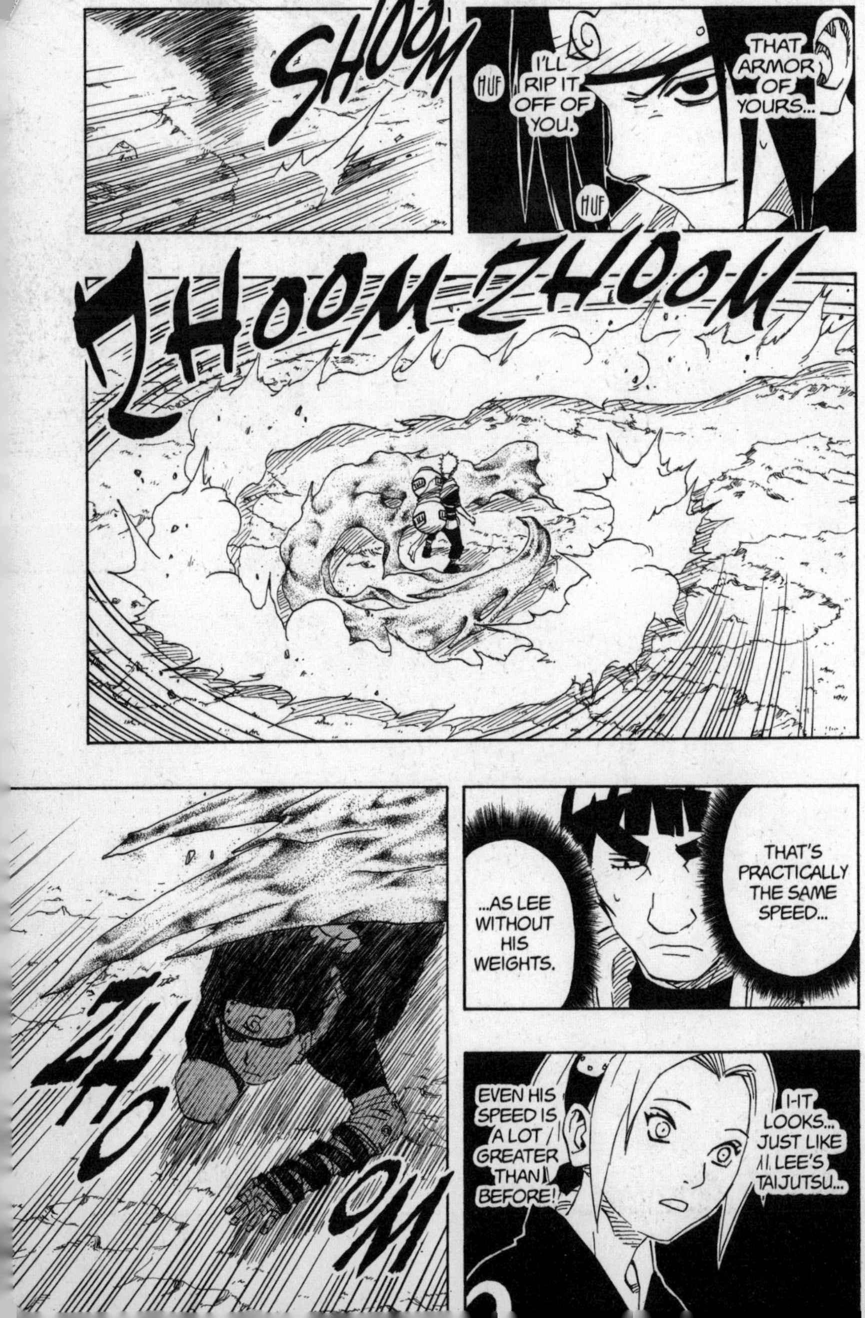
THAT ARMOR OF YOURS...
HUF
I'LL RIP IT OFF OF YOU.
HUF
SHOOM
ZHOOM ZHOOM
THAT'S PRACTICALLY THE SAME SPEED...
...AS LEE WITHOUT HIS WEIGHTS.
I-IT LOOKS... JUST LIKE LEE'S TAIJUTSU...
EVEN HIS SPEED IS A LOT GREATER THAN BEFORE!
ZHOOM

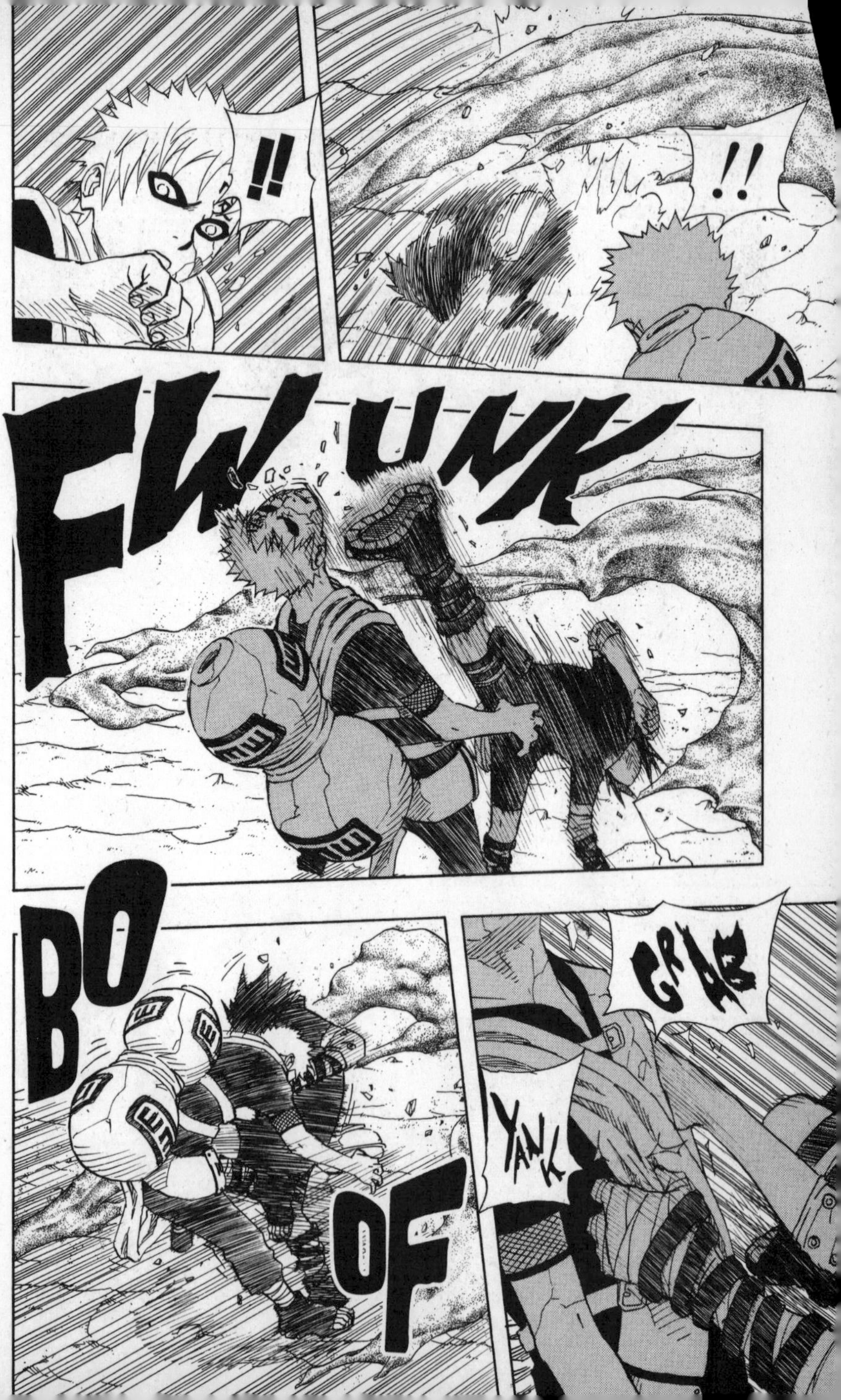
!!
!!
FWUMK
GRAB
YANK
BOOF

READ THIS WAY

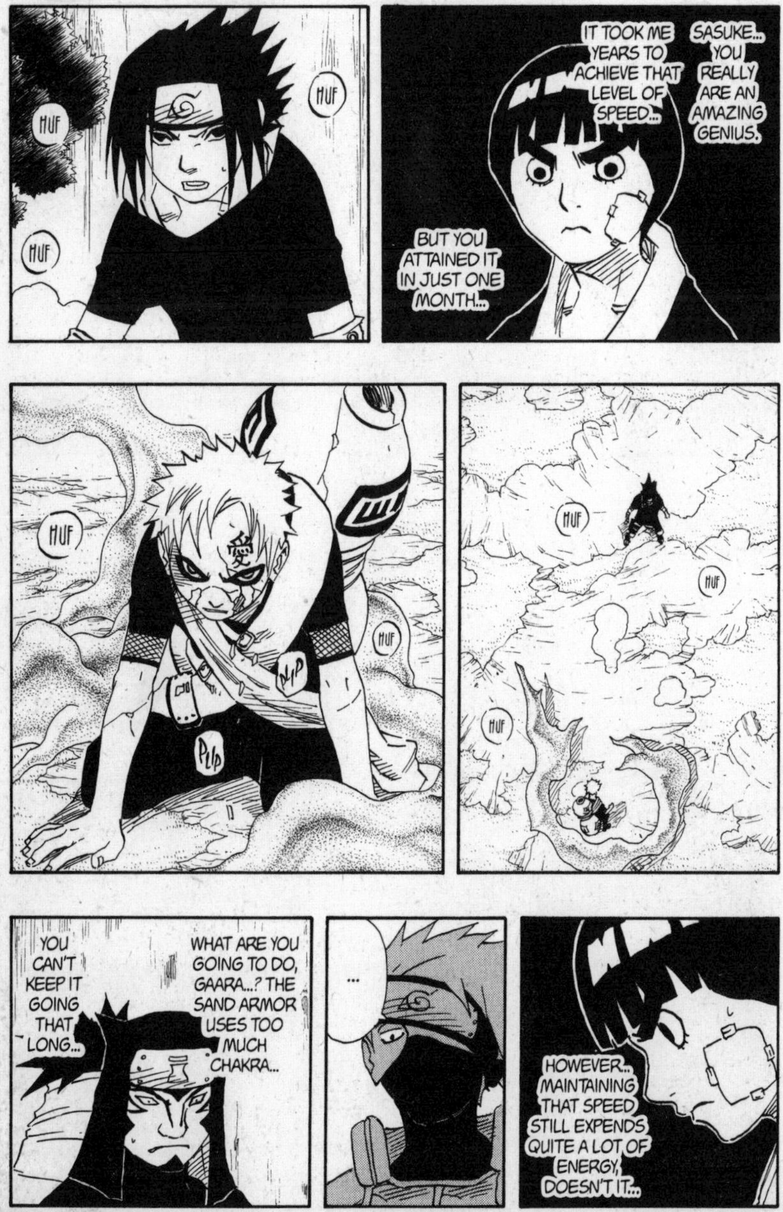

SASUKE... YOU REALLY ARE AN AMAZING GENIUS.
IT TOOK ME YEARS TO ACHIEVE THAT LEVEL OF SPEED...
BUT YOU ATTAINED IT IN JUST ONE MONTH...
HUF
HUF
HUF
HUF
HUF
HUF
HUF
PLIP
PLIP
HUF
HOWEVER... MAINTAINING THAT SPEED STILL EXPENDS QUITE A LOT OF ENERGY, DOESN'T IT...
...
WHAT ARE YOU GOING TO DO, GAARA...? THE SAND ARMOR USES TOO MUCH CHAKRA...
YOU CAN'T KEEP IT GOING THAT LONG...

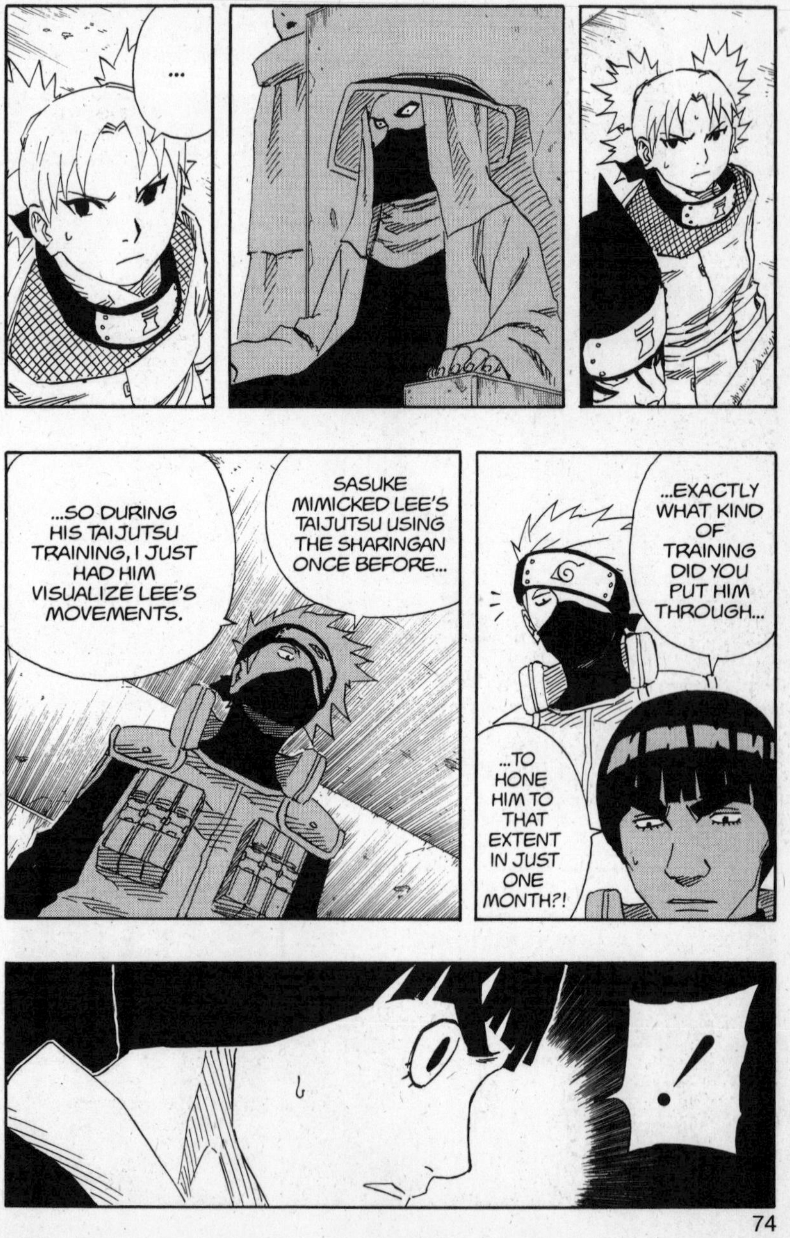
...
...EXACTLY WHAT KIND OF TRAINING DID YOU PUT HIM THROUGH...
...TO HONE HIM TO THAT EXTENT IN JUST ONE MONTH?!
SASUKE MIMICKED LEE'S TAIJUTSU USING THE SHARINGAN ONCE BEFORE...
...SO DURING HIS TAIJUTSU TRAINING, I JUST HAD HIM VISUALIZE LEE'S MOVEMENTS.
!

READ THIS WAY

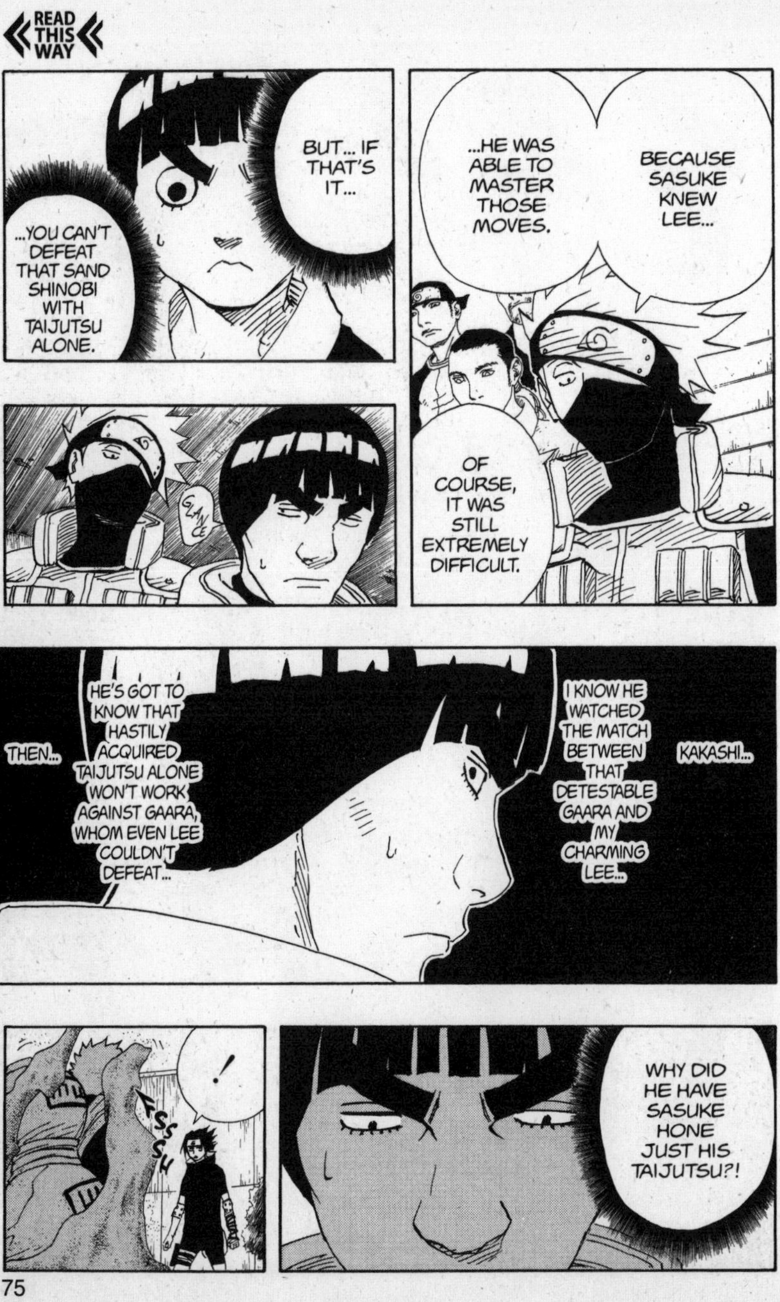

BECAUSE SASUKE KNEW LEE...
...HE WAS ABLE TO MASTER THOSE MOVES.
OF COURSE, IT WAS STILL EXTREMELY DIFFICULT.
BUT... IF THAT'S IT...
...YOU CAN'T DEFEAT THAT SAND SHINOBI WITH TAIJUTSU ALONE.
GLANCE
KAKASHI...
I KNOW HE WATCHED THE MATCH BETWEEN THAT DETESTABLE GAARA AND MY CHARMING LEE...
HE'S GOT TO KNOW THAT HASTILY ACQUIRED TAIJUTSU ALONE WON'T WORK AGAINST GAARA, WHOM EVEN LEE COULDN'T DEFEAT...
THEN...
WHY DID HE HAVE SASUKE HONE JUST HIS TAIJUTSU?!
!
FSSSH

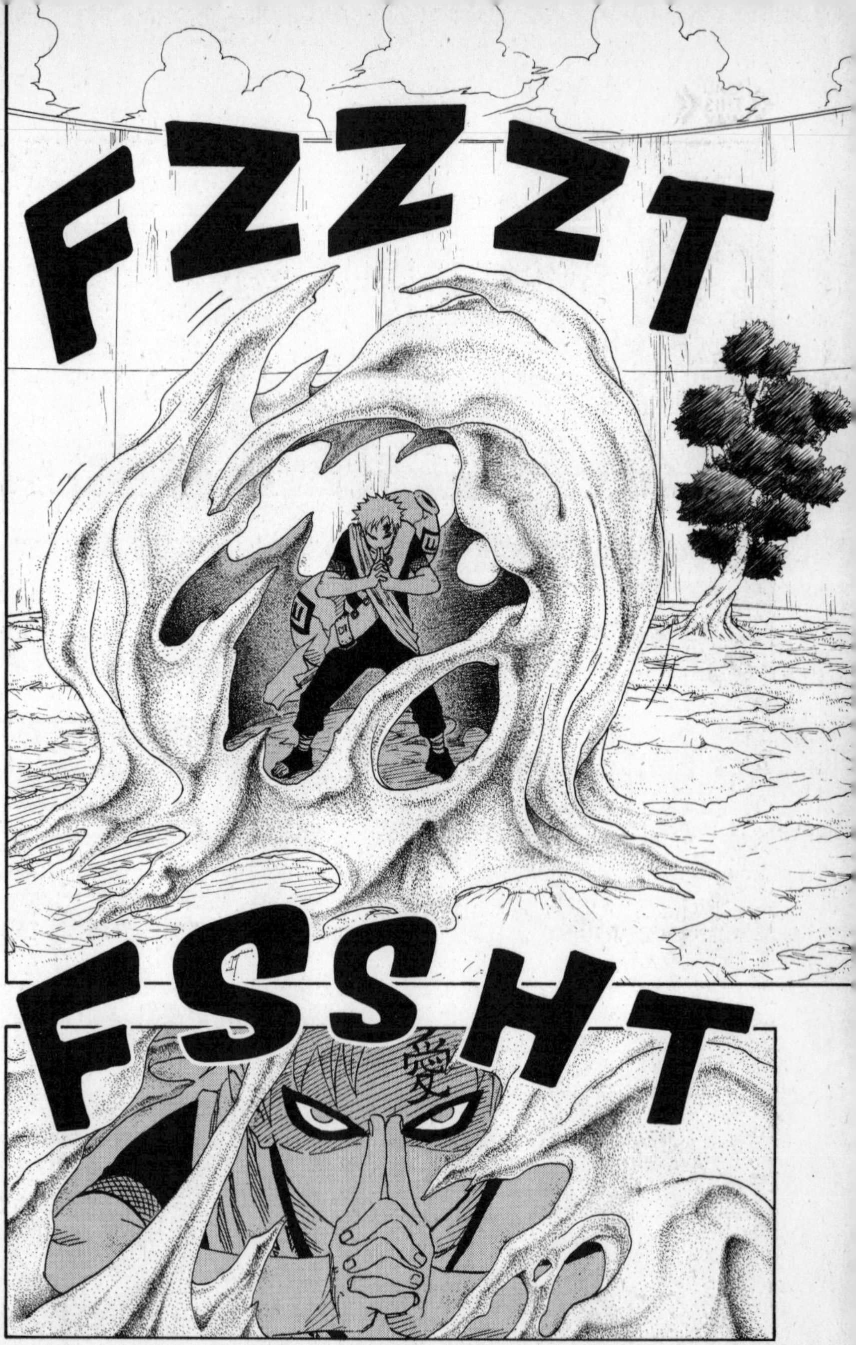
FZZZT
FSSHT

READ THIS WAY

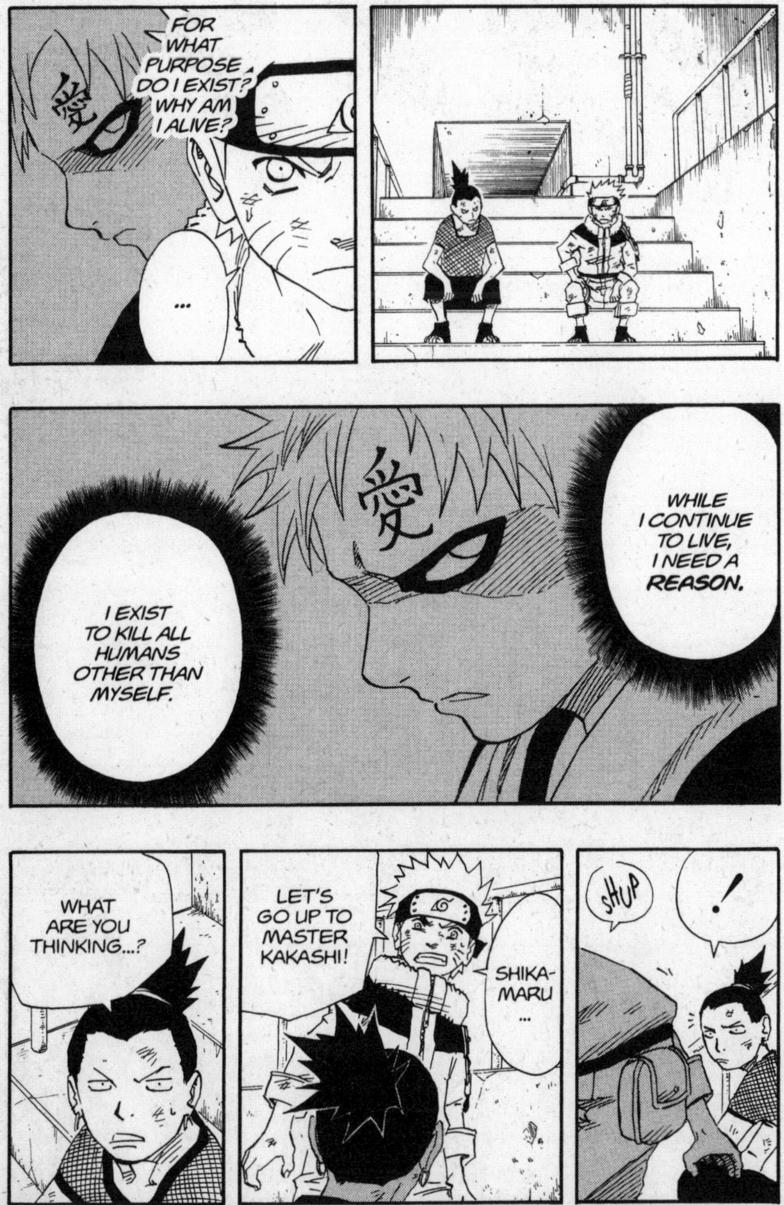
FOR WHAT PURPOSE DO I EXIST? WHY AM I ALIVE?
...
WHILE I CONTINUE TO LIVE, I NEED A REASON.
I EXIST TO KILL ALL HUMANS OTHER THAN MYSELF.
!
SHUP
SHIKA-MARU ...
LET'S GO UP TO MASTER KAKASHI!
WHAT ARE YOU THINKING...?

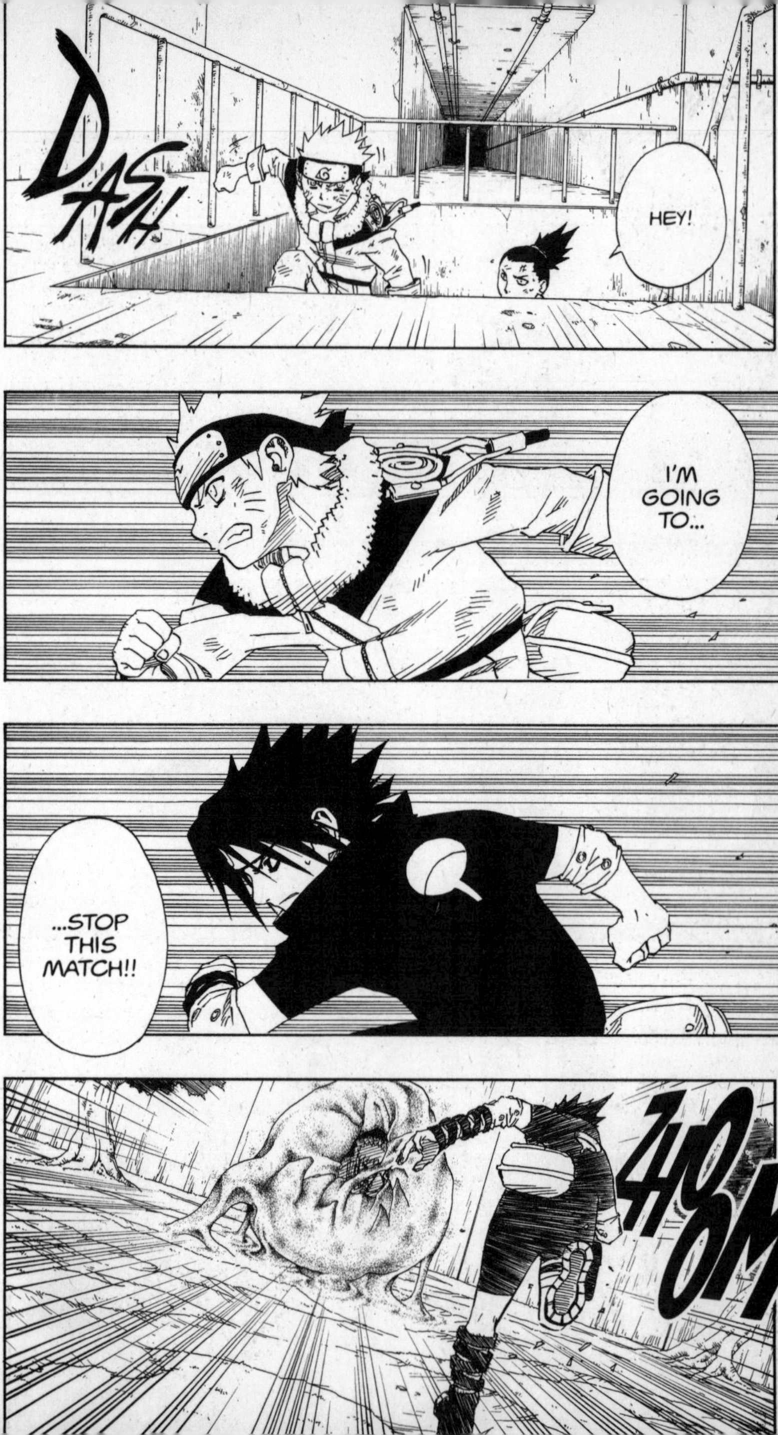
DASH
HEY!
I'M GOING TO...
...STOP THIS MATCH!!
WHOOM

READ THIS WAY

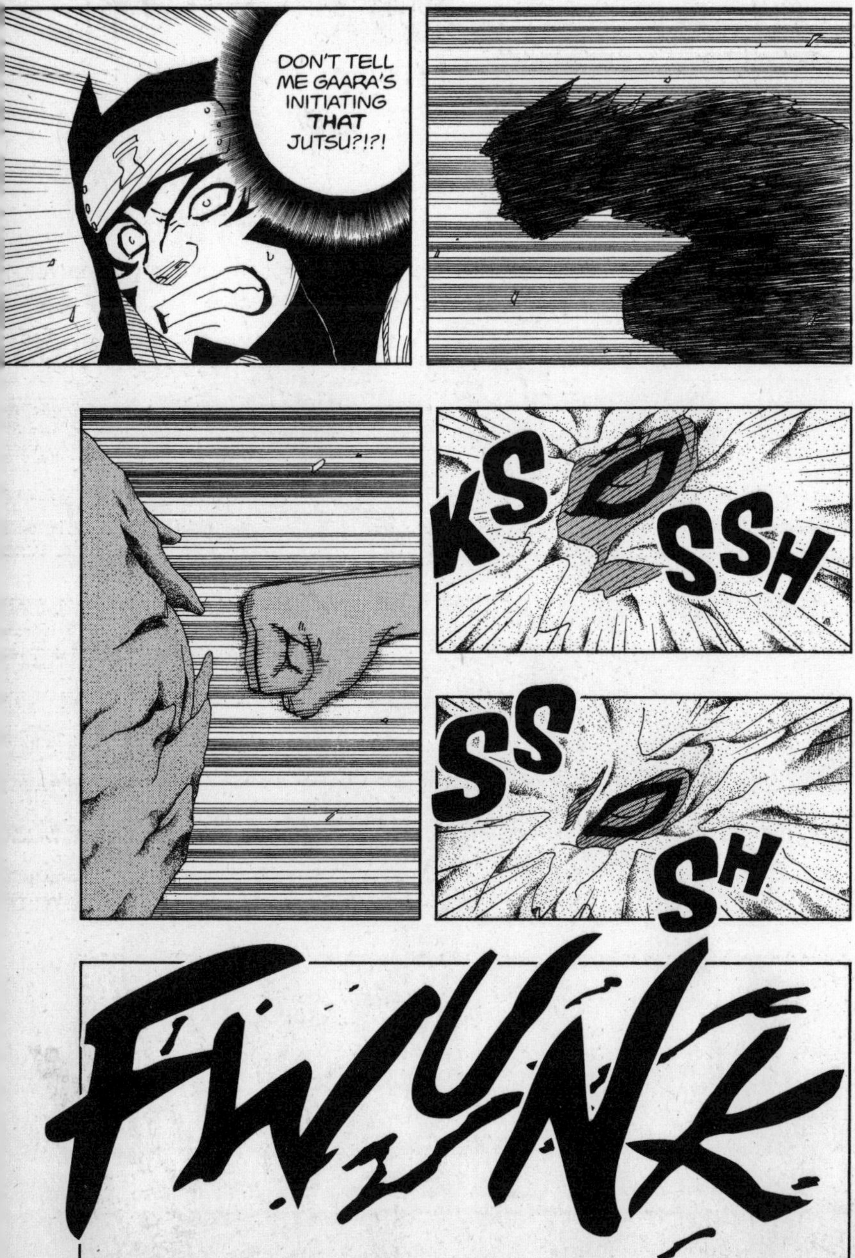
DON'T TELL ME GAARA'S INITIATING THAT JUTSU?!?!
KSSSH
SSSH
FWUNK

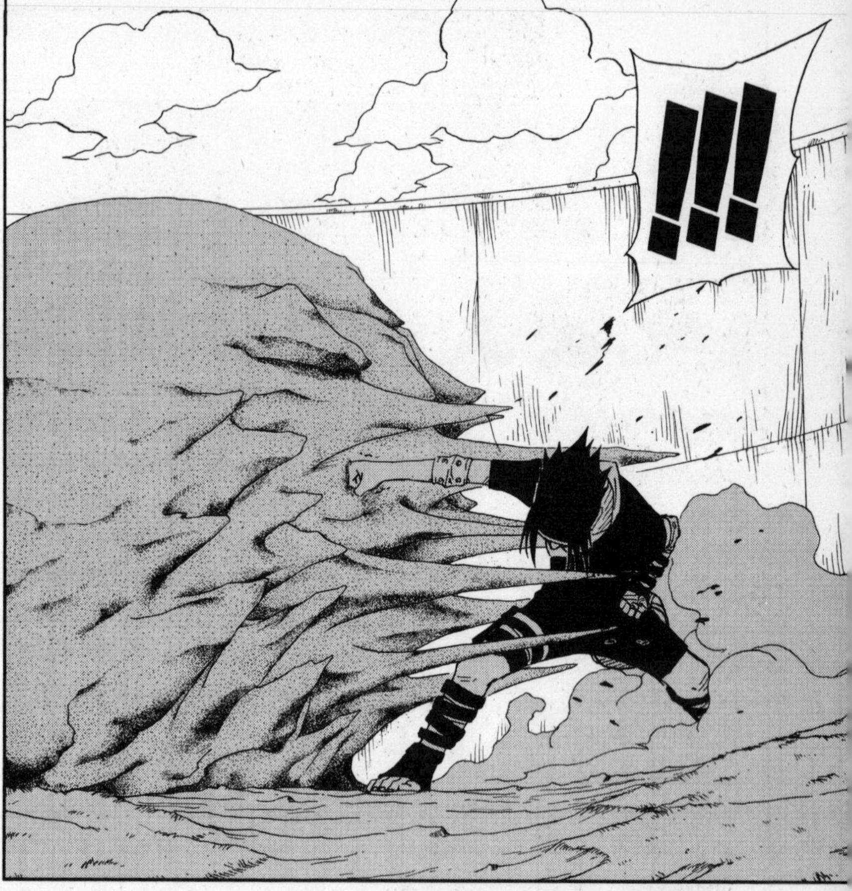
!!!

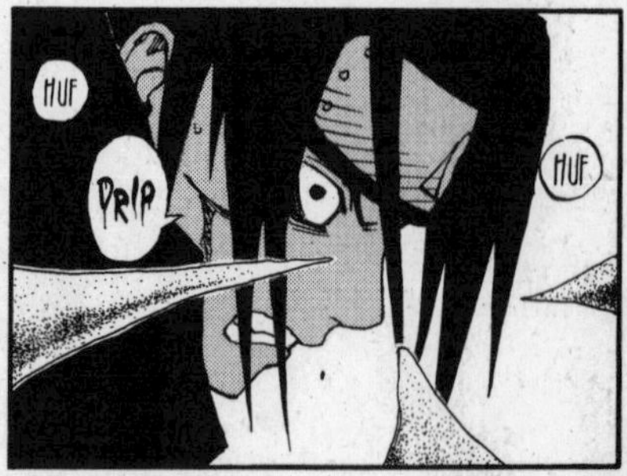
HUF
HUF
DRIP

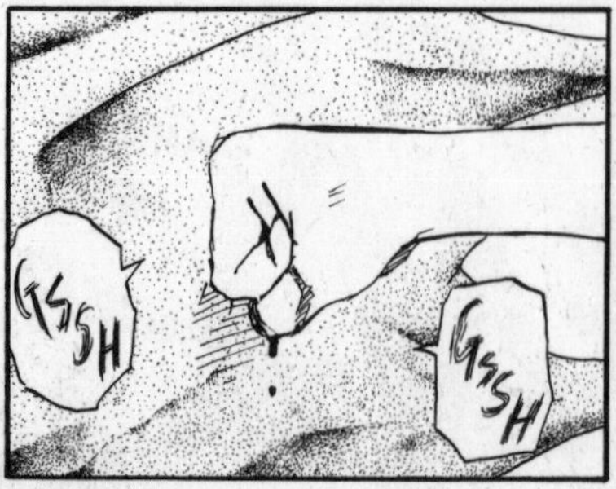
GSSH
GSSH

READ THIS WAY

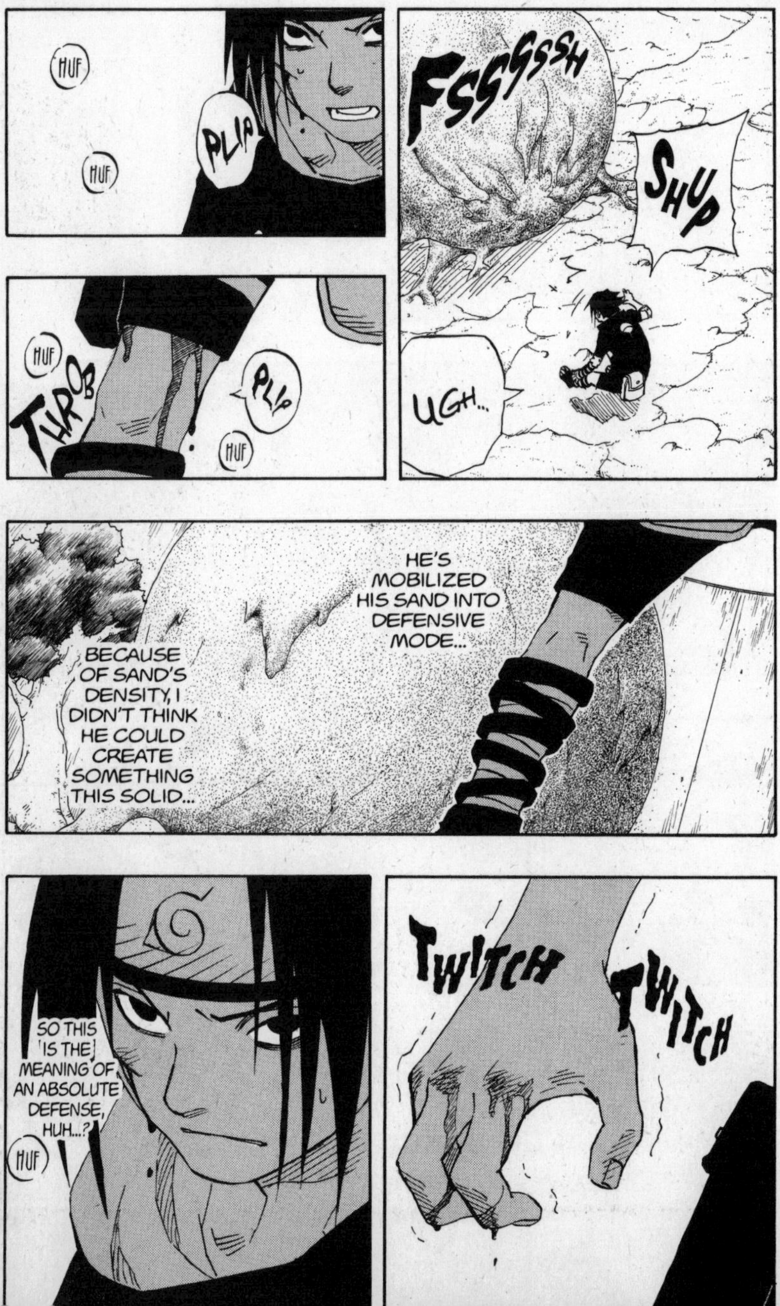
FSSSSSH
SHUP
UGH...
HUF
PLIP
HUF
THROB
HUF
PLIP
HUF
HE'S MOBILIZED HIS SAND INTO DEFENSIVE MODE...
BECAUSE OF SAND'S DENSITY, I DIDN'T THINK HE COULD CREATE SOMETHING THIS SOLID...
TWITCH
TWITCH
SO THIS IS THE MEANING OF AN ABSOLUTE DEFENSE, HUH...?
HUF

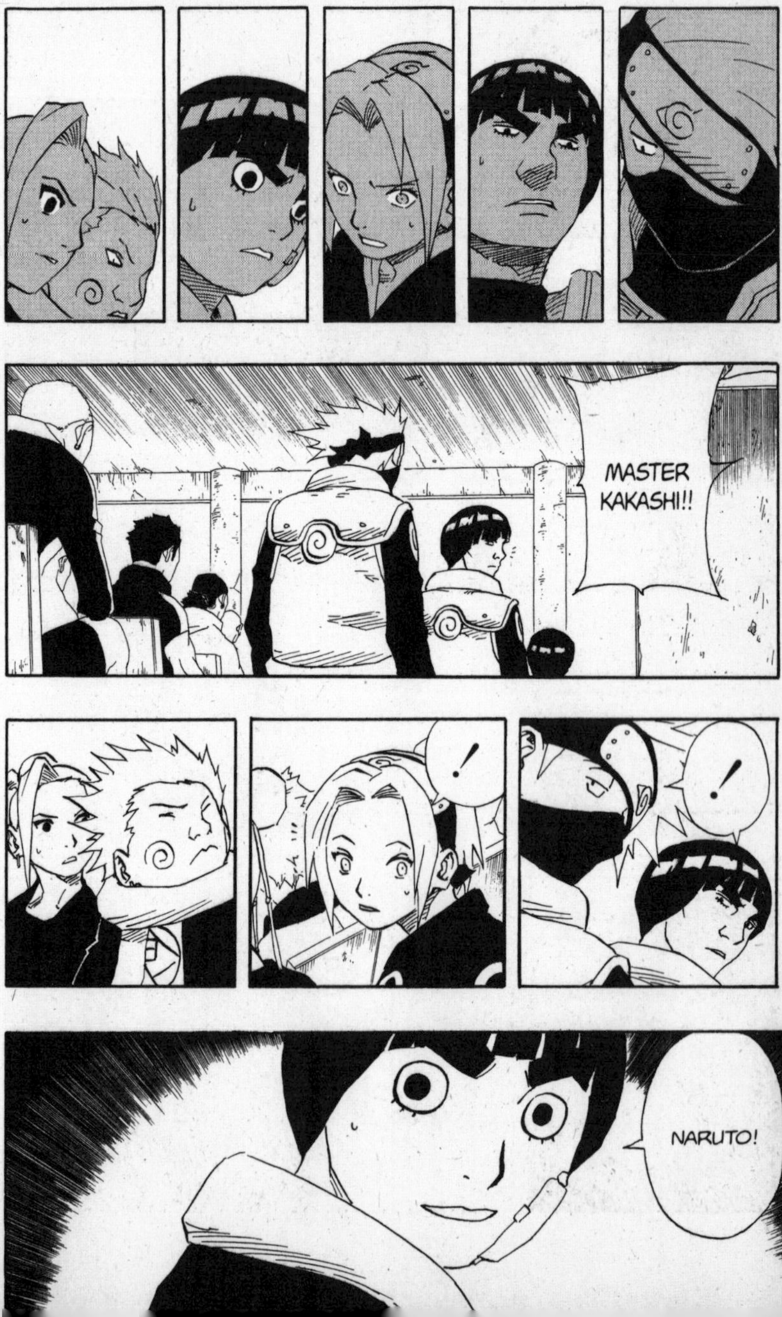
MASTER KAKASHI!!
!
!
NARUTO!

READ THIS WAY

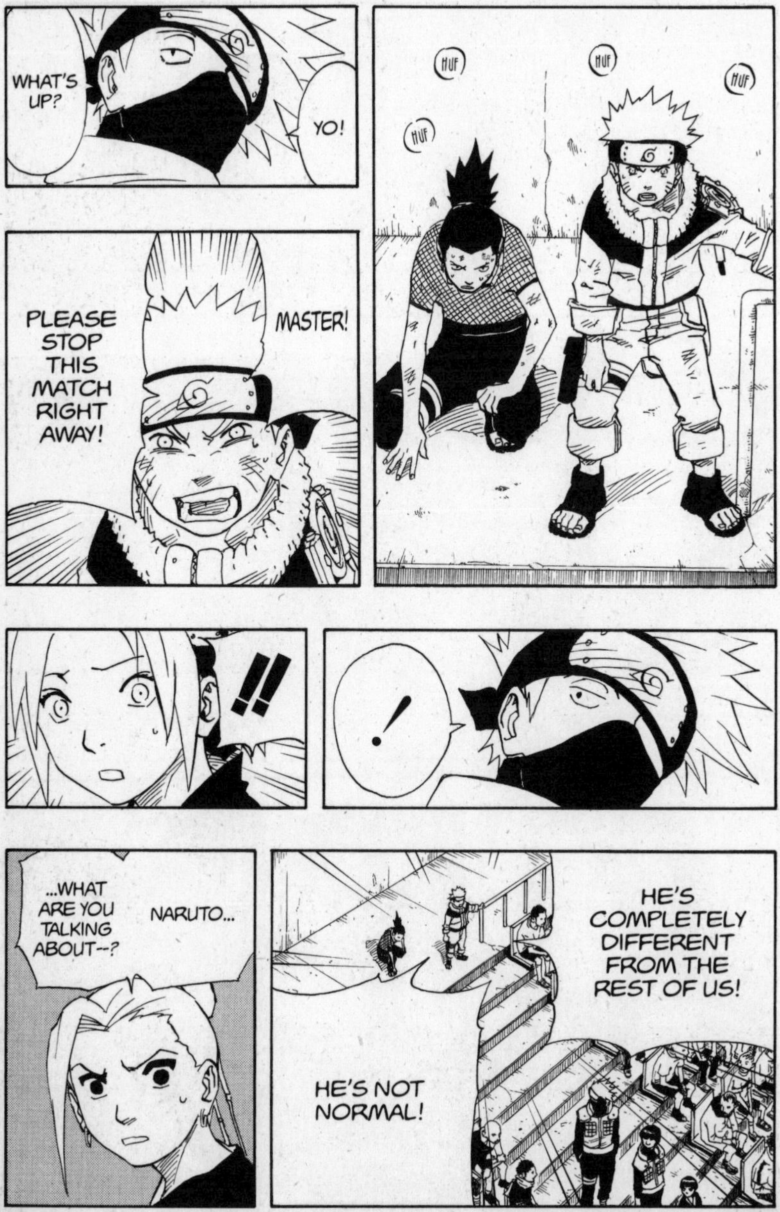
HUF
HUF
HUF
HUF
YO!
WHAT'S UP?
MASTER!
PLEASE STOP THIS MATCH RIGHT AWAY!
!
!!
HE'S COMPLETELY DIFFERENT FROM THE REST OF US!
HE'S NOT NORMAL!
NARUTO...
...WHAT ARE YOU TALKING ABOUT--?

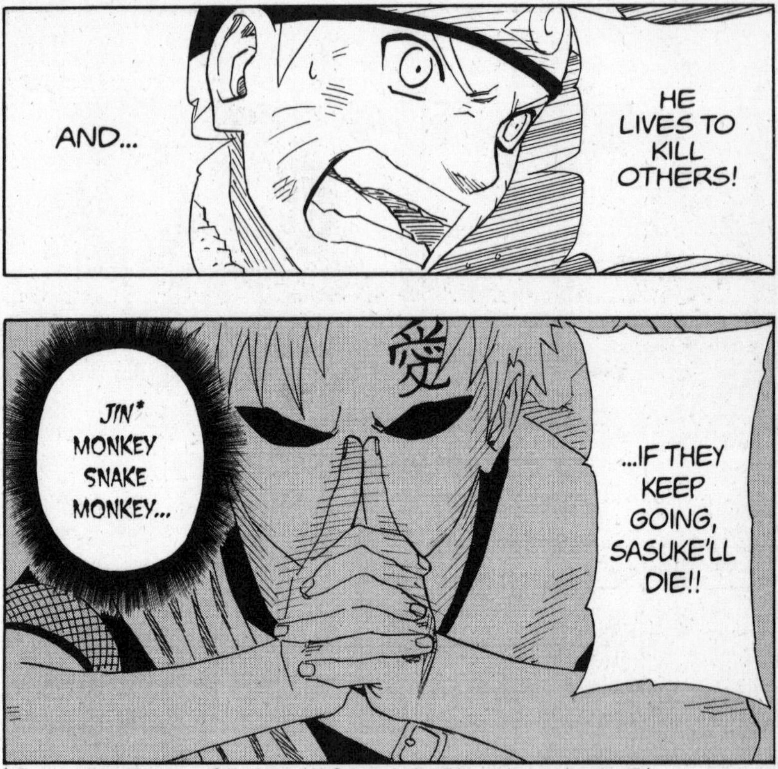
HE LIVES TO KILL OTHERS!
AND...
...IF THEY KEEP GOING, SASUKE'LL DIE!!
JIN* MONKEY SNAKE MONKEY...

* *Jin* means Yang Water, one of the elemental influences in the Chinese sexagenary cycle. -Ed.

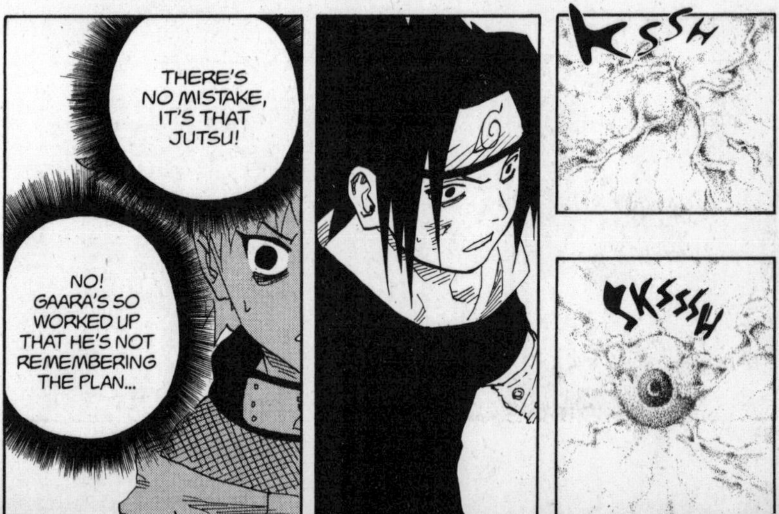
KSSH
SKSSSH
THERE'S NO MISTAKE, IT'S THAT JUTSU!
NO! GAARA'S SO WORKED UP THAT HE'S NOT REMEMBERING THE PLAN...

READ THIS WAY

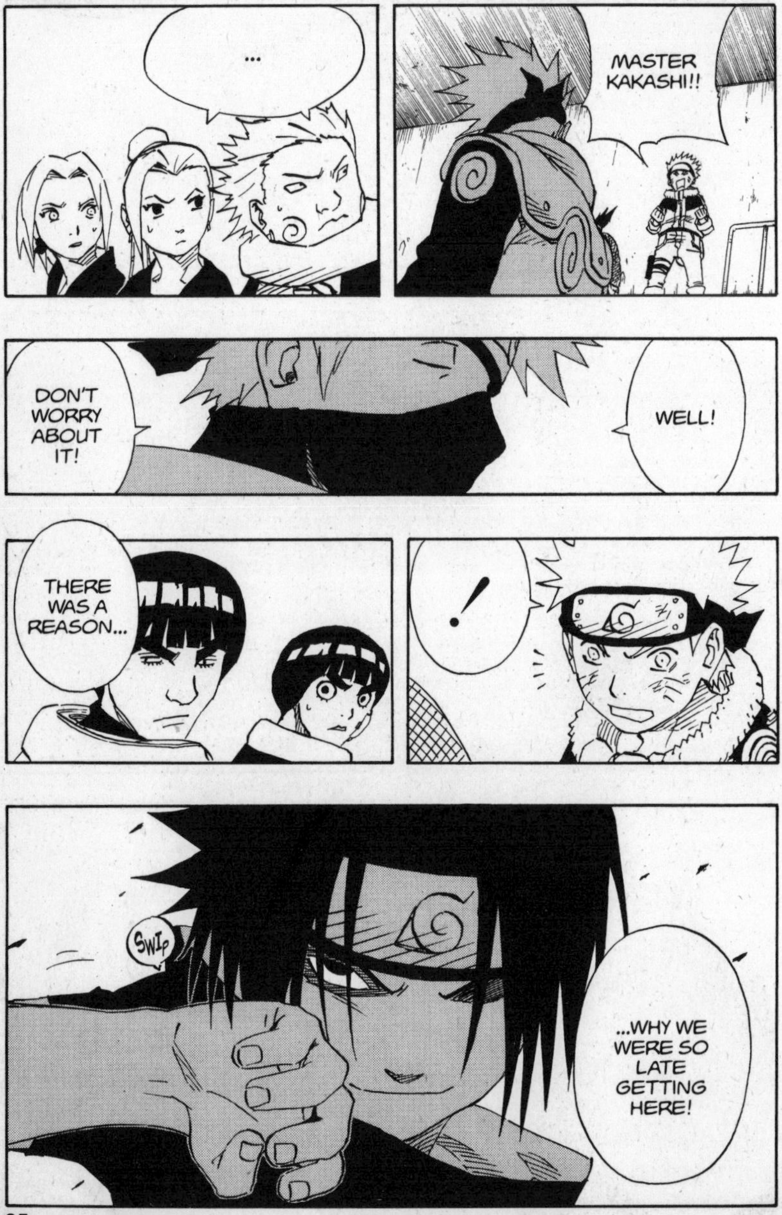
MASTER KAKASHI!!
...
WELL!
DON'T WORRY ABOUT IT!
!
THERE WAS A REASON...
...WHY WE WERE SO LATE GETTING HERE!
SWIP

THE WORLD OF KISHIMOTO MASASHI
MY PERSONAL HISTORY, PART 18

I DIDN'T WIN THE CONTEST, SO I ENDED UP SPENDING MY FIRST YEAR OF COLLEGE PRETTY DISGRUNTLED.

ONE DAY, SOMEONE APPROACHED ME SAYING "I DRAW MANGA TOO" AND PROFFERED THIS: "IF YOU'LL DRAW MANGA FOR MY NEW COLLECTION, I'LL PAY YOU." "WELL, IF I CAN GET MONEY FOR MY OWN PIECE, MIGHT AS WELL," I THOUGHT, SO I QUICKLY PUT TOGETHER ROUGHLY EIGHT PAGES OF A RANDOM STAND-ALONE SHORT AND GAVE IT TO HIM. HE WAS PUTTING TOGETHER A DÔJINSHI [SELF-PUBLISHED WORK] WITH ABOUT FIVE PEOPLE IN TOTAL, AND HAD COME TO COMMISSION ME TO BE ONE OF THE FIVE, HAVING HEARD A RUMOR THAT I DREW MANGA. SINCE THE DEAL WAS THAT I WOULD GET AN EQUAL SHARE OF THE PROFIT, I PLEASANTLY LOOKED FORWARD TO THE BOOK'S COMPLETION. BUT NO MATTER HOW LONG I WAITED, NO BOOK!

AFTER I HAD WAITED A LONG WHILE, I ASKED THE FELLOW "SO WHEN IS THE BOOK COMING OUT?" BUT HE ANSWERED, "THREE OTHER MANGA, INCLUDING MY OWN, ARE STILL NOT DONE..." I REALLY WANTED TO SHOUT BACK, "HOW CAN IT TAKE YOU MORE THAN FOUR MONTHS TO COMPLETE EIGHT PAGES!" BUT INSTEAD I JUST MUTTERED "AH, I SEE" AND ENTERED A STATE OF RESIGNATION. THE NEXT TIME I SAW HIM HE HAD HIS BACK TO ME, FURIOUSLY PLAYING VIDEO GAMES AT THE ARCADE. THAT'S WHEN IT FINALLY HIT ME (AAH! HE'S A SHAM MANGA ARTIST).

HOWEVER, THIS WORLD IS NOT MADE UP OF JUST SHAM MANGA ARTISTS! A CERTAIN PAIR OF SENPAI [UPPERCLASSMEN] WOULD END UP TRANSFORMING MY DISGRUNTLED LIFE WHEN I ENTERED MY SECOND YEAR OF COLLEGE! THOSE TWO COMPETED AGAINST EACH OTHER, COLLECTING NEWCOMER AWARDS LEFT AND RIGHT, AND WERE VETERANS ENOUGH TO ALREADY HAVE ASSIGNED EDITORS, EVEN CUTTING BACK ON SLEEP TO INCREASE THEIR TIME SPENT DRAWING MANGA. "YES! FINALLY, I'VE MET GENUINE MANGA ARTISTS!" I JOYFULLY SAID TO MYSELF, FREQUENTLY RUNNING OVER TO MY SENPAI'S HOUSES TO HANG OUT AND LEARN ALL ABOUT MANGA PRODUCTION! THEY WERE ALSO WILLING TO READ MY MANGA AND GIVE ME ALL SORTS OF CRITIQUES SO THAT MY SKILLS WERE HONED! I AM SO ETERNALLY GRATEFUL TO THOSE TWO. EVEN NOW, THEY LET ME CALL THEM ON OCCASION... HOWEVER, I FEEL BAD ABOUT BOTHERING THEM, SO IT'S STILL HARD FOR ME TO PICK UP THE PHONE. FOR THEY'RE BOTH SLEEP-DEPRIVED PROFESSIONAL MANGA ARTISTS LEADING IRREGULAR LIVES!

Number 113:

The Reason He Was Late...!!

URGH... GAARA!

THE THIRD EYE... THERE'S NO MISTAKE, IT'S THAT JUTSU!!

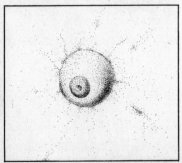

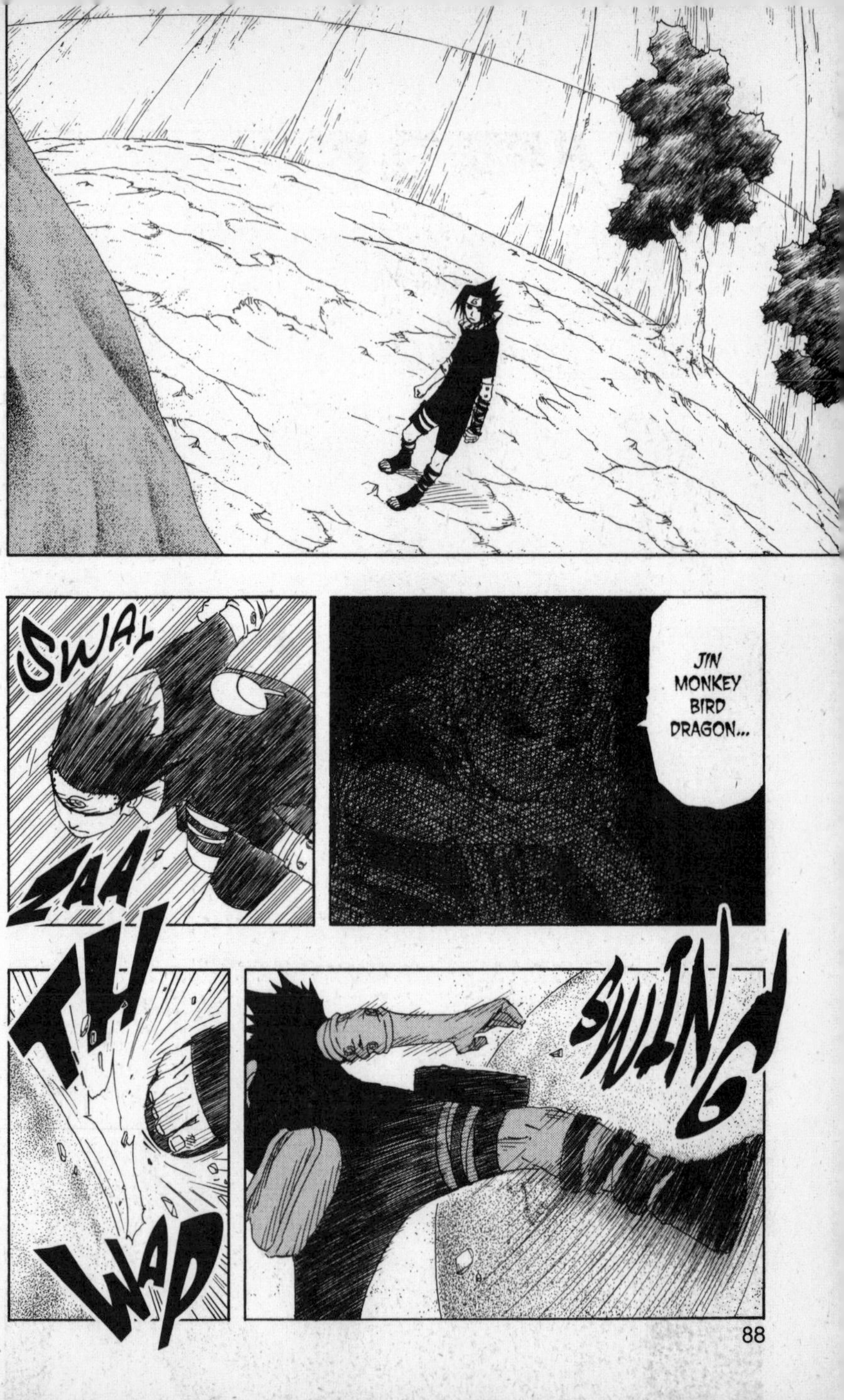
JIN
MONKEY
BIRD
DRAGON...
SWAY
ZAA
SWING
THWAP

READ THIS WAY

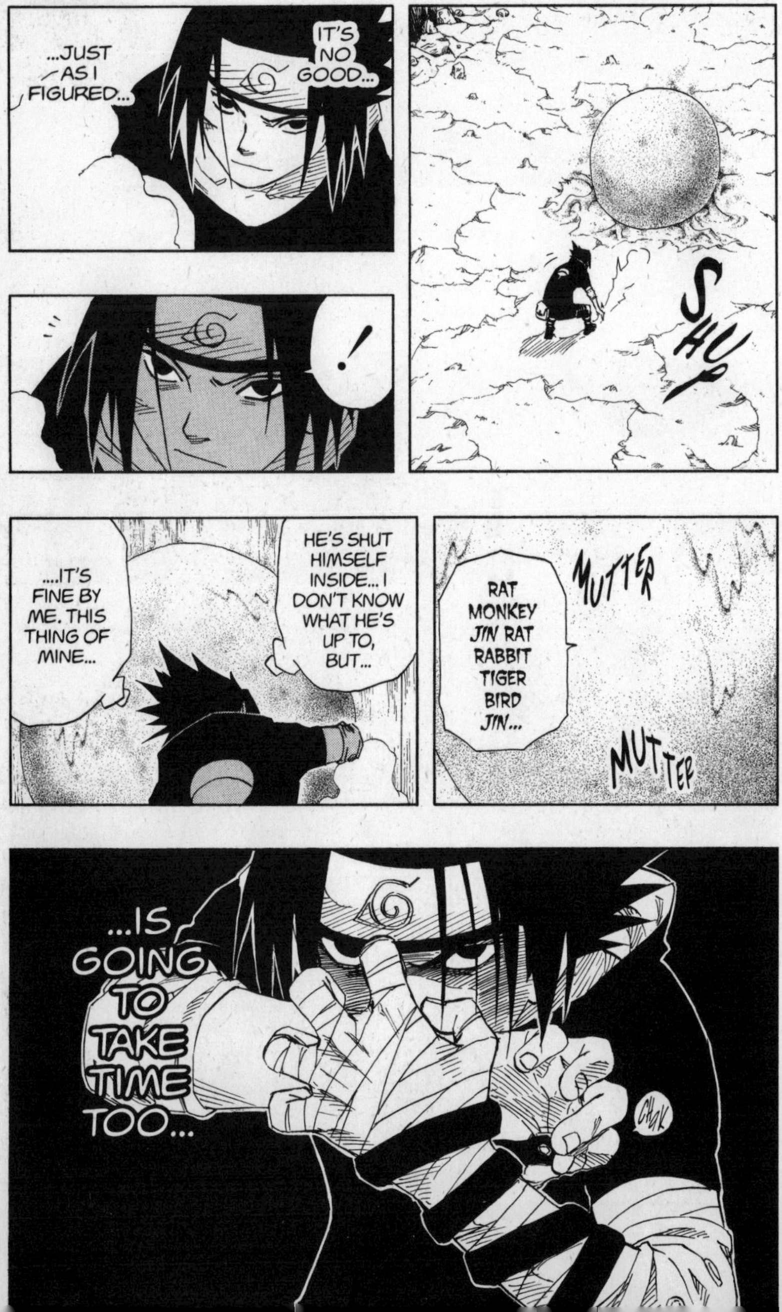
SHUP
IT'S NO GOOD...
...JUST AS I FIGURED...
!
MUTTER
RAT MONKEY JIN RAT RABBIT TIGER BIRD JIN...
MUTTER
HE'S SHUT HIMSELF INSIDE... I DON'T KNOW WHAT HE'S UP TO, BUT...
....IT'S FINE BY ME. THIS THING OF MINE...
...IS GOING TO TAKE TIME TOO...
CHAK

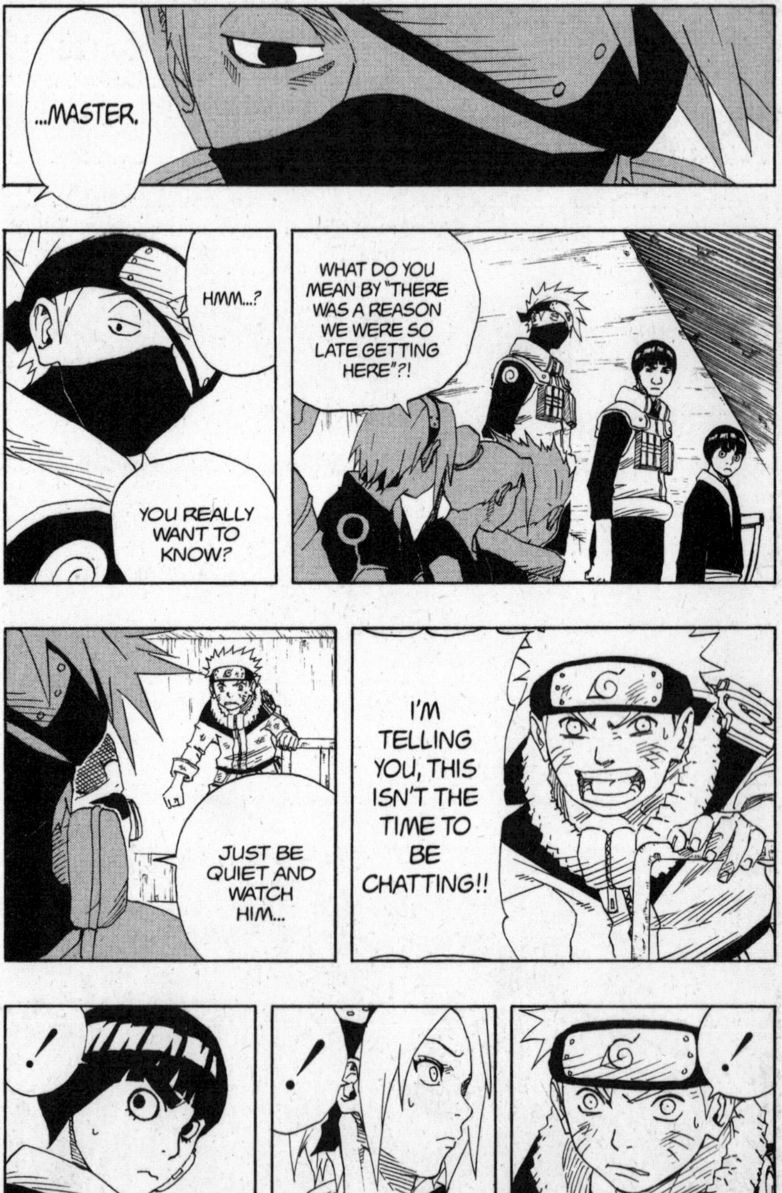
...MASTER.
WHAT DO YOU MEAN BY "THERE WAS A REASON WE WERE SO LATE GETTING HERE"?!
HMM...?
YOU REALLY WANT TO KNOW?
I'M TELLING YOU, THIS ISN'T THE TIME TO BE CHATTING!!
JUST BE QUIET AND WATCH HIM...
!
!
!

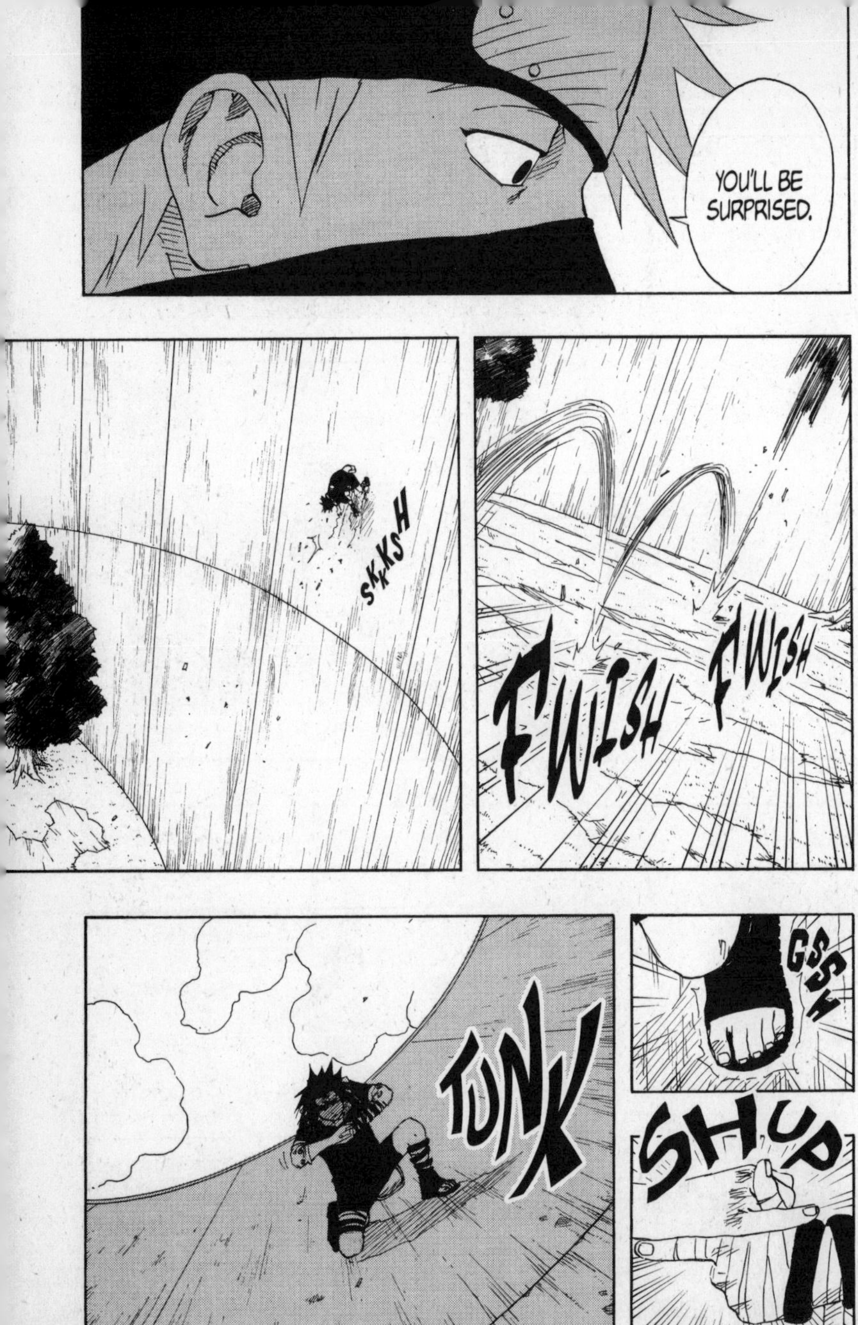

YOU'LL BE SURPRISED.
FWISH
FWISH
SKKSH
GSSH
SHUP
TUNK

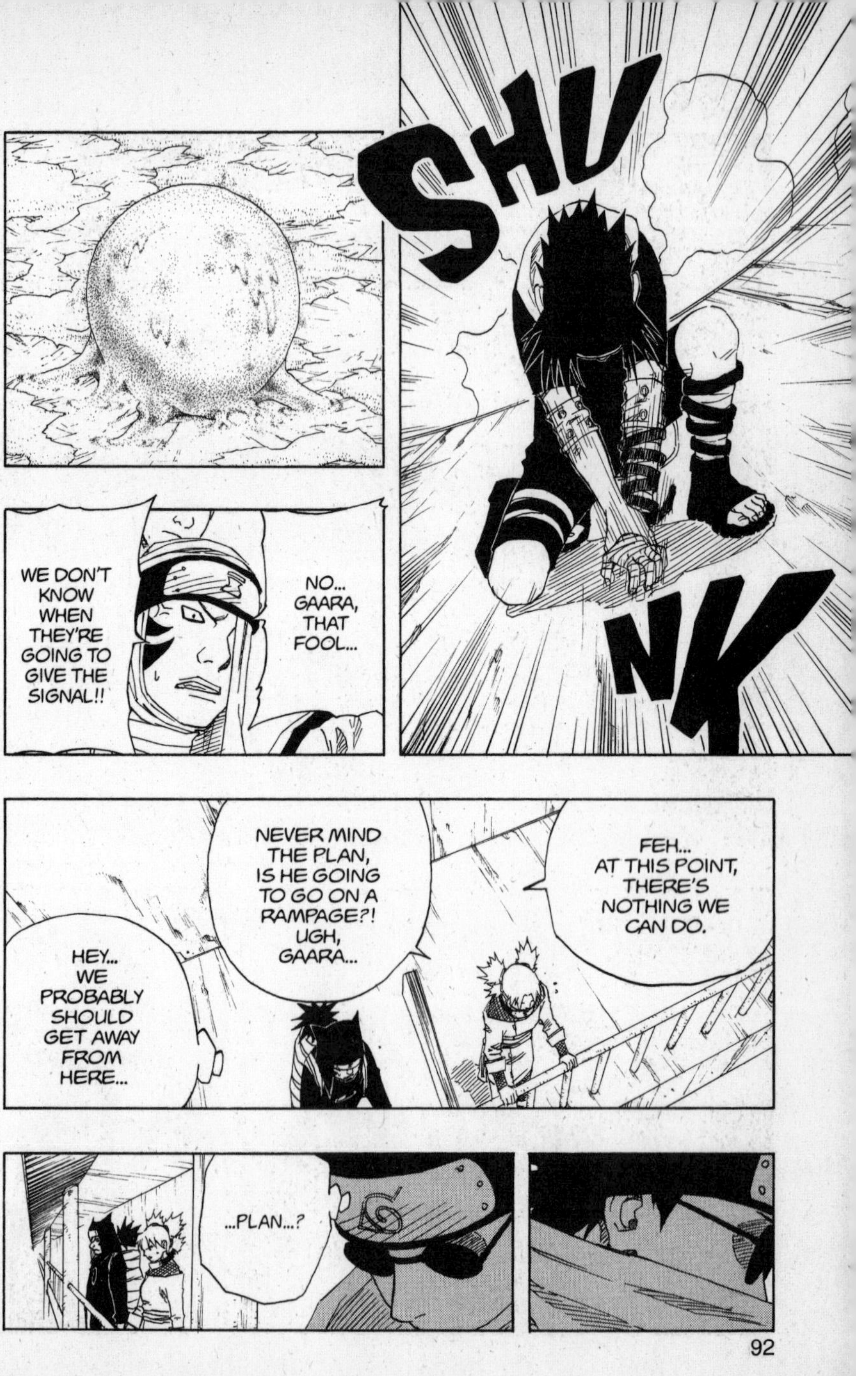
SHUNK
NO... GAARA, THAT FOOL...
WE DON'T KNOW WHEN THEY'RE GOING TO GIVE THE SIGNAL!!
FEH... AT THIS POINT, THERE'S NOTHING WE CAN DO.
NEVER MIND THE PLAN, IS HE GOING TO GO ON A RAMPAGE?! UGH, GAARA...
HEY... WE PROBABLY SHOULD GET AWAY FROM HERE...
...PLAN...?

READ THIS WAY

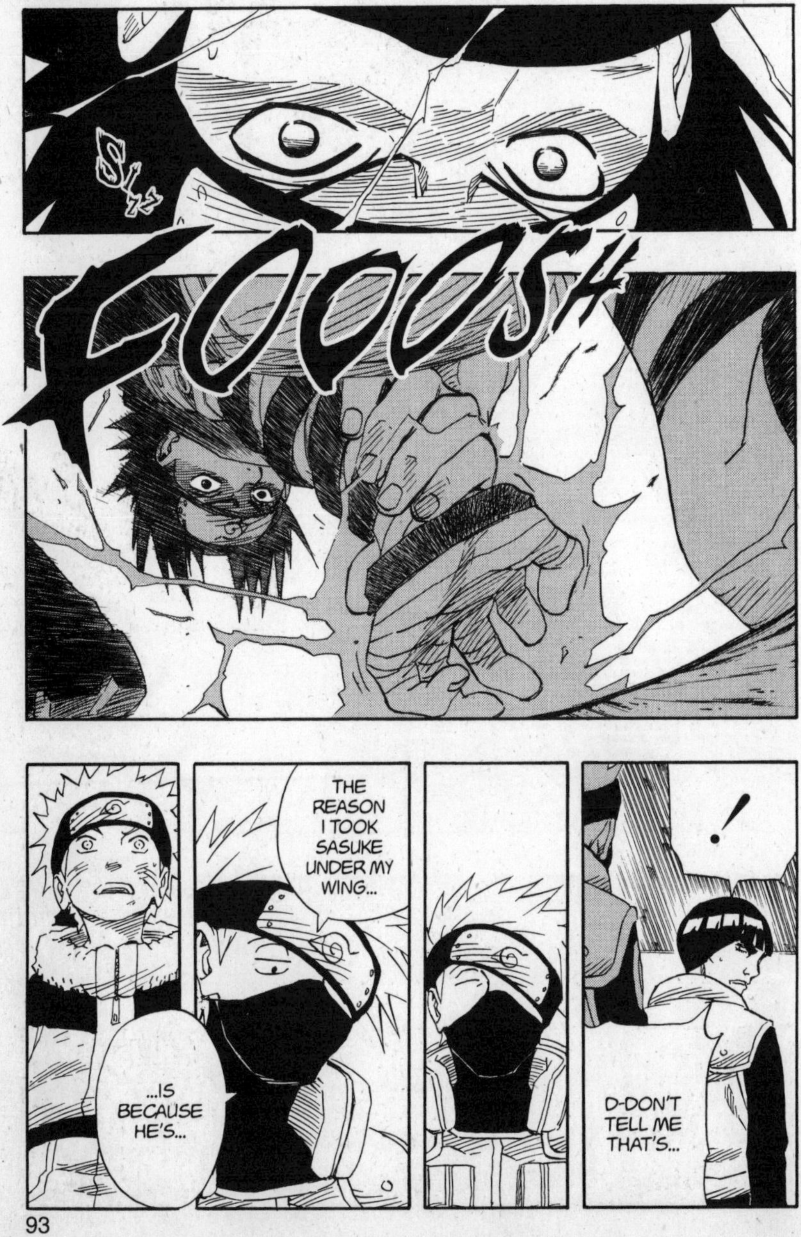
SIZZ
COOOSH
!
D-DON'T TELL ME THAT'S...
THE REASON I TOOK SASUKE UNDER MY WING...
...IS BECAUSE HE'S...

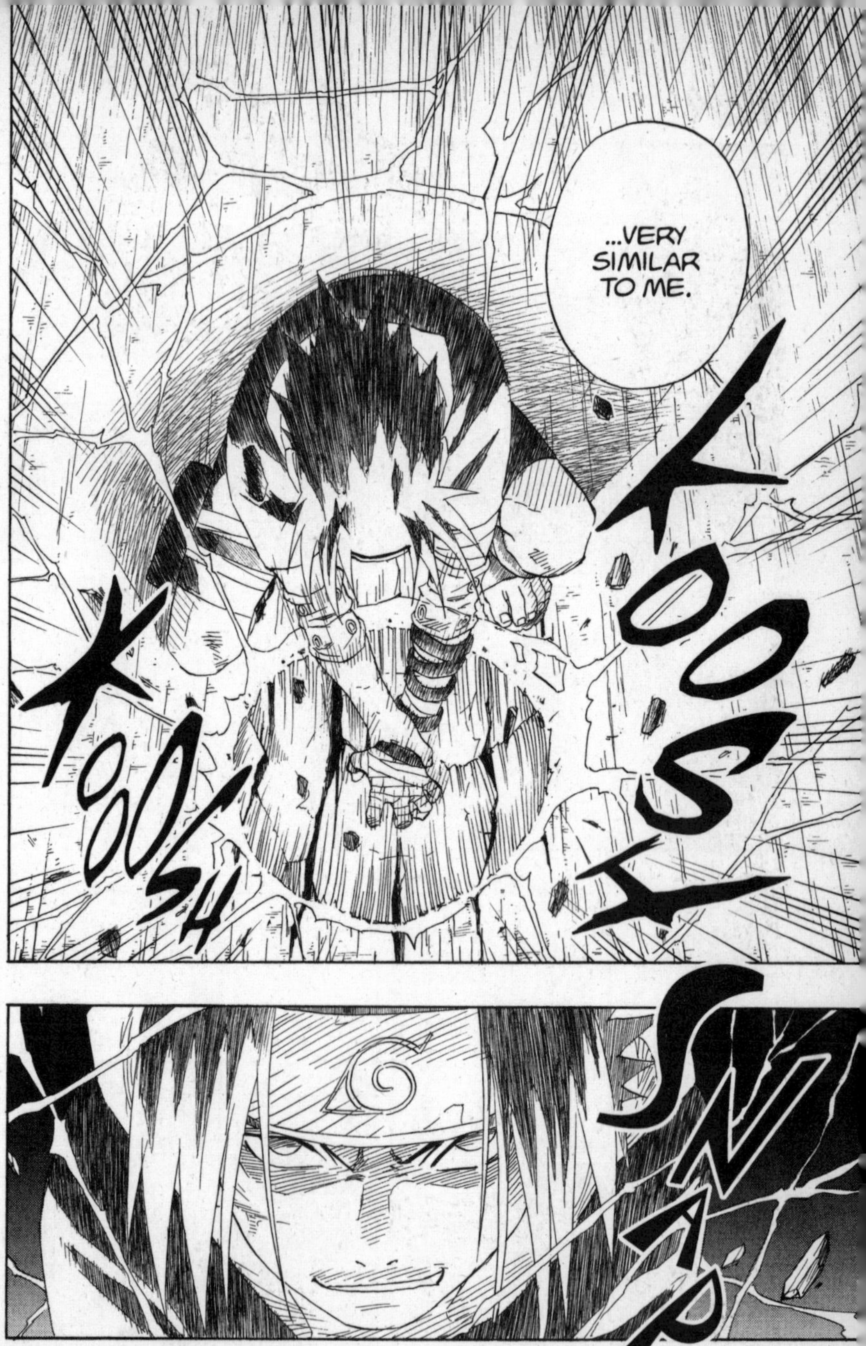
...VERY SIMILAR TO ME.
KOOSH
KOOSH
SNAP

READ THIS WAY

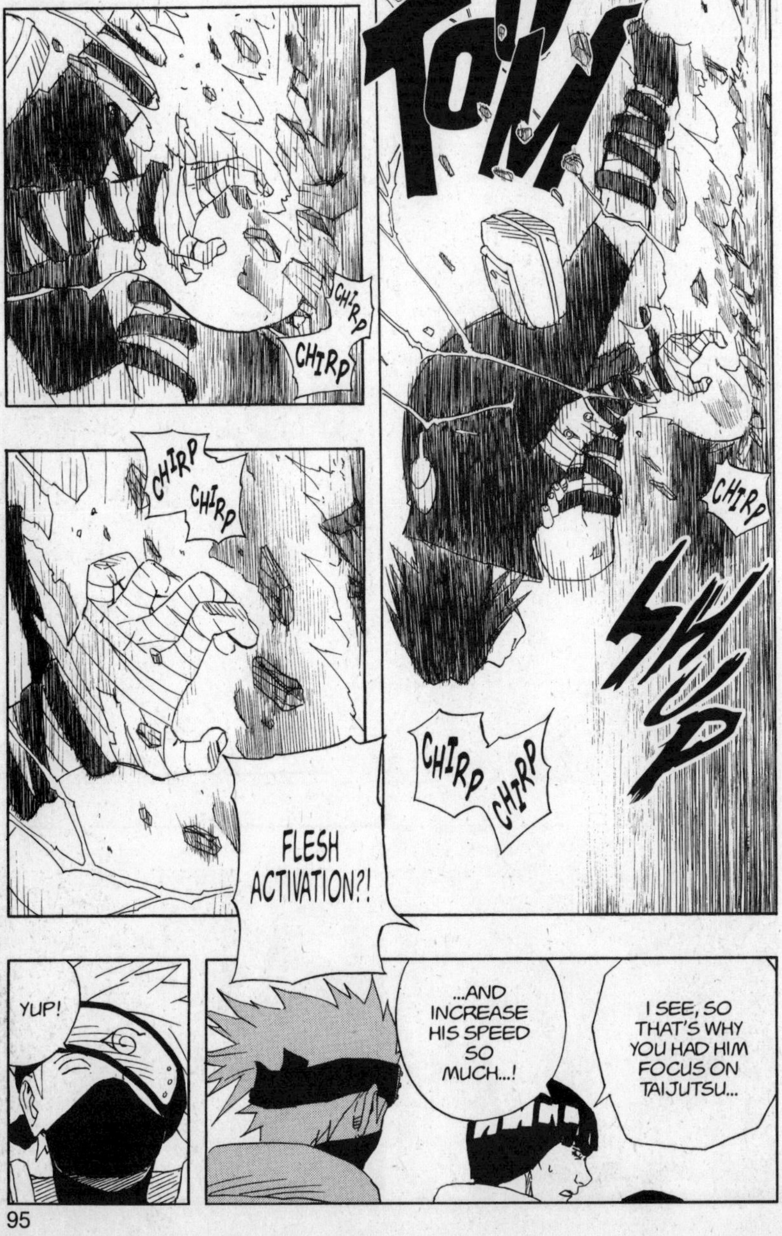

TOOM
CHIRP
SHUP
CHIRP CHIRP
CHIRP CHIRP
CHIRP CHIRP
FLESH ACTIVATION?!
I SEE, SO THAT'S WHY YOU HAD HIM FOCUS ON TAIJUTSU...
...AND INCREASE HIS SPEED SO MUCH...!
YUP!

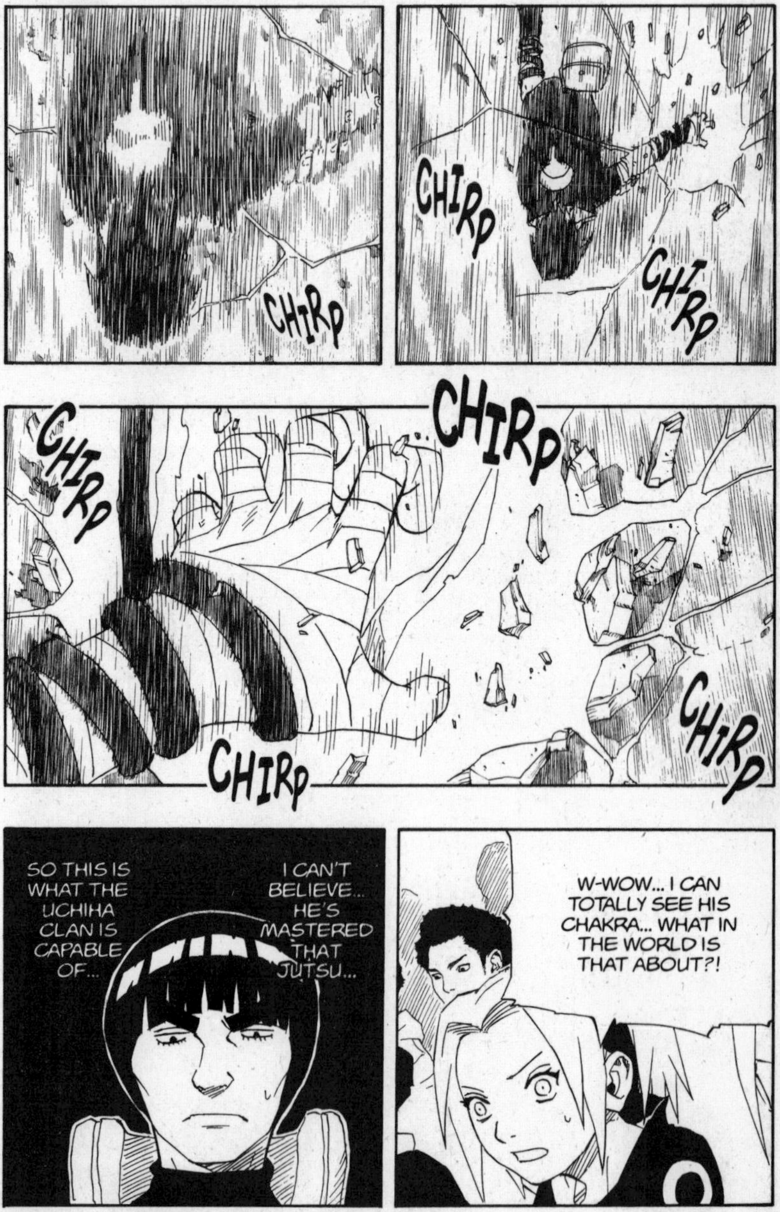
CHIRP
CHIRP
CHIRP
CHIRP
CHIRP
CHIRP
CHIRP
W-WOW... I CAN TOTALLY SEE HIS CHAKRA... WHAT IN THE WORLD IS THAT ABOUT?!
I CAN'T BELIEVE... HE'S MASTERED THAT JUTSU...
SO THIS IS WHAT THE UCHIHA CLAN IS CAPABLE OF...

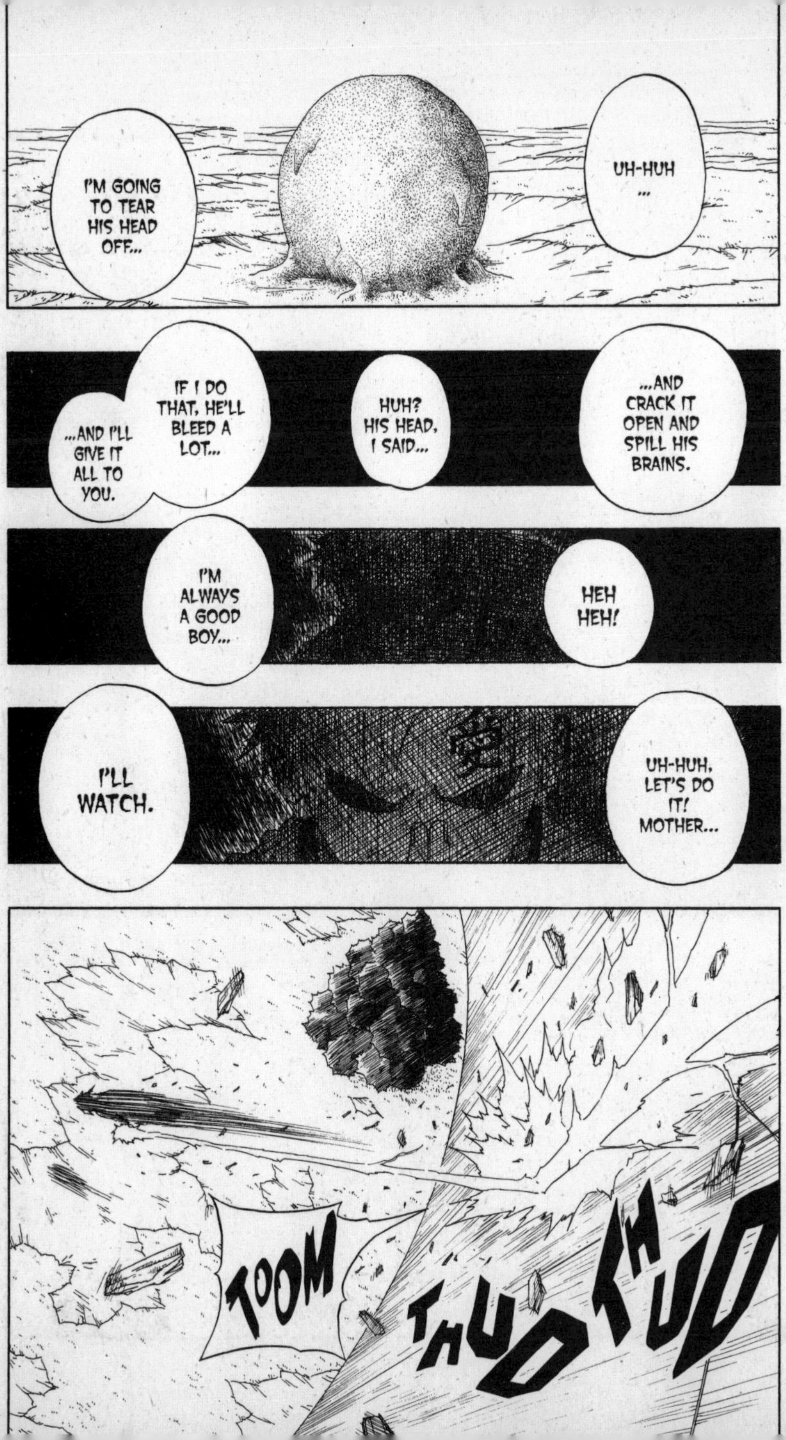
UH-HUH ...
I'M GOING TO TEAR HIS HEAD OFF...
...AND CRACK IT OPEN AND SPILL HIS BRAINS.
HUH? HIS HEAD, I SAID...
IF I DO THAT, HE'LL BLEED A LOT...
...AND I'LL GIVE IT ALL TO YOU.
HEH HEH!
I'M ALWAYS A GOOD BOY...
UH-HUH, LET'S DO IT! MOTHER...
I'LL WATCH.
THUD
THUD
TOOM

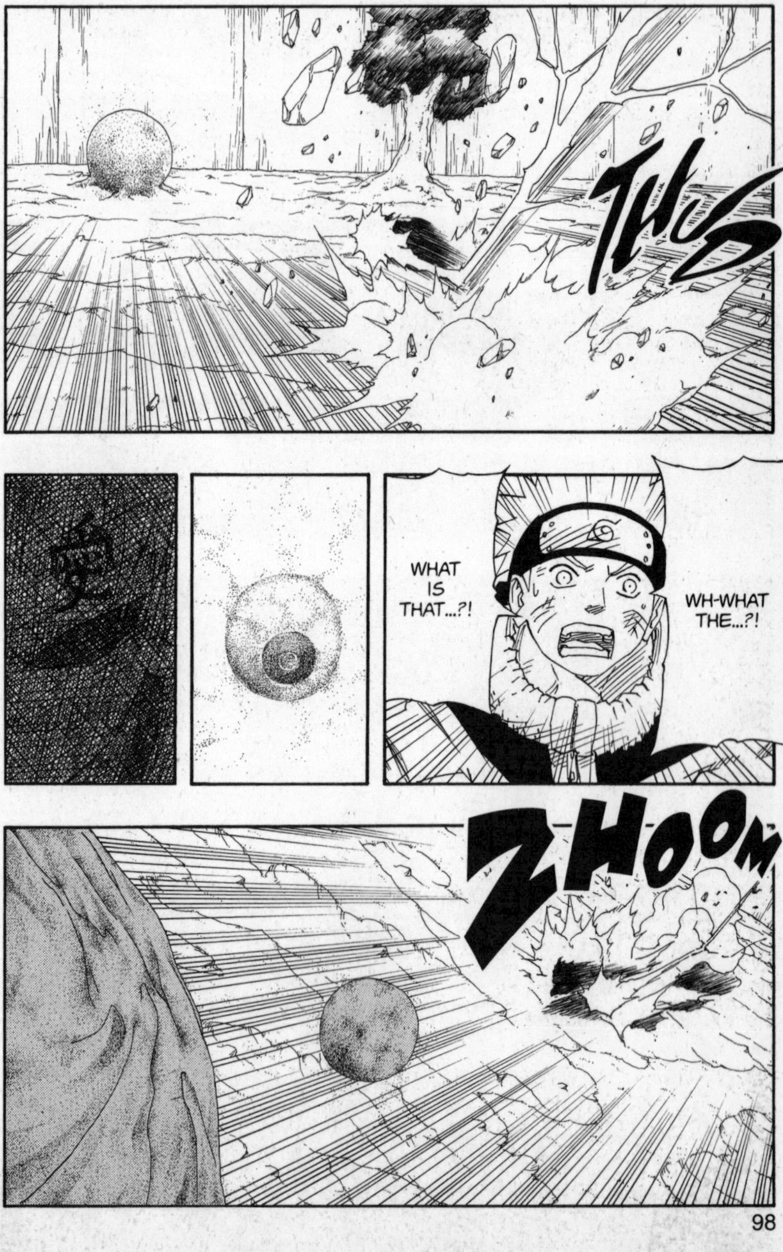
THWUD
WH-WHAT THE...?!
WHAT IS THAT...?!
ZHOOM

TRULY...

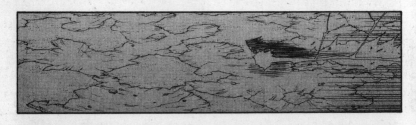

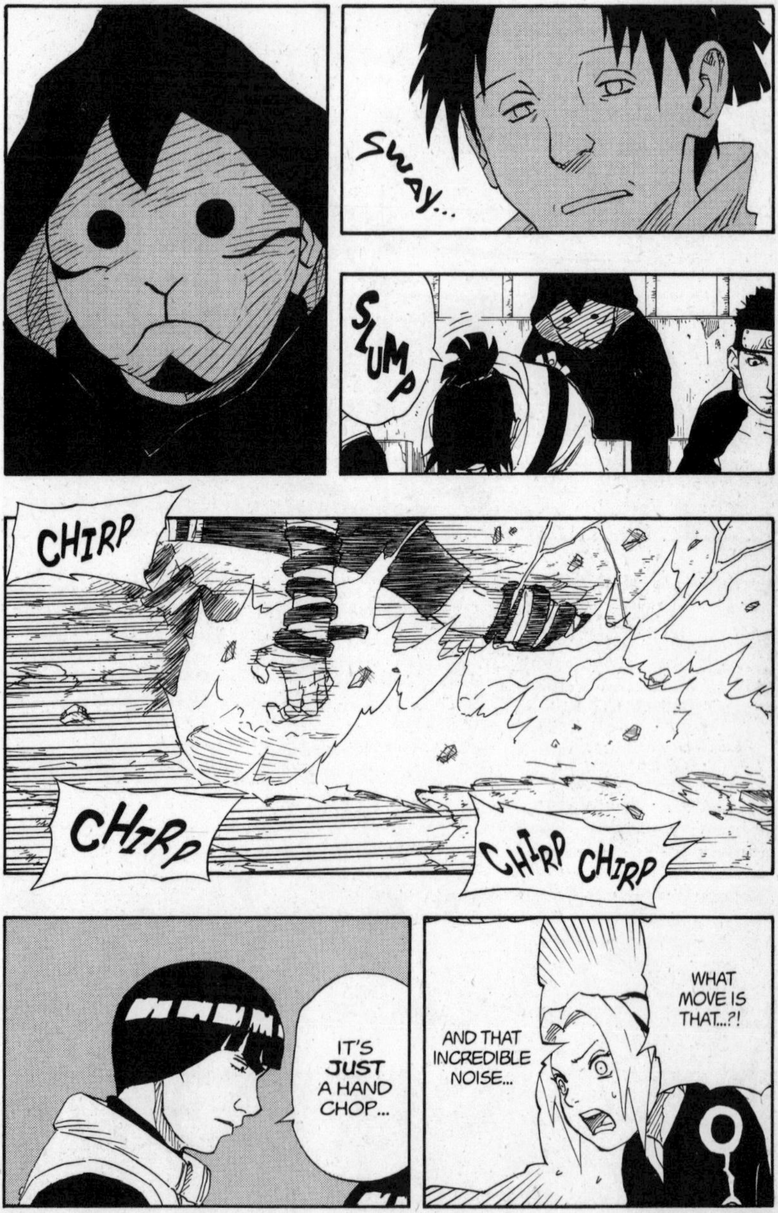
SWAY...
SLUMP
CHIRP
CHIRP CHIRP
CHIRP
WHAT MOVE IS THAT...?!
AND THAT INCREDIBLE NOISE...
IT'S **JUST** A HAND CHOP...

READ THIS WAY

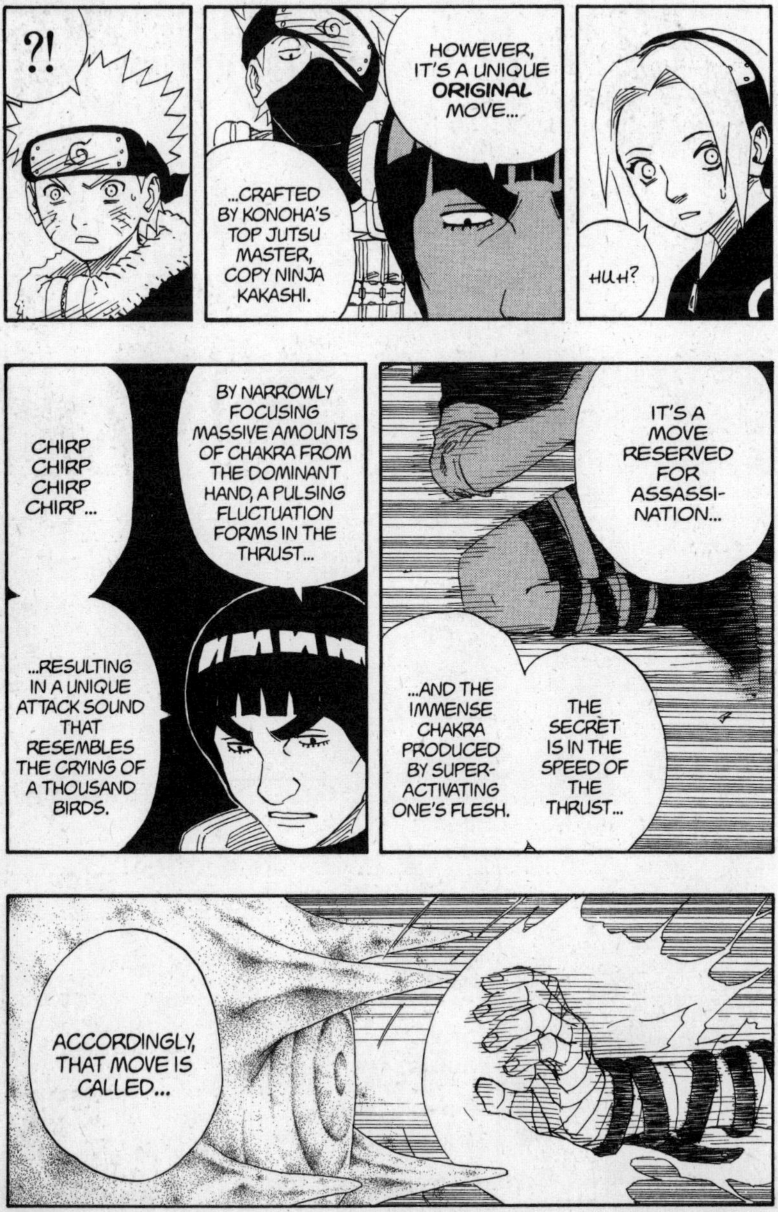
HUH?
HOWEVER, IT'S A UNIQUE **ORIGINAL** MOVE...
...CRAFTED BY KONOHA'S TOP JUTSU MASTER, COPY NINJA KAKASHI.
?!
IT'S A MOVE RESERVED FOR ASSASSI-NATION...
THE SECRET IS IN THE SPEED OF THE THRUST...
...AND THE IMMENSE CHAKRA PRODUCED BY SUPER-ACTIVATING ONE'S FLESH.
BY NARROWLY FOCUSING MASSIVE AMOUNTS OF CHAKRA FROM THE DOMINANT HAND, A PULSING FLUCTUATION FORMS IN THE THRUST...
CHIRP CHIRP CHIRP CHIRP...
...RESULTING IN A UNIQUE ATTACK SOUND THAT RESEMBLES THE CRYING OF A THOUSAND BIRDS.
ACCORDINGLY, THAT MOVE IS CALLED...

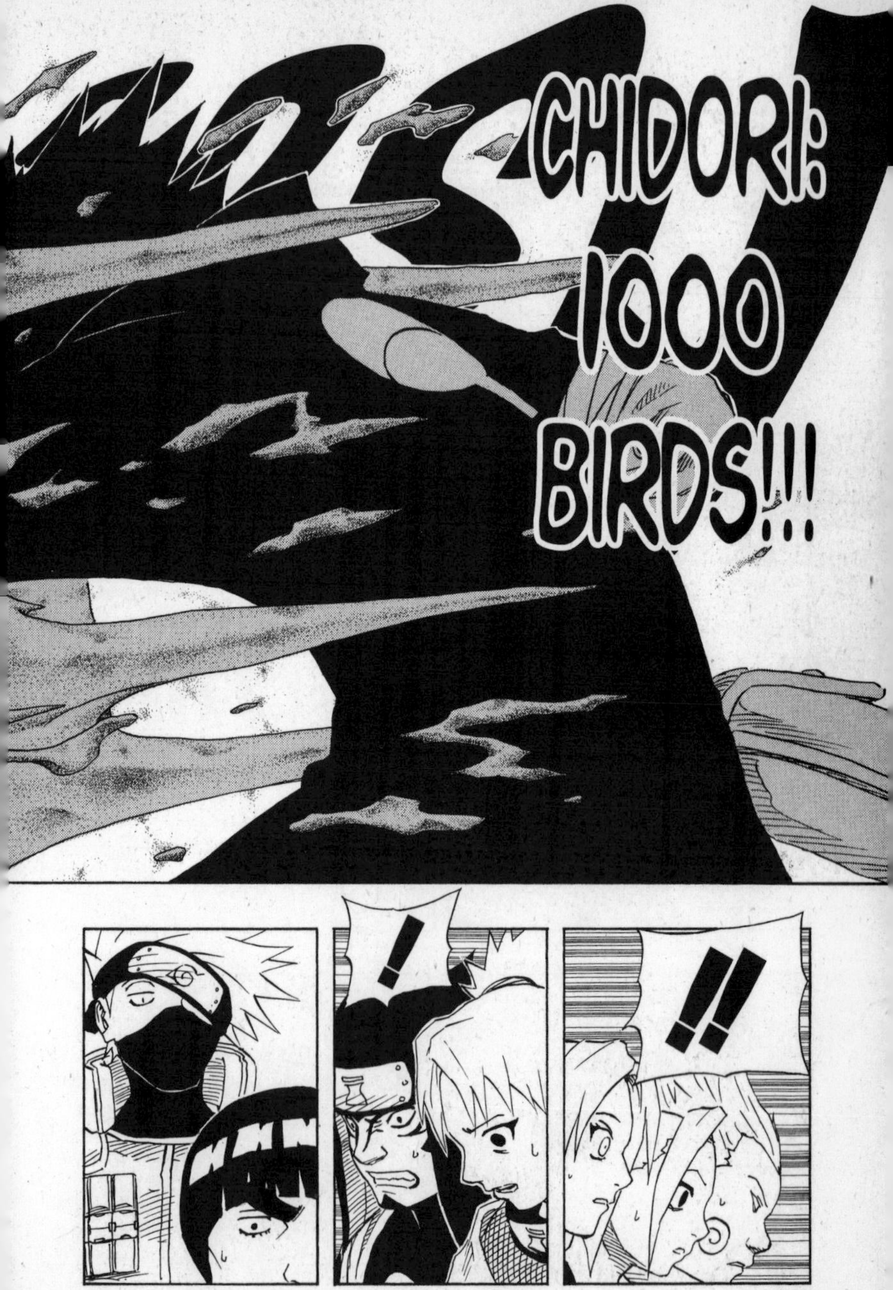
CHIDORI: 1000 BIRDS!!!
!!
!

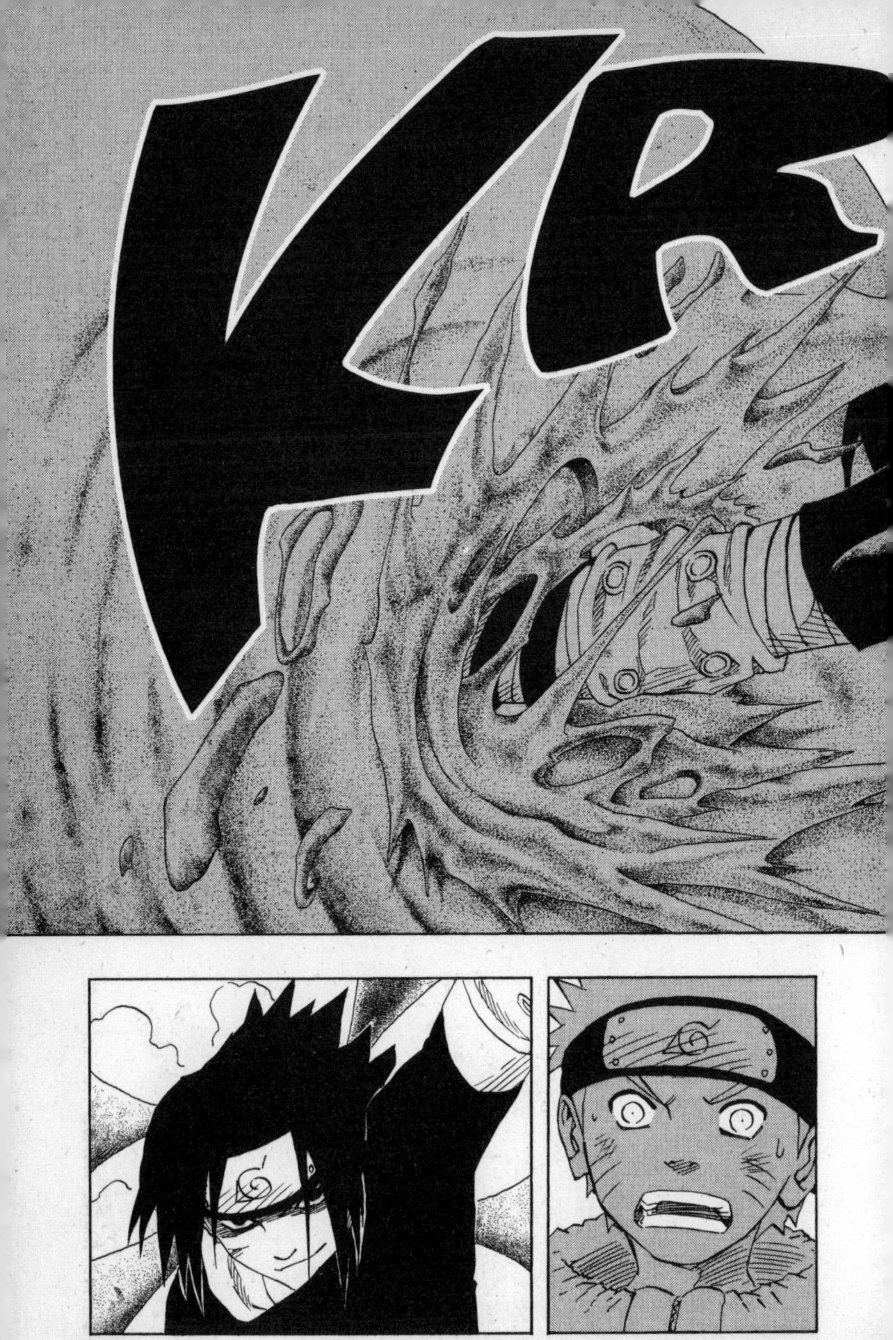

Number 114: Violent Assault...!!

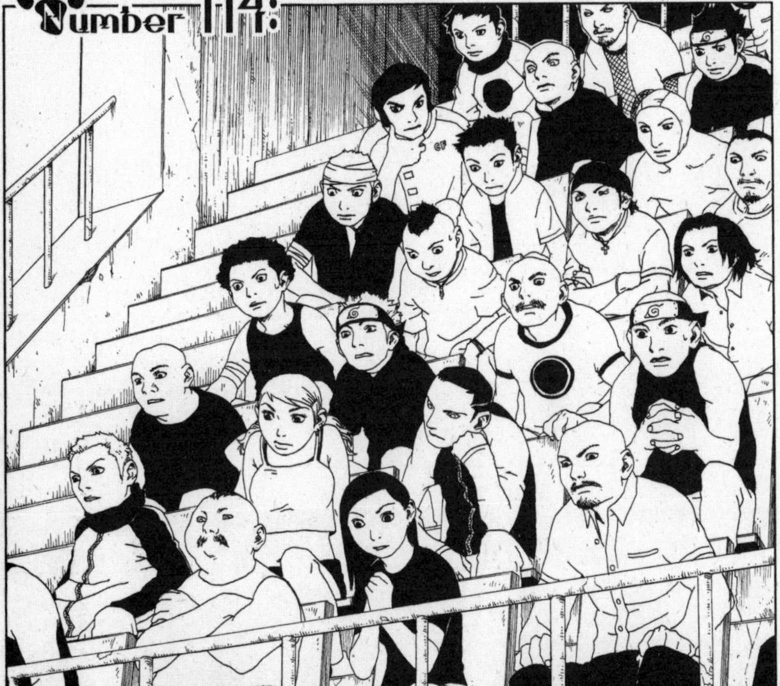

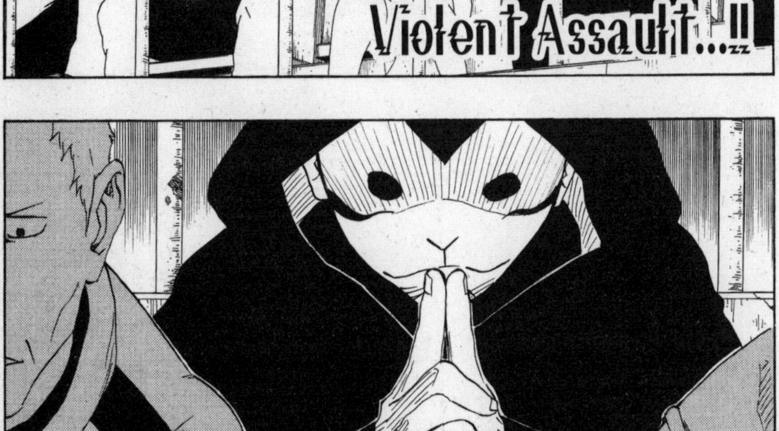

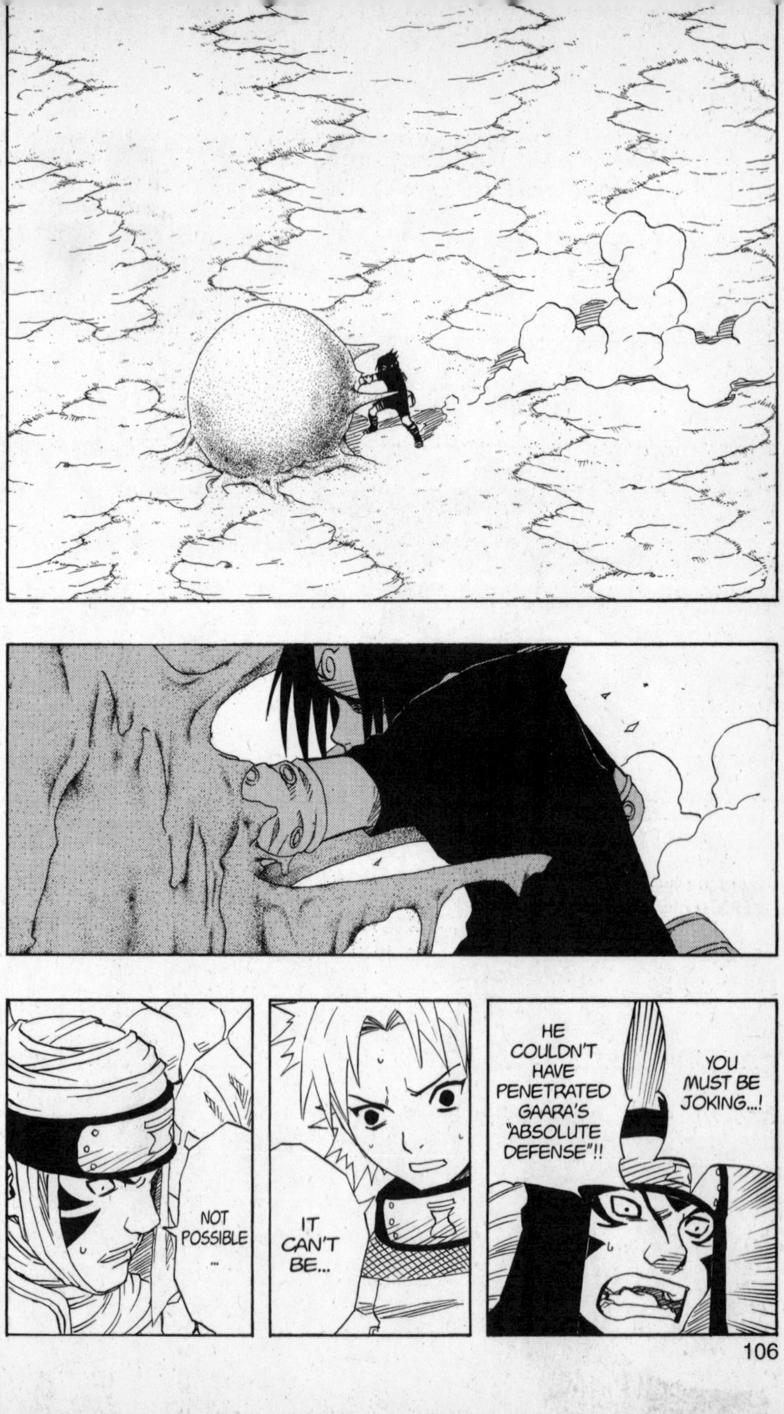
YOU MUST BE JOKING...!
HE COULDN'T HAVE PENETRATED GAARA'S "ABSOLUTE DEFENSE"!!
IT CAN'T BE...
NOT POSSIBLE ...

READ THIS WAY

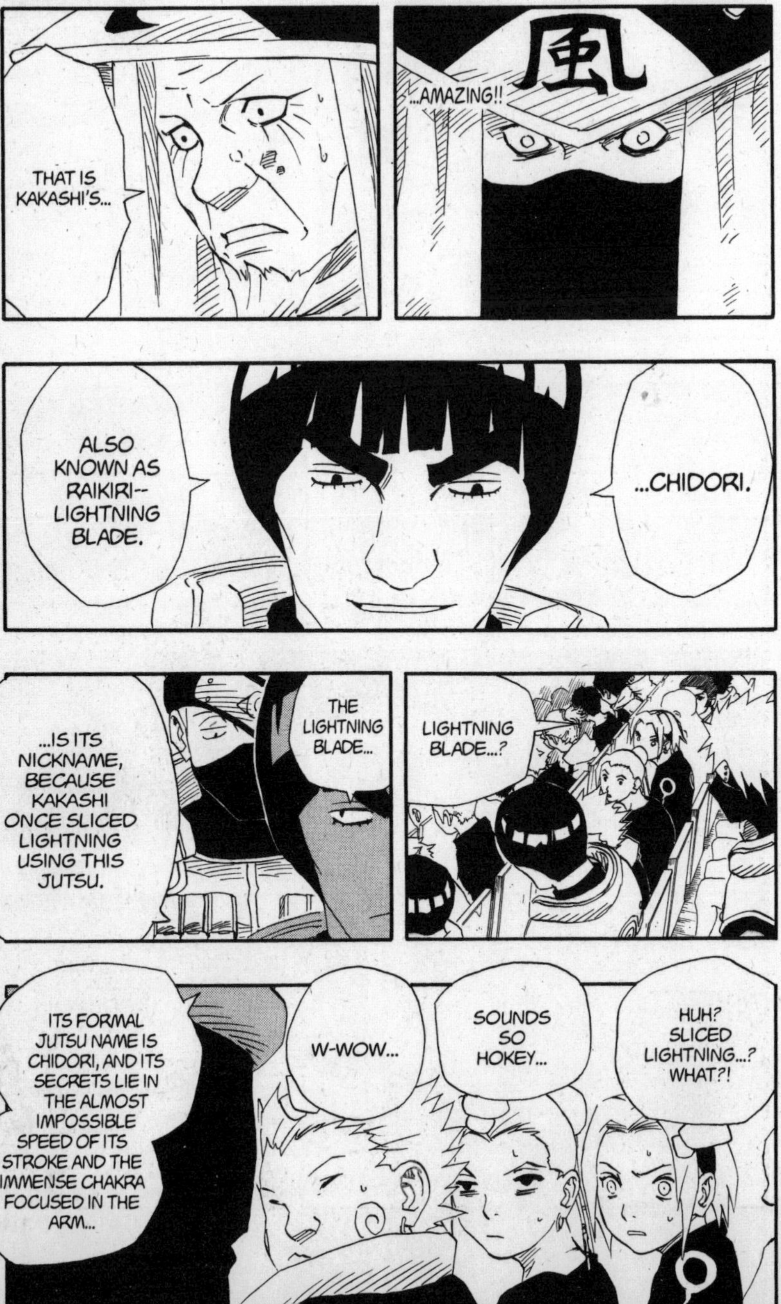
風
...AMAZING!!
THAT IS KAKASHI'S...
...CHIDORI.
ALSO KNOWN AS RAIKIRI-- LIGHTNING BLADE.
LIGHTNING BLADE...?
THE LIGHTNING BLADE...
...IS ITS NICKNAME, BECAUSE KAKASHI ONCE SLICED LIGHTNING USING THIS JUTSU.
HUH? SLICED LIGHTNING...? WHAT?!
SOUNDS SO HOKEY...
W-WOW...
ITS FORMAL JUTSU NAME IS CHIDORI, AND ITS SECRETS LIE IN THE ALMOST IMPOSSIBLE SPEED OF ITS STROKE AND THE IMMENSE CHAKRA FOCUSED IN THE ARM...

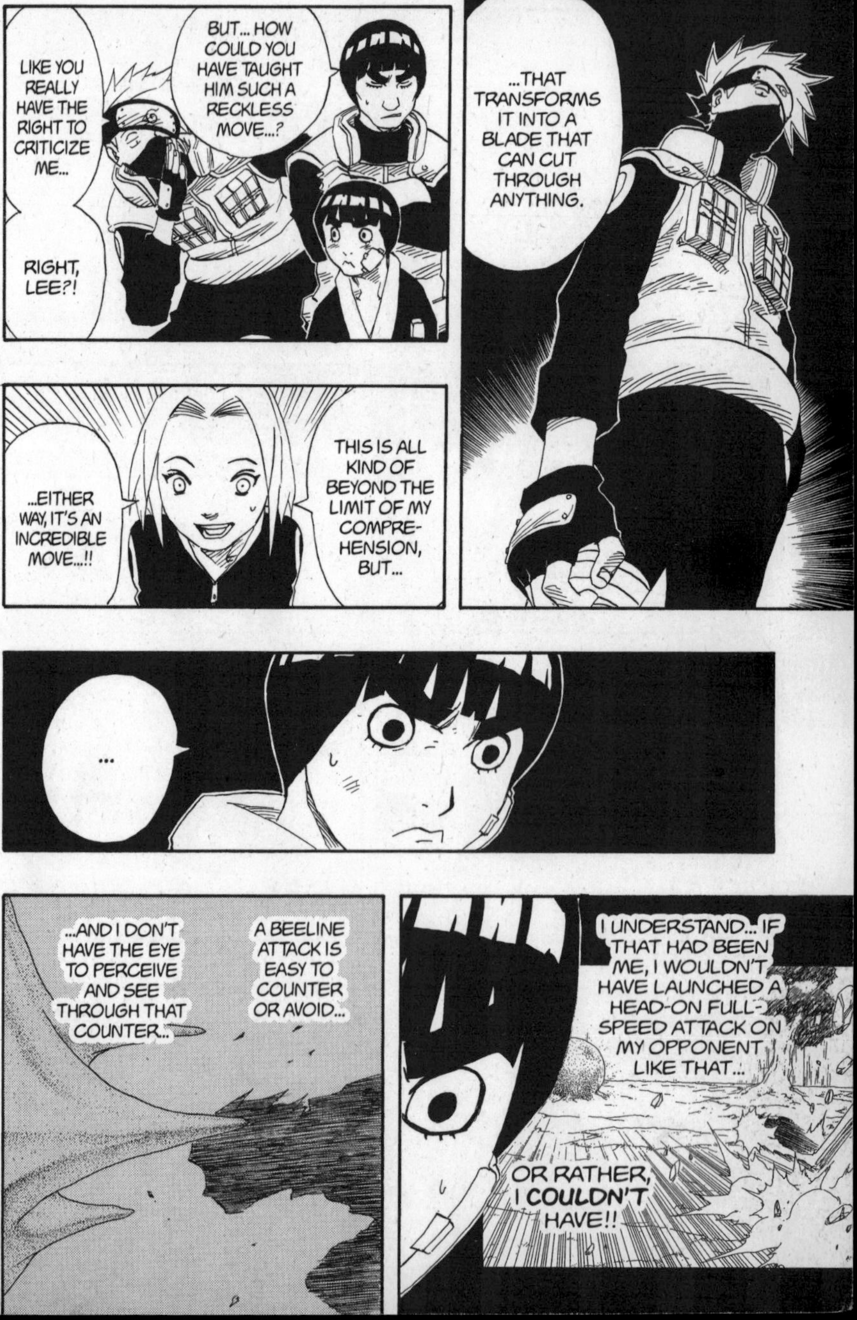
...THAT TRANSFORMS IT INTO A BLADE THAT CAN CUT THROUGH ANYTHING.
BUT... HOW COULD YOU HAVE TAUGHT HIM SUCH A RECKLESS MOVE...?
LIKE YOU REALLY HAVE THE RIGHT TO CRITICIZE ME...
RIGHT, LEE?!
THIS IS ALL KIND OF BEYOND THE LIMIT OF MY COMPRE-HENSION, BUT...
...EITHER WAY, IT'S AN INCREDIBLE MOVE...!!
...
I UNDERSTAND... IF THAT HAD BEEN ME, I WOULDN'T HAVE LAUNCHED A HEAD-ON FULL-SPEED ATTACK ON MY OPPONENT LIKE THAT...
OR RATHER, I **COULDN'T** HAVE!!
A BEELINE ATTACK IS EASY TO COUNTER OR AVOID...
...AND I DON'T HAVE THE EYE TO PERCEIVE AND SEE THROUGH THAT COUNTER...

READ THIS WAY

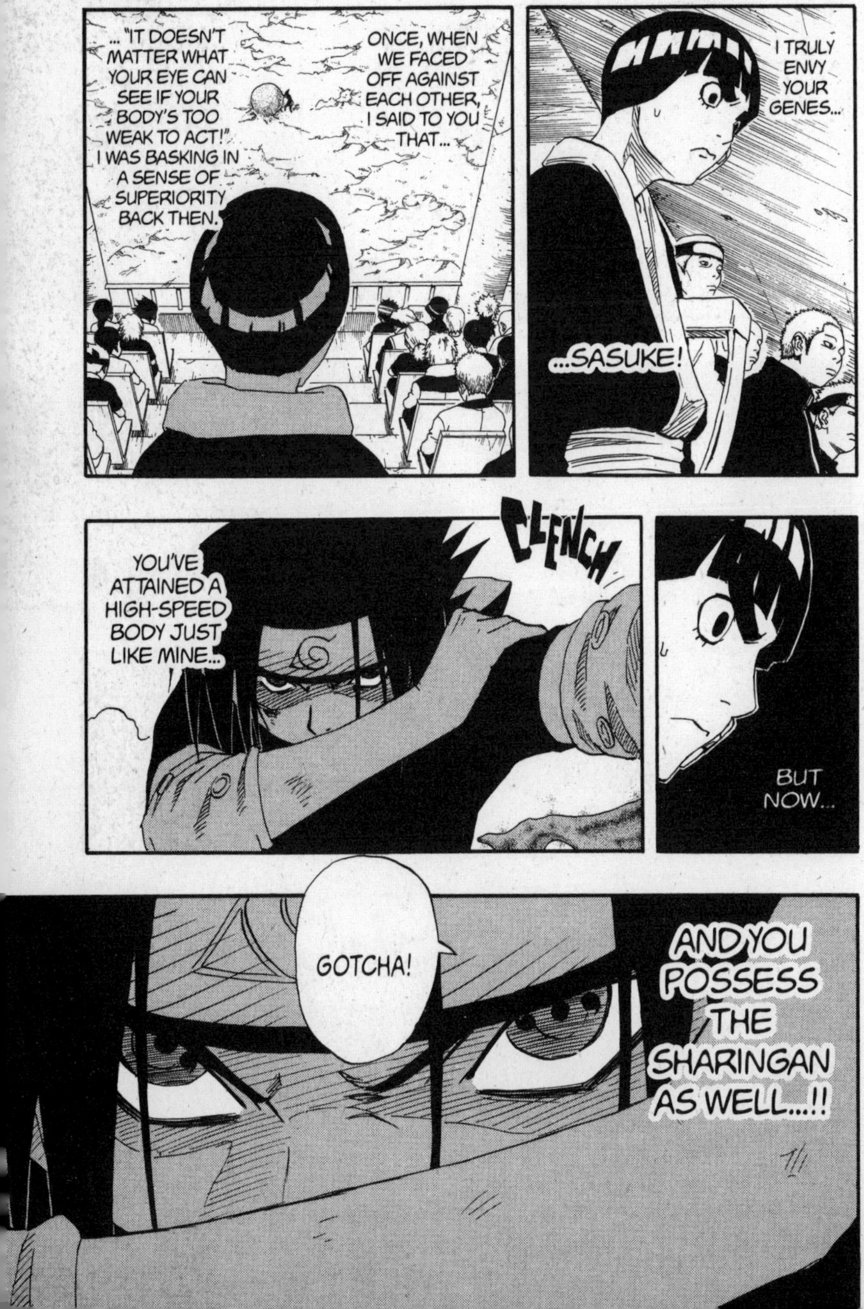
I TRULY ENVY YOUR GENES...
...SASUKE!
ONCE, WHEN WE FACED OFF AGAINST EACH OTHER, I SAID TO YOU THAT...
..."IT DOESN'T MATTER WHAT YOUR EYE CAN SEE IF YOUR BODY'S TOO WEAK TO ACT!" I WAS BASKING IN A SENSE OF SUPERIORITY BACK THEN.
BUT NOW...
CLENCH
YOU'VE ATTAINED A HIGH-SPEED BODY JUST LIKE MINE...
AND YOU POSSESS THE SHARINGAN AS WELL...!!
GOTCHA!

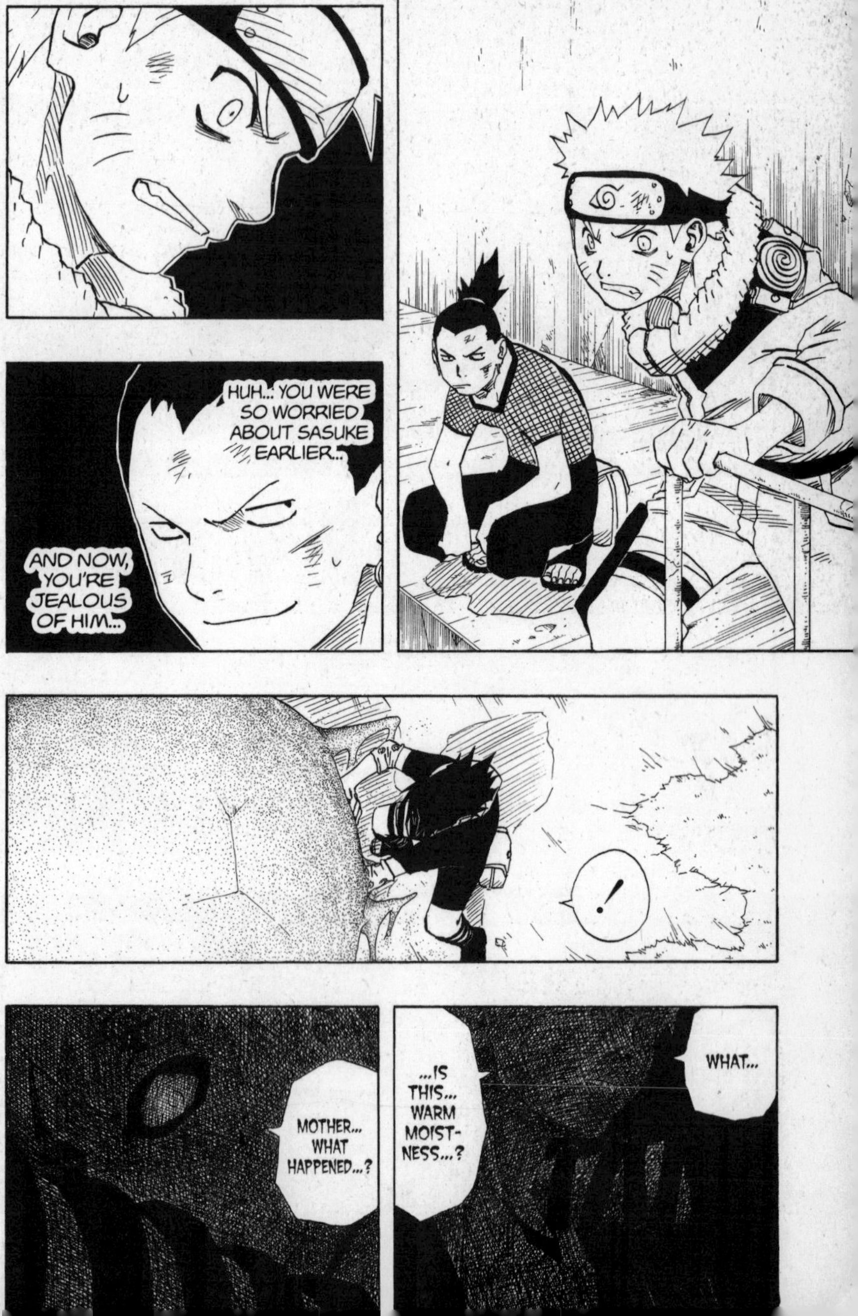
HUH... YOU WERE SO WORRIED ABOUT SASUKE EARLIER...
AND NOW, YOU'RE JEALOUS OF HIM...
!
WHAT...
...IS THIS... WARM MOIST-NESS...?
MOTHER... WHAT HAPPENED...?

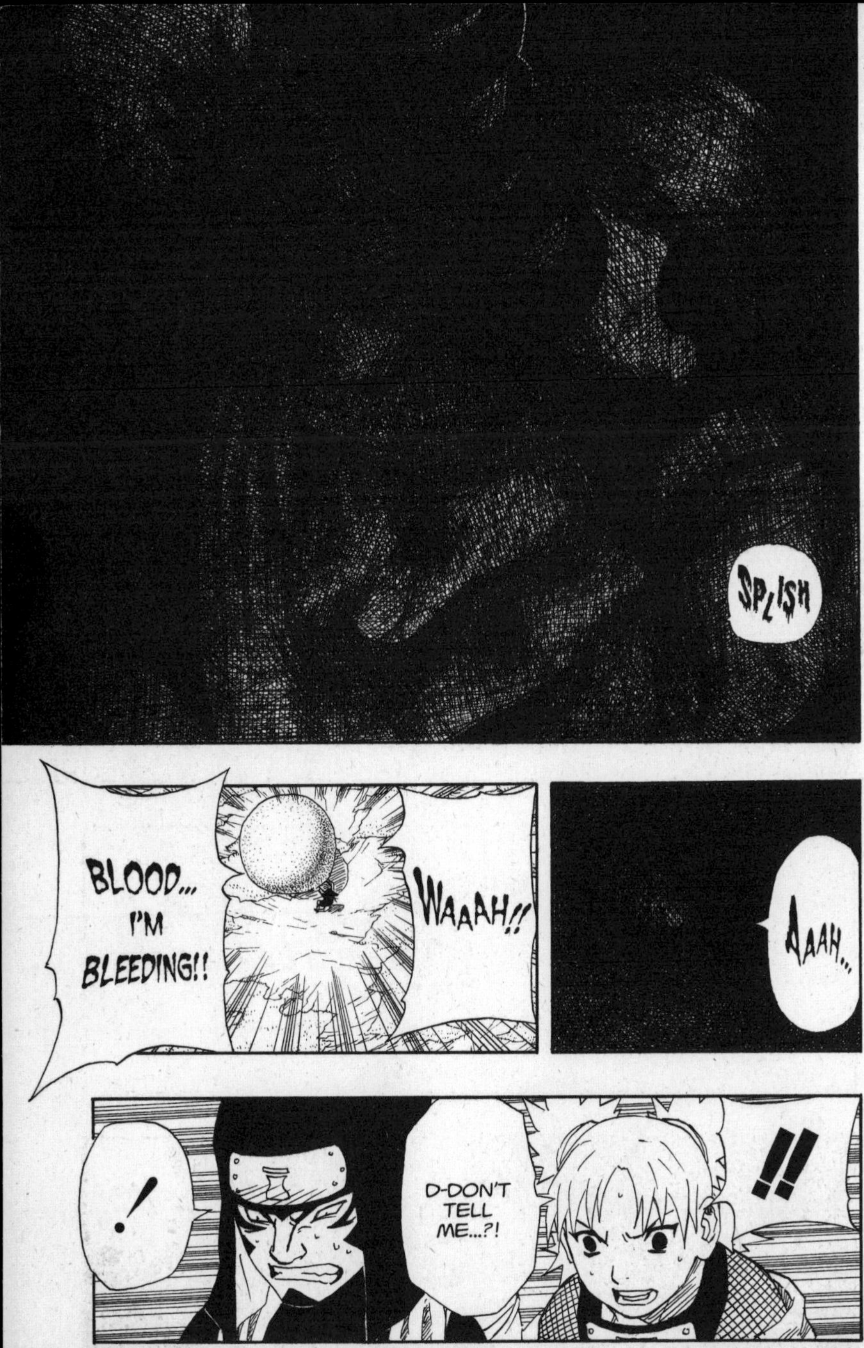
SPLISH
AAAH...
WAAAH!!
BLOOD... I'M BLEEDING!!
!!
D-DON'T TELL ME...?!
!

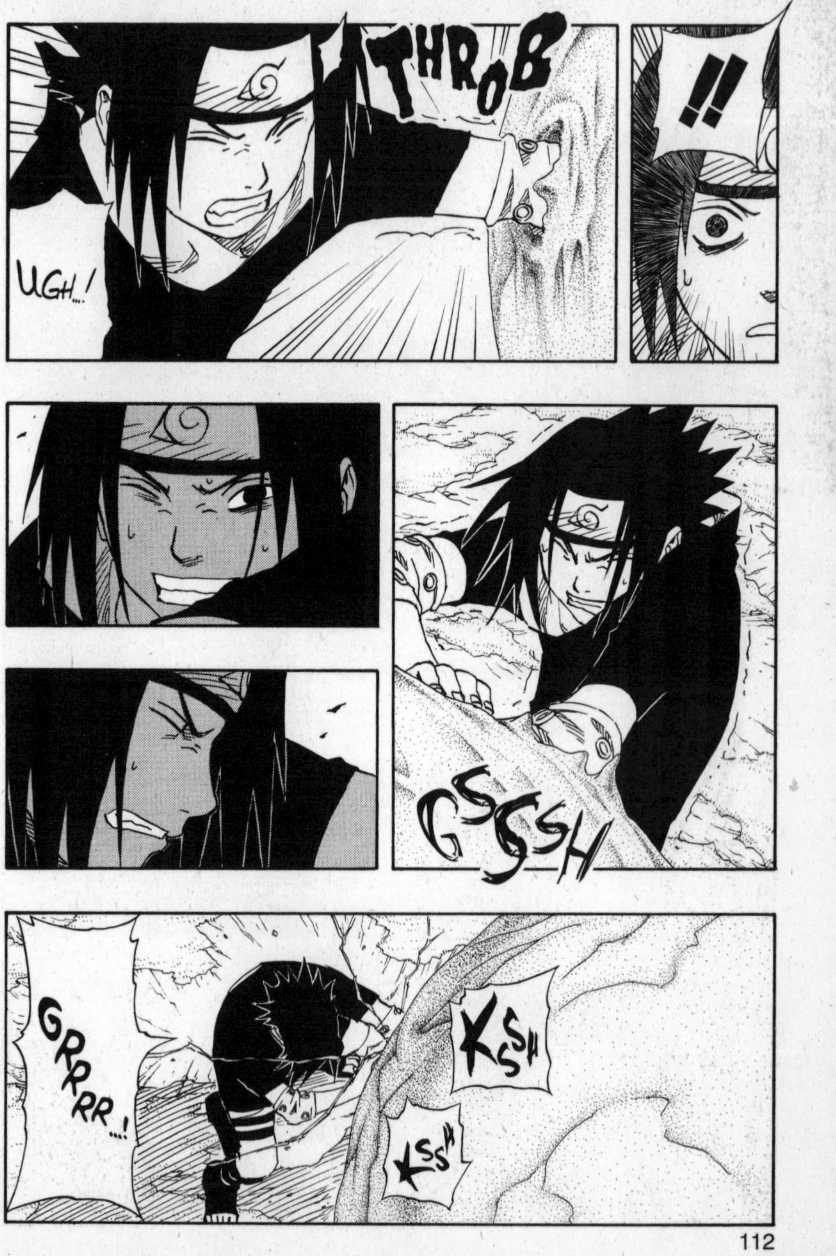
!!
THROB
UGH...!
GSSSH
KSSH
KSSH
GRRRR...!

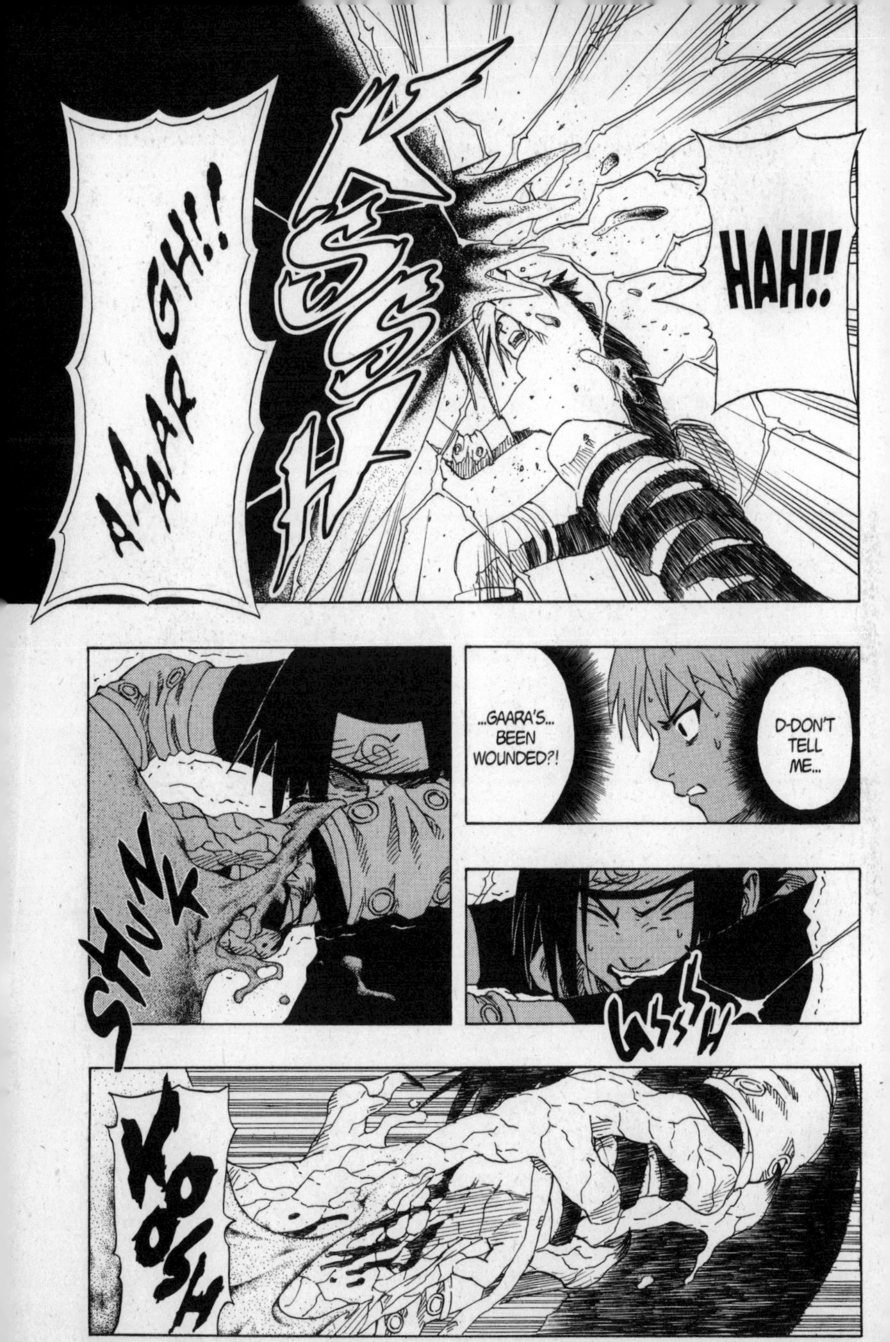
HAH!!
KSSSH
AAARRGH!!
D-DON'T TELL ME...
...GAARA'S... BEEN WOUNDED?!
GSSSH
SHUNK
KOOSH

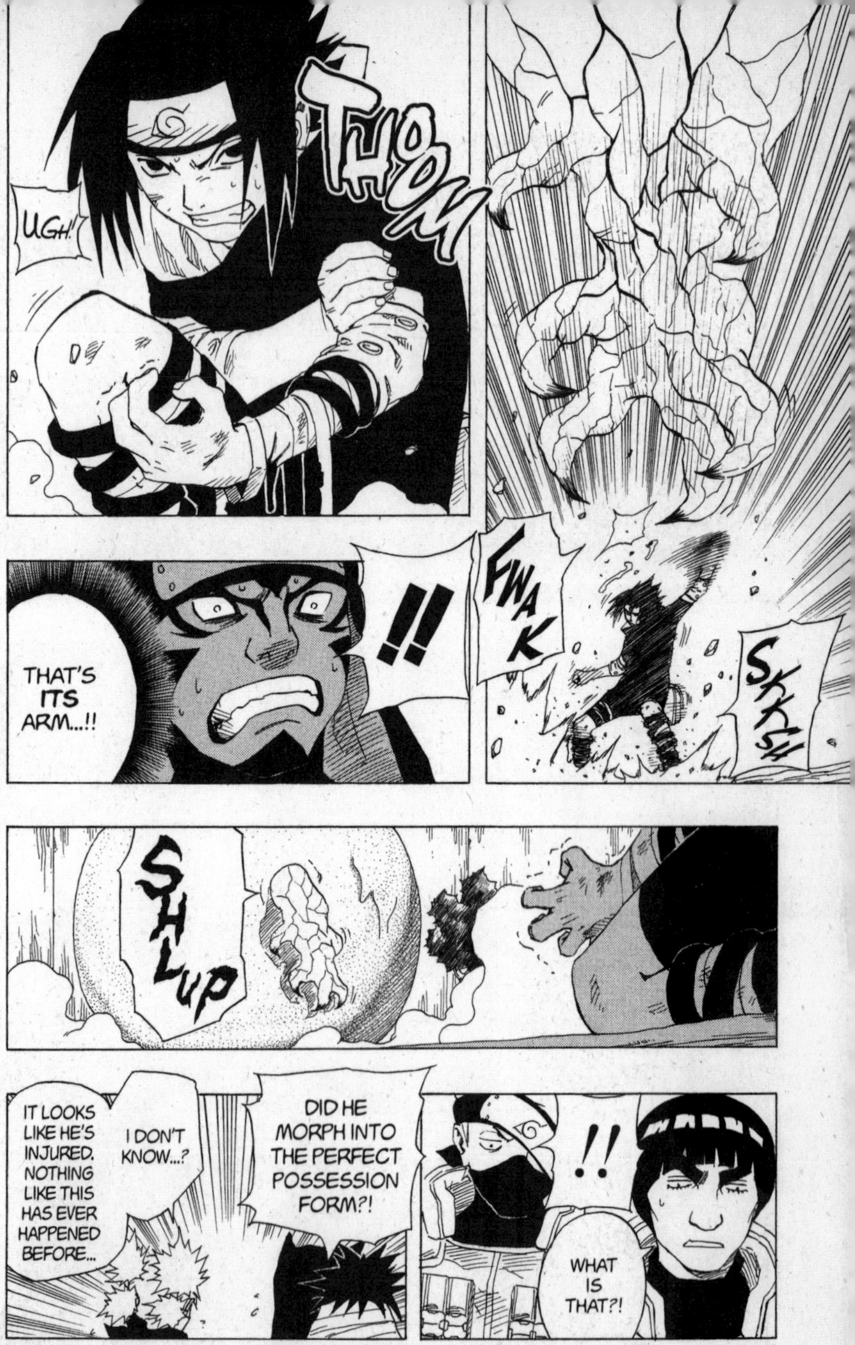
THOOM
UGH!
FWAK
SKKSH
!!
THAT'S ITS ARM...!!
SHLUP
!!
WHAT IS THAT?!
DID HE MORPH INTO THE PERFECT POSSESSION FORM?!
I DON'T KNOW...?
IT LOOKS LIKE HE'S INJURED. NOTHING LIKE THIS HAS EVER HAPPENED BEFORE...

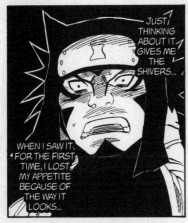

READ THIS WAY

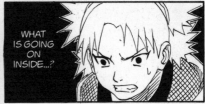

WHAT IS GOING ON INSIDE...?
DARN... WHAT HAS HE GONE AND DONE NOW...
JUST THINKING ABOUT IT GIVES ME THE SHIVERS...
WHEN I SAW IT FOR THE FIRST TIME, I LOST MY APPETITE BECAUSE OF THE WAY IT LOOKS...
...!

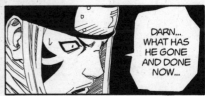

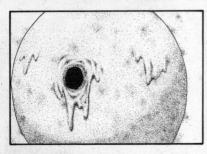

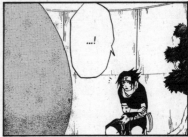

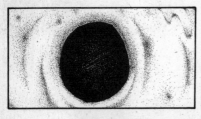

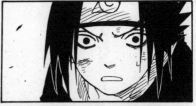

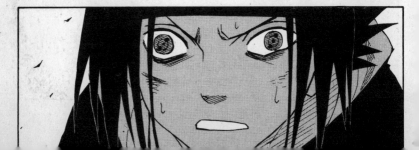

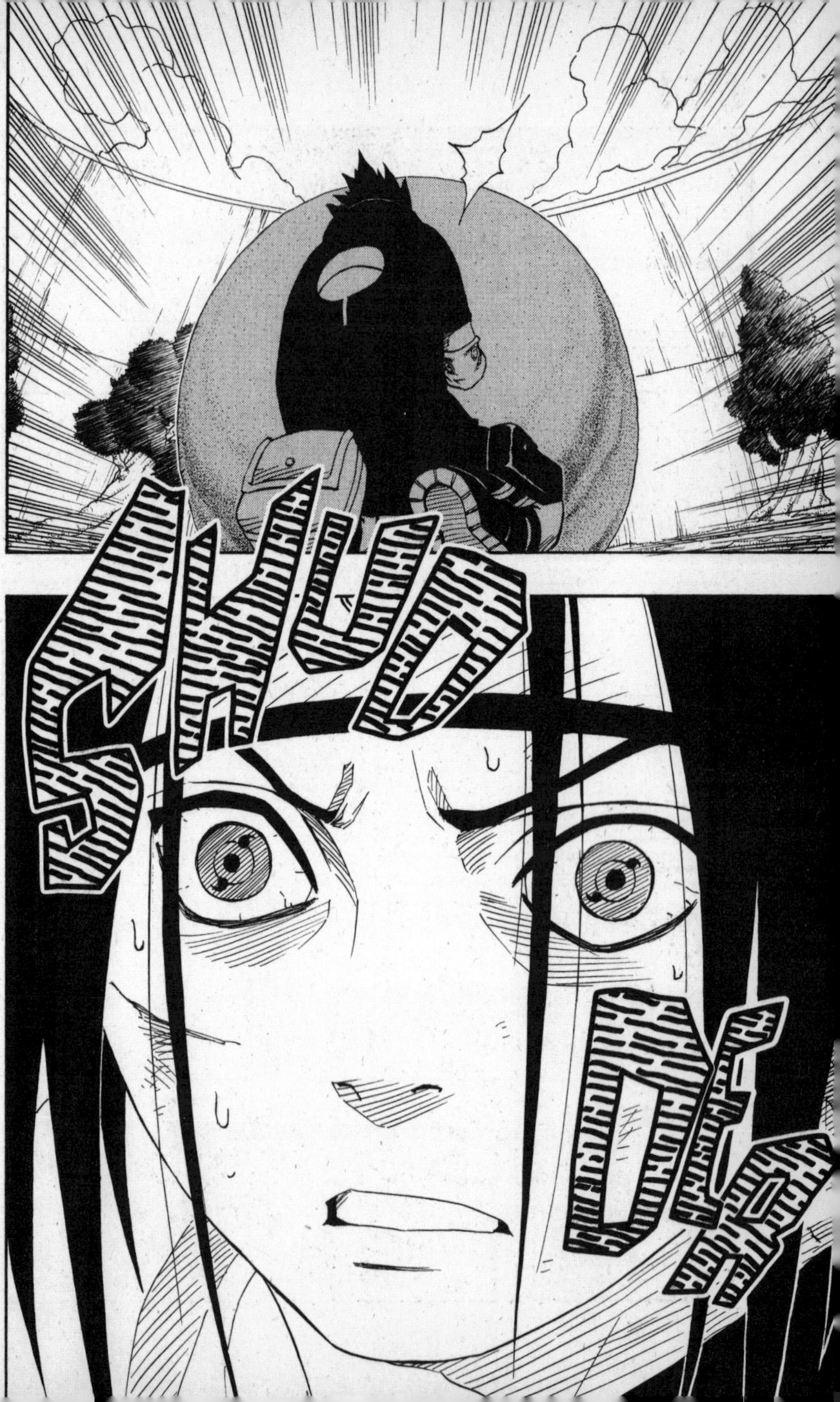

READ THIS WAY

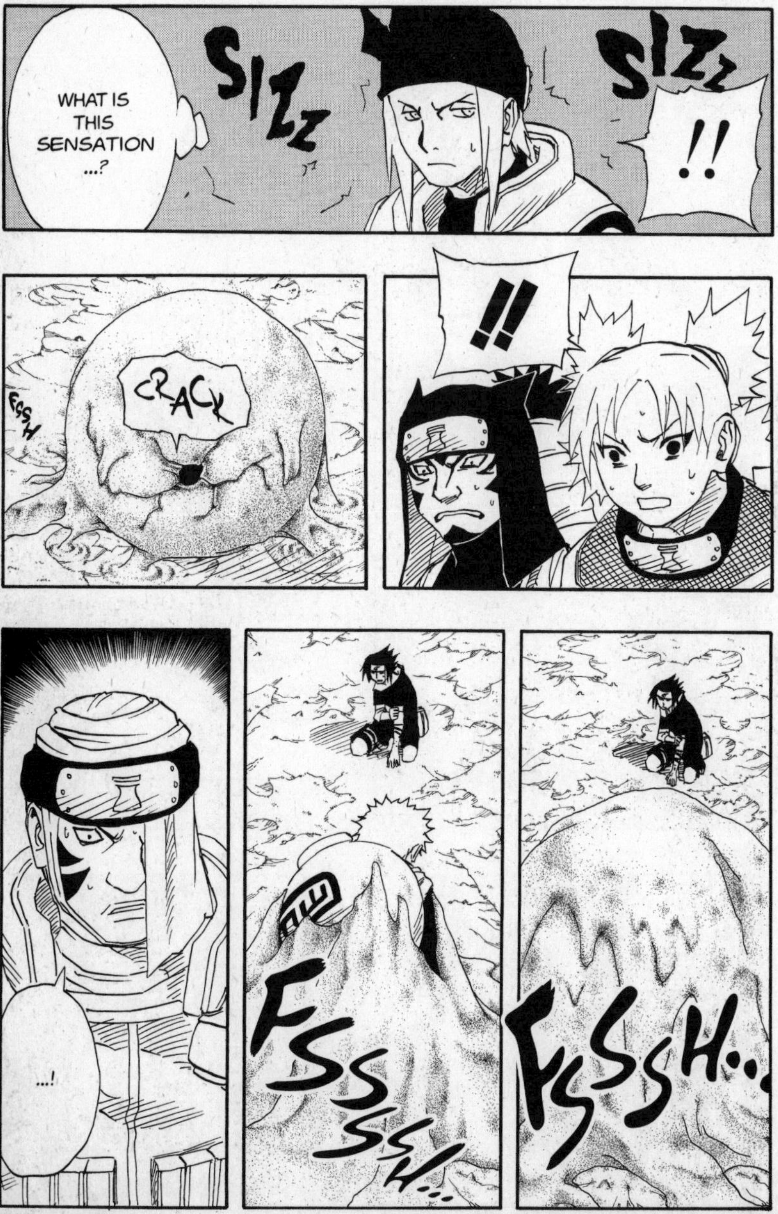

SIZZ
!!
SIZZ
WHAT IS THIS SENSATION ...?
!!
CRACK
FSSH
FSSSH...
FSSSSH...
...!

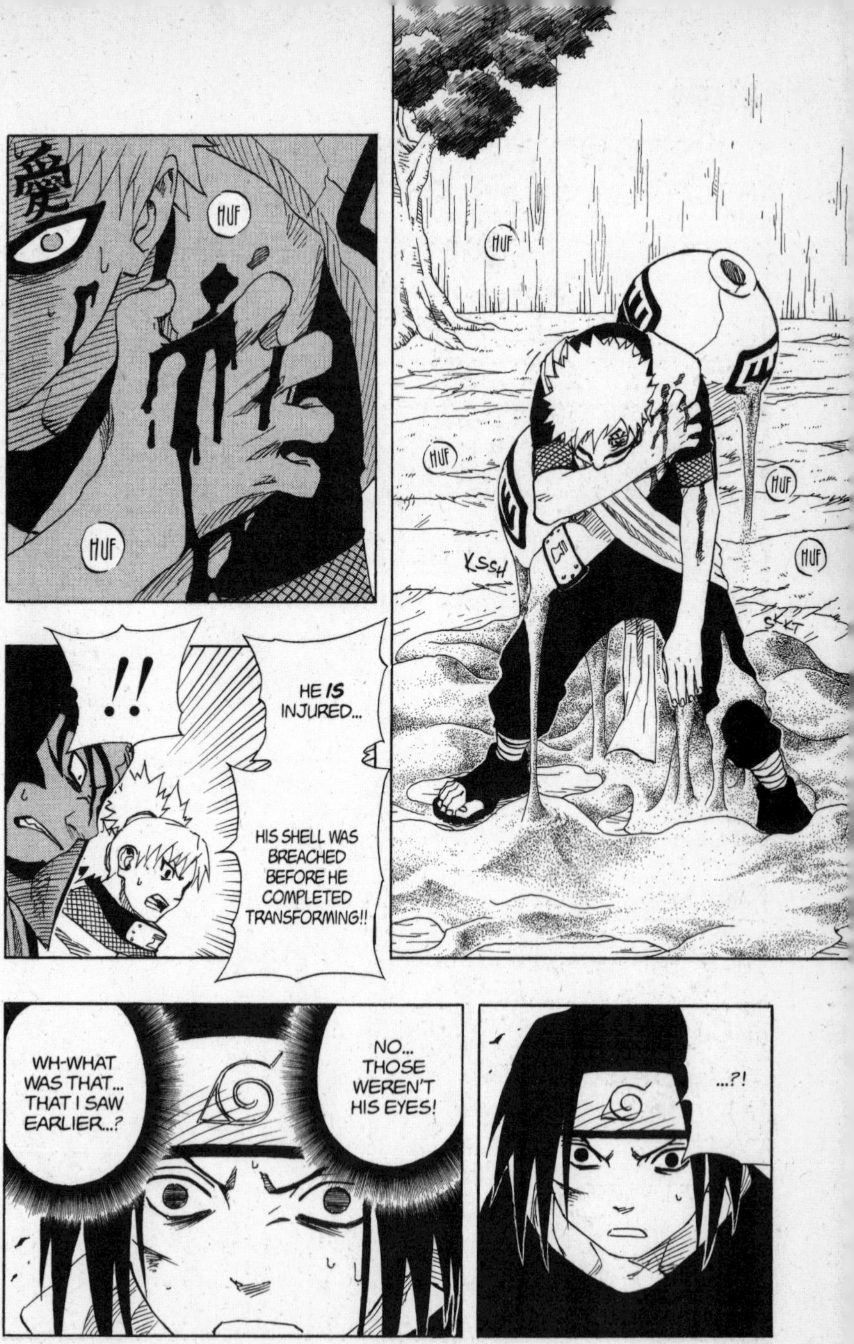
HUF
HUF
HUF
HUF
KSSH
SKKT
HUF
HUF
HE IS INJURED...
!!
HIS SHELL WAS BREACHED BEFORE HE COMPLETED TRANSFORMING!!
...?!
NO... THOSE WEREN'T HIS EYES!
WH-WHAT WAS THAT... THAT I SAW EARLIER...?

READ THIS WAY

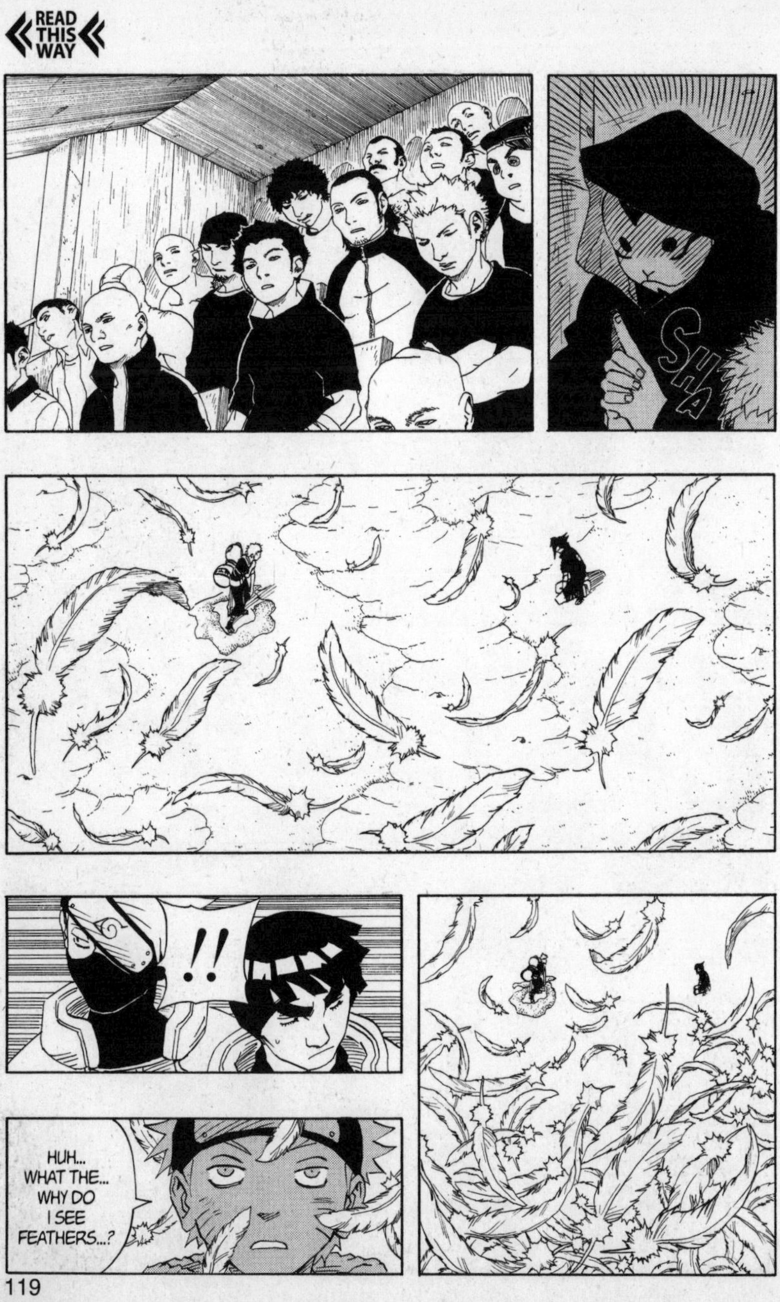

SHA
!!
HUH... WHAT THE... WHY DO I SEE FEATHERS...?

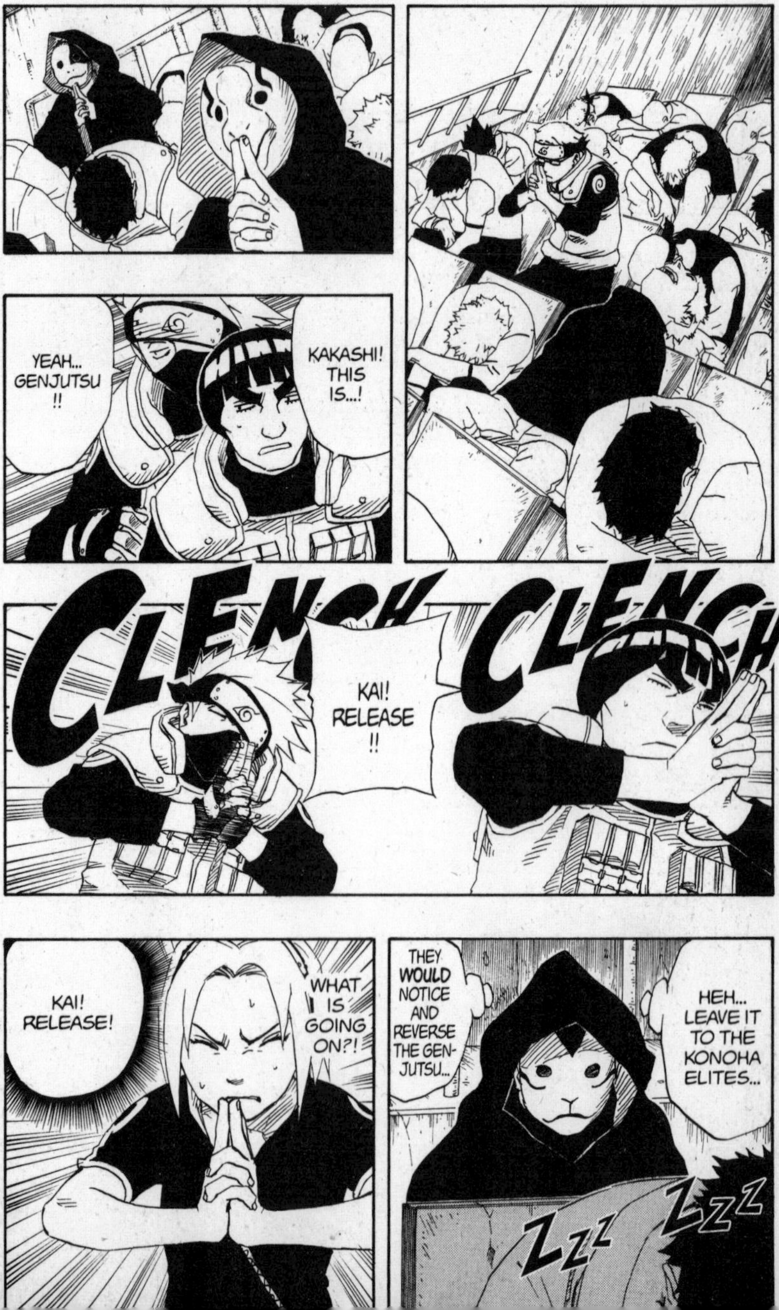
KAKASHI! THIS IS...!
YEAH... GENJUTSU !!
CLENCH
KAI! RELEASE !!
CLENCH
HEH... LEAVE IT TO THE KONOHA ELITES...
THEY **WOULD** NOTICE AND REVERSE THE GEN-JUTSU...
ZZZ
ZZZ
WHAT IS GOING ON?!
KAI! RELEASE!

READ THIS WAY

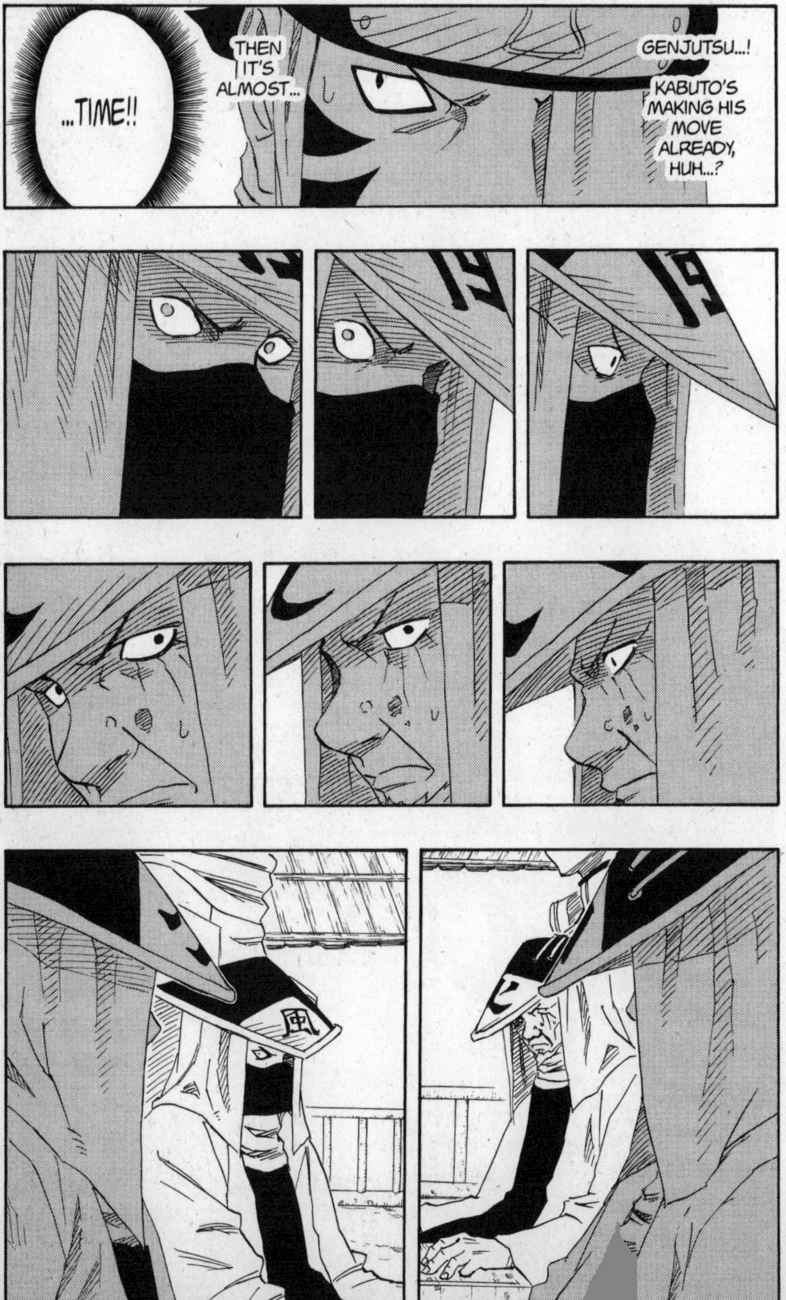
GENJUTSU...!
KABUTO'S MAKING HIS MOVE ALREADY, HUH...?
THEN IT'S ALMOST...
...TIME!!

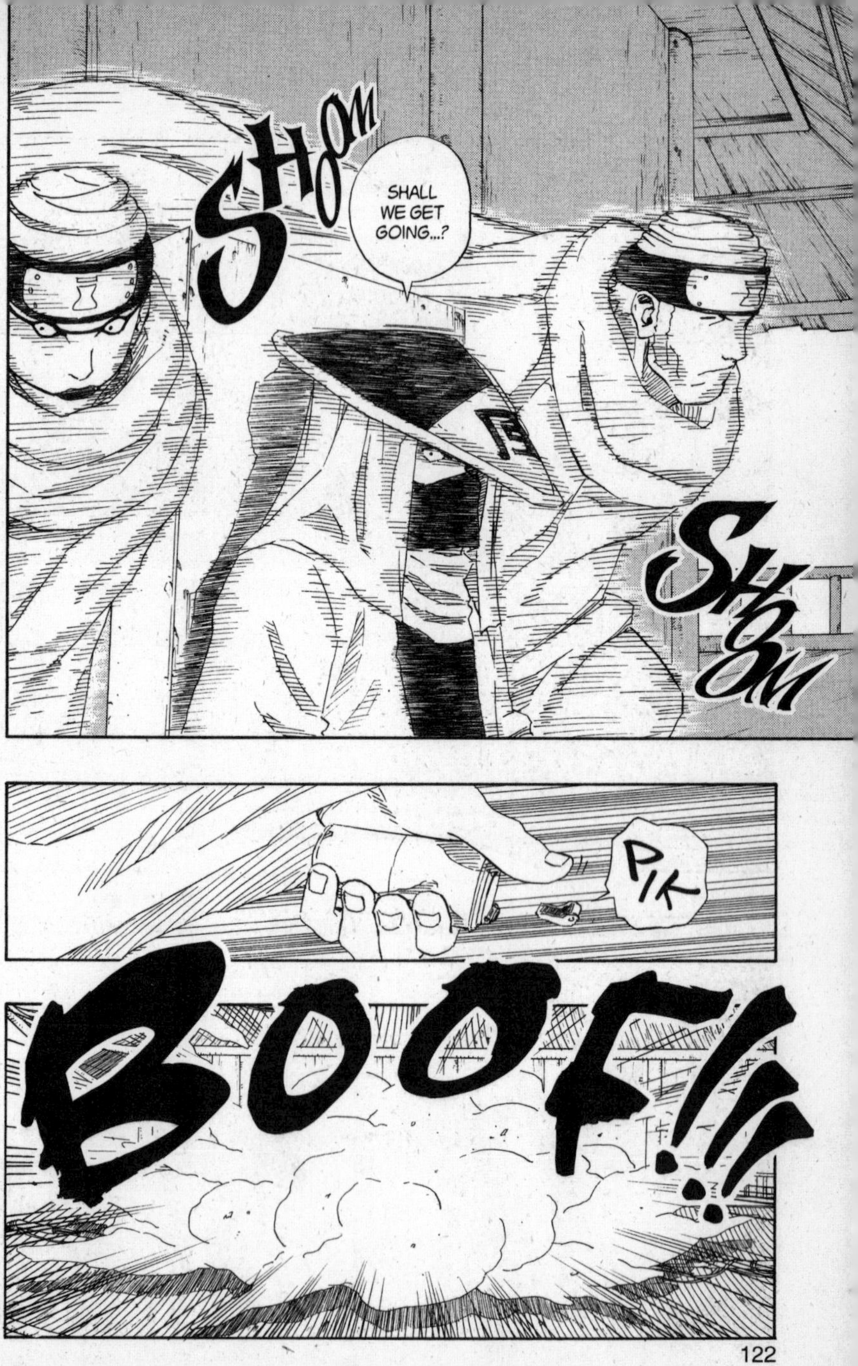
SHALL WE GET GOING...?
SHOOM
SHOOM
PIK
BOOF!!

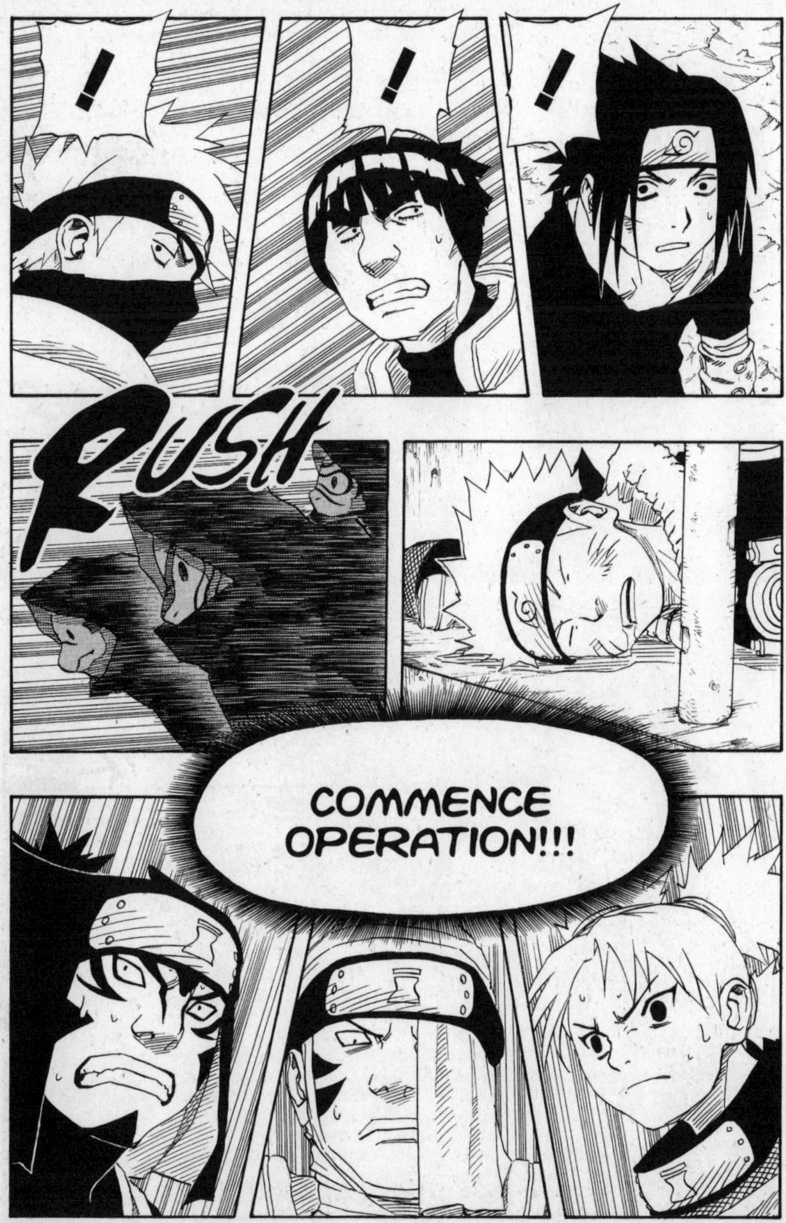
!
!
!
RUSH
COMMENCE OPERATION!!!

NARUTO IS IN ITS THIRD YEAR. AND ASSISTANTS HAVE COME AND GONE. ASSISTANT NO. 1, THE DUMB-ACTING SUPER-COOL KYUSHU NATIVE TAKAHASHI-SAN, WHO WAS THERE FROM THE VERY BEGINNING OF *NARUTO* (SEE VOLUME 6, PAGE 26) HAS LEFT OUR OFFICE, AND TWO NEW ASSISTANTS HAVE STARTED. AND SO...

MEET KISHIMOTO MASASHI'S ASSISTANTS
PART 5
ASSISTANT NO. 5: NISHIYA KOUICHI

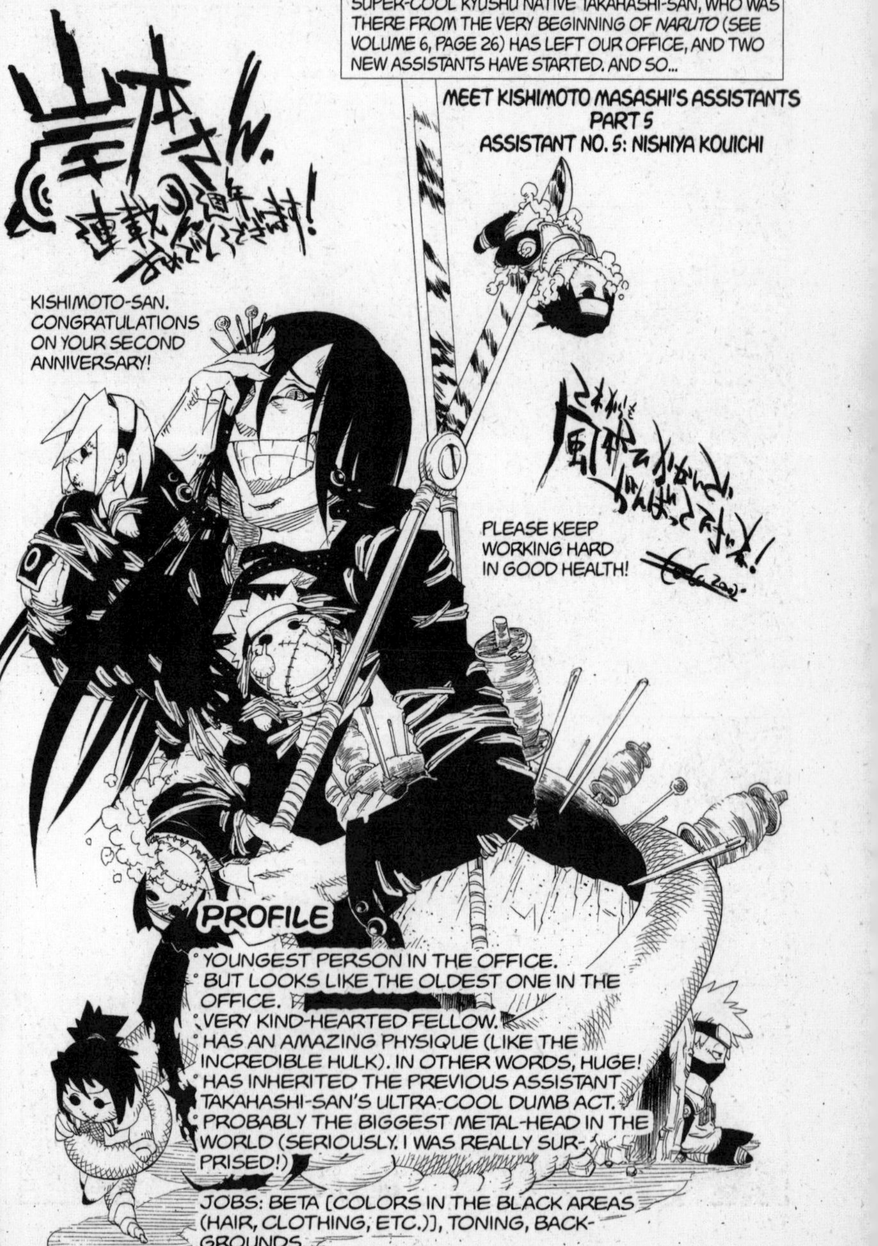
KISHIMOTO-SAN. CONGRATULATIONS ON YOUR SECOND ANNIVERSARY!
PLEASE KEEP WORKING HARD IN GOOD HEALTH!

PROFILE

- YOUNGEST PERSON IN THE OFFICE.
- BUT LOOKS LIKE THE OLDEST ONE IN THE OFFICE. [redacted]
- VERY KIND-HEARTED FELLOW.
- HAS AN AMAZING PHYSIQUE (LIKE THE INCREDIBLE HULK). IN OTHER WORDS, HUGE!
- HAS INHERITED THE PREVIOUS ASSISTANT TAKAHASHI-SAN'S ULTRA-COOL DUMB ACT.
- PROBABLY THE BIGGEST METAL-HEAD IN THE WORLD (SERIOUSLY. I WAS REALLY SURPRISED!)

JOBS: BETA [COLORS IN THE BLACK AREAS (HAIR, CLOTHING, ETC.)], TONING, BACKGROUNDS.

Number 115: The Chûnin Exam, Concluded...!!

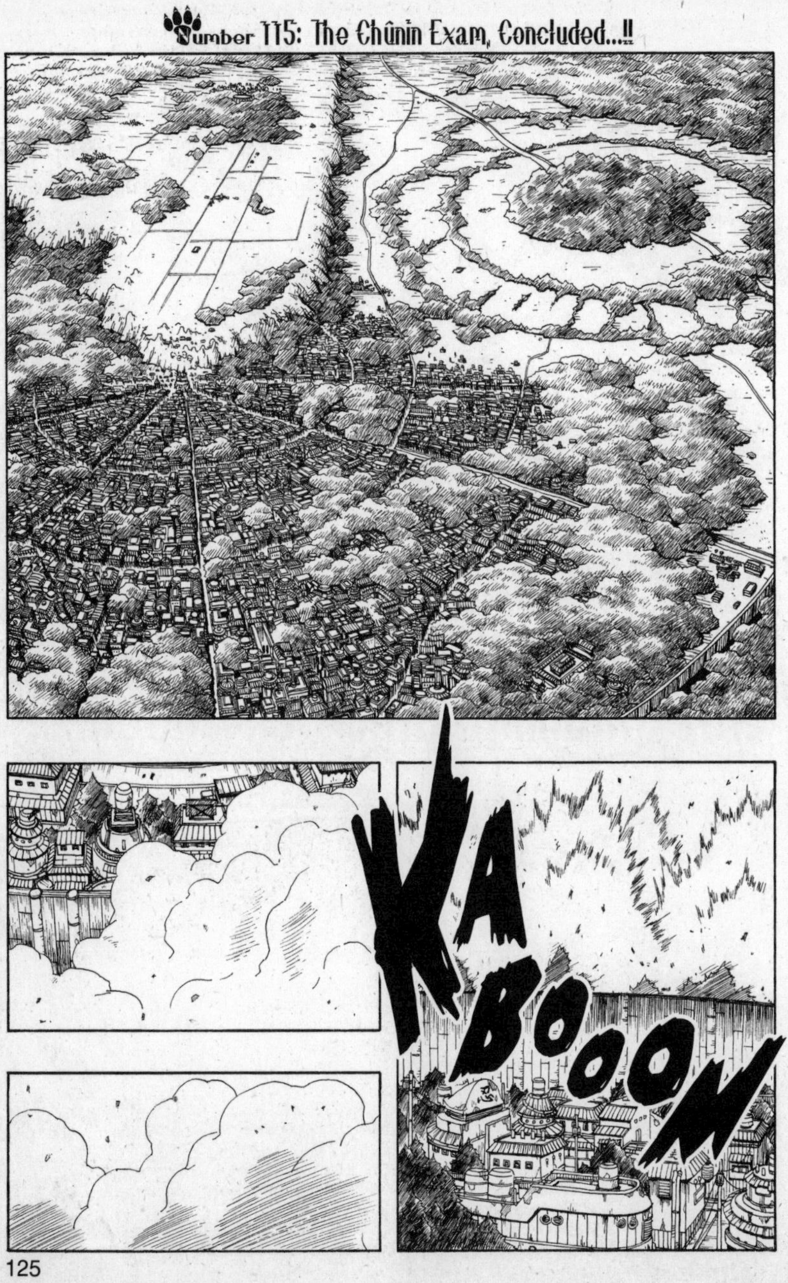
KABOOOM

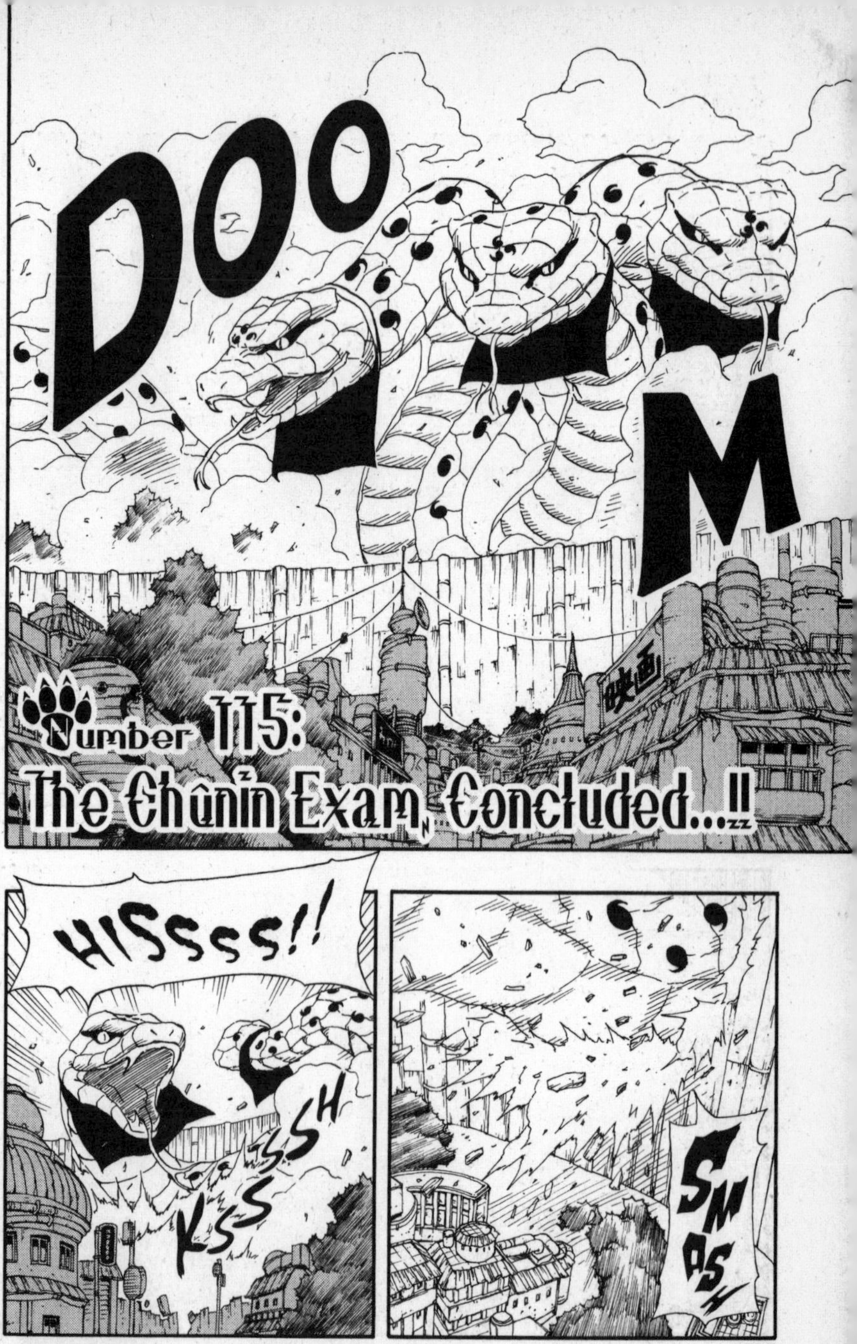
DOOM
Number 115:
The Chûnin Exam Concluded...!!
SMASH
HISSSS!!
KSSSH

FOOSH

FOOSH

FOOSH

SHOOM

SHOOM

THUS

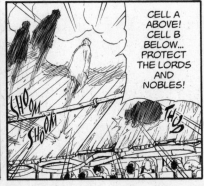

CELL A ABOVE! CELL B BELOW... PROTECT THE LORDS AND NOBLES!

!!

BOOF

BOOF

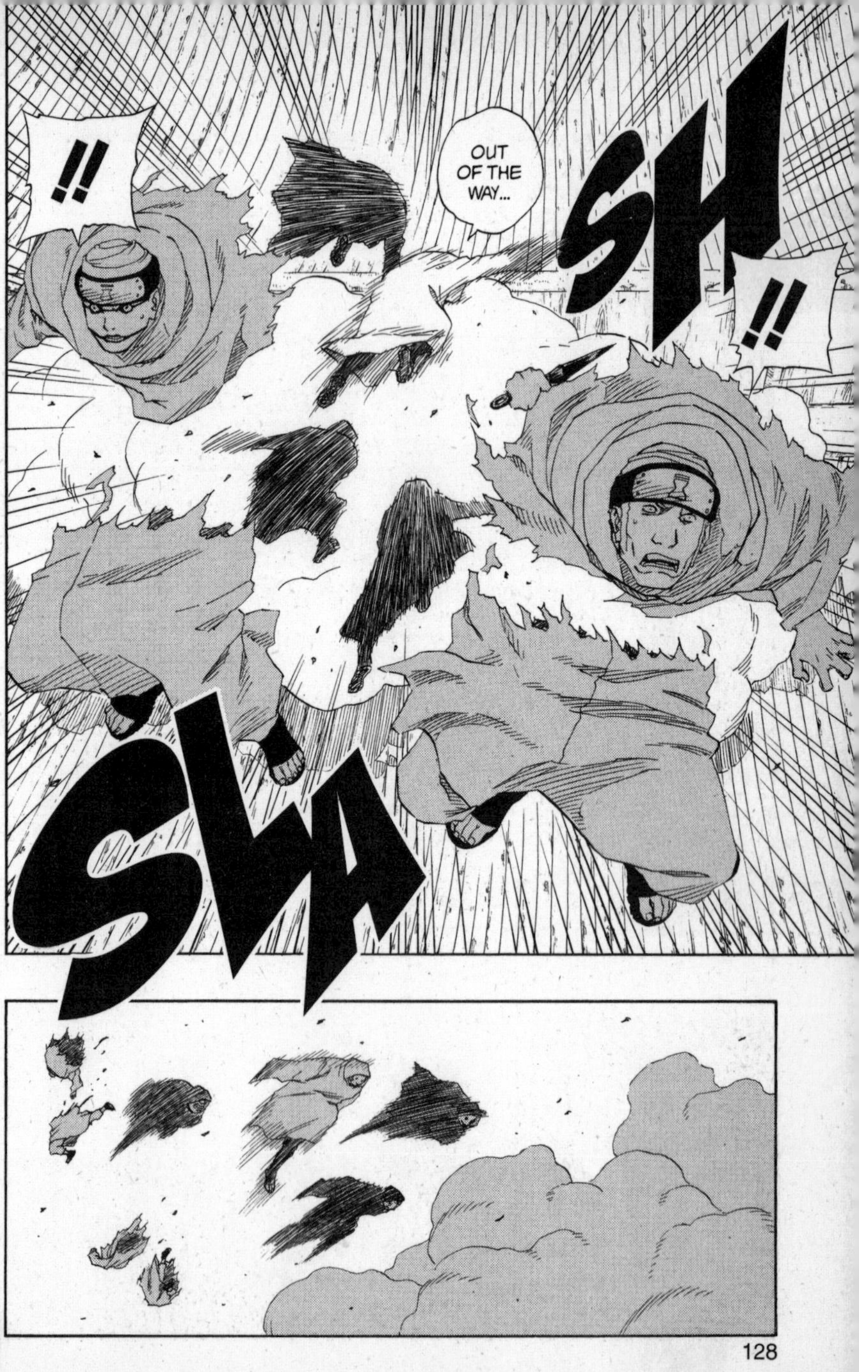

!!
SH
OUT OF THE WAY...
!!
SLA

READ THIS WAY

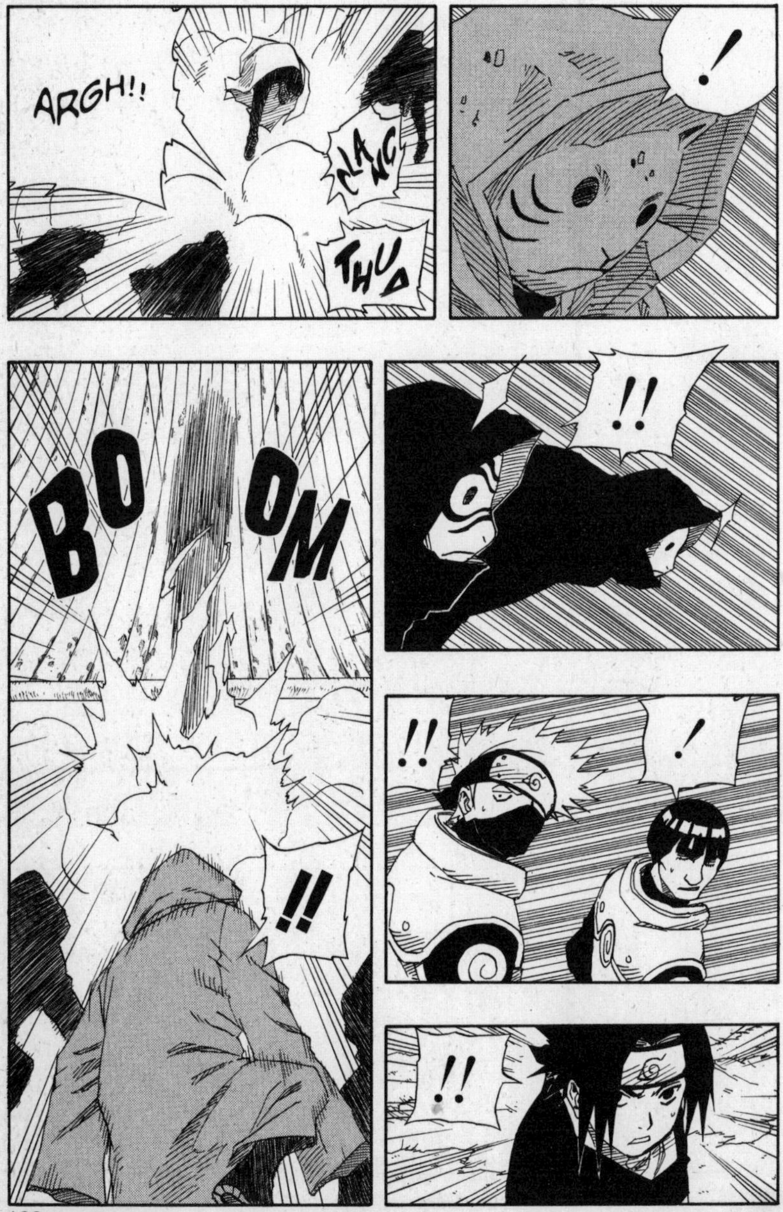
!
CLANG
THUD
ARGH!!
!!
!
!!
!!
BOOM
!!

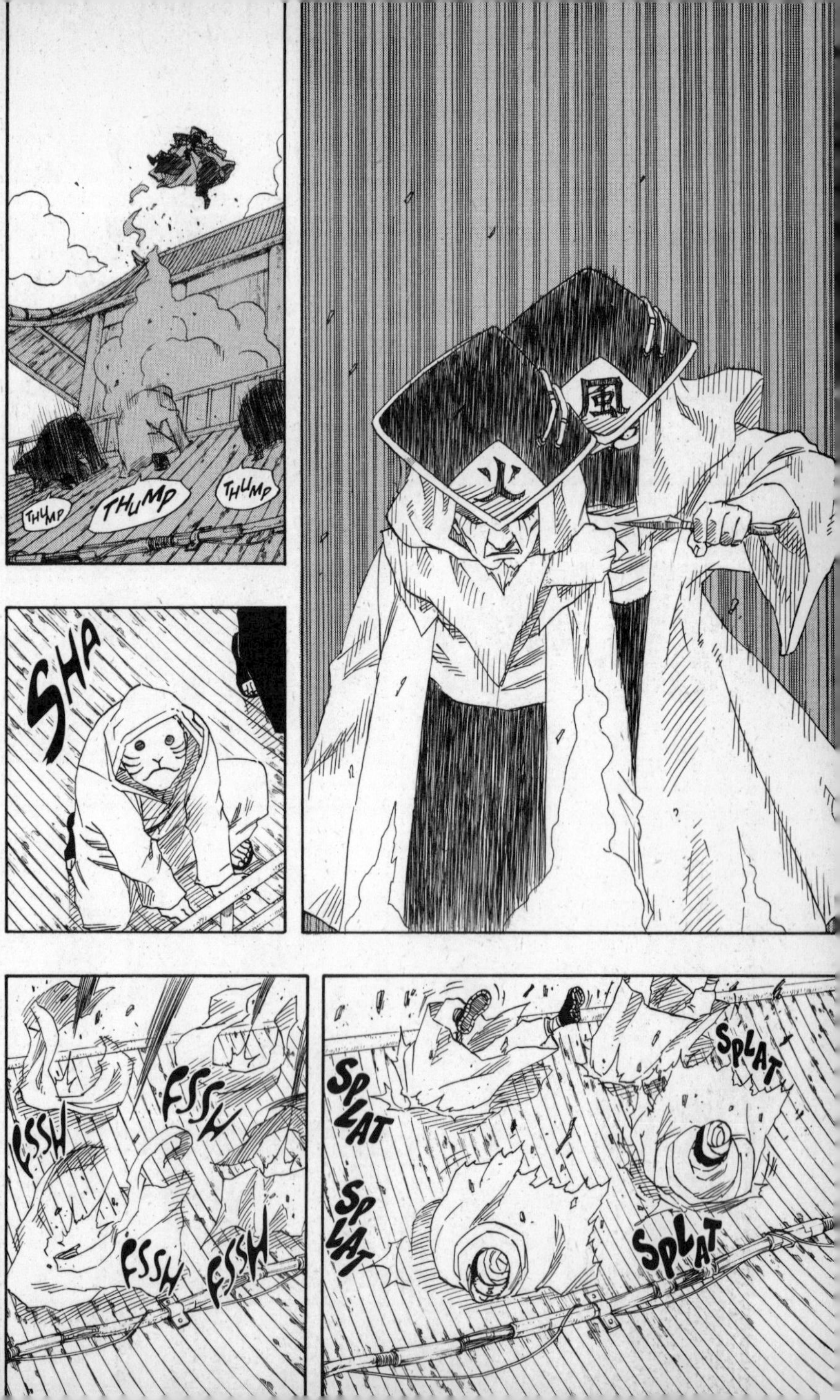
THUMP
THUMP
THUMP
SHA
SPLAT
SPLAT
SPLAT
SPLAT
FSSH
FSSH
FSSH
FSSH

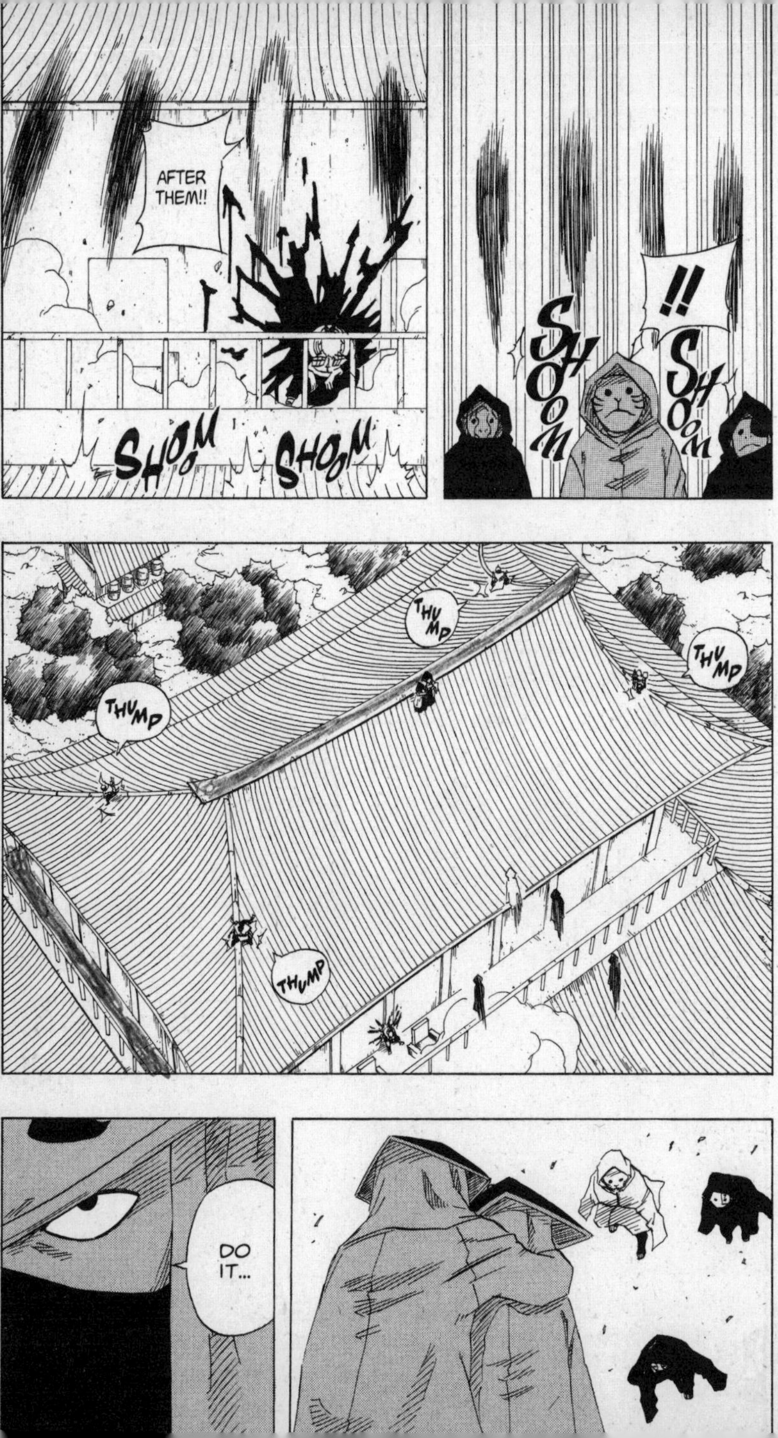
!!
SHOOM
SHOOM
AFTER THEM!!
SHOOM
SHOOM
THUMP
THUMP
THUMP
THUMP
DO IT...

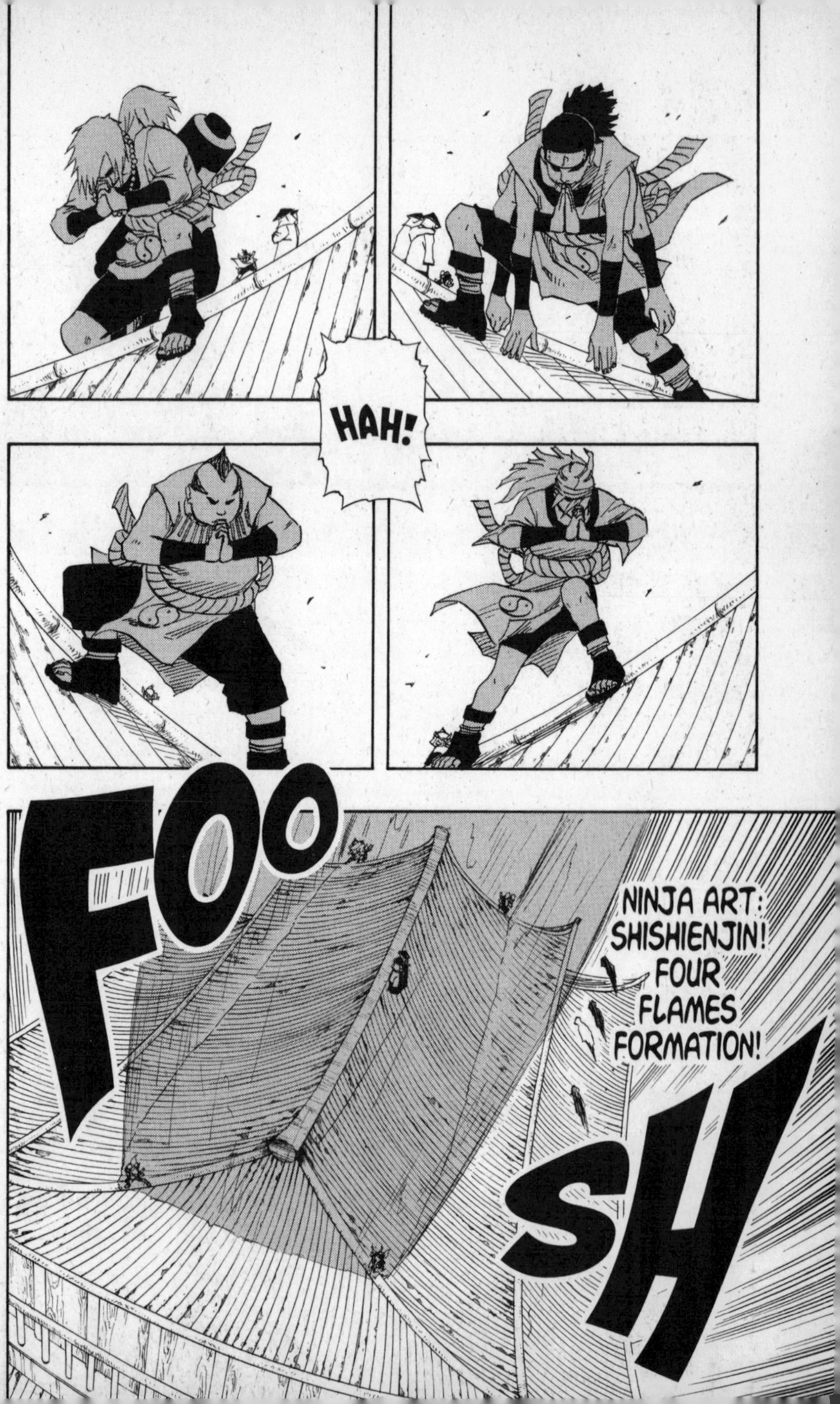
HAH!
NINJA ART: SHISHIENJIN! FOUR FLAMES FORMATION!
FOOSH

READ THIS WAY

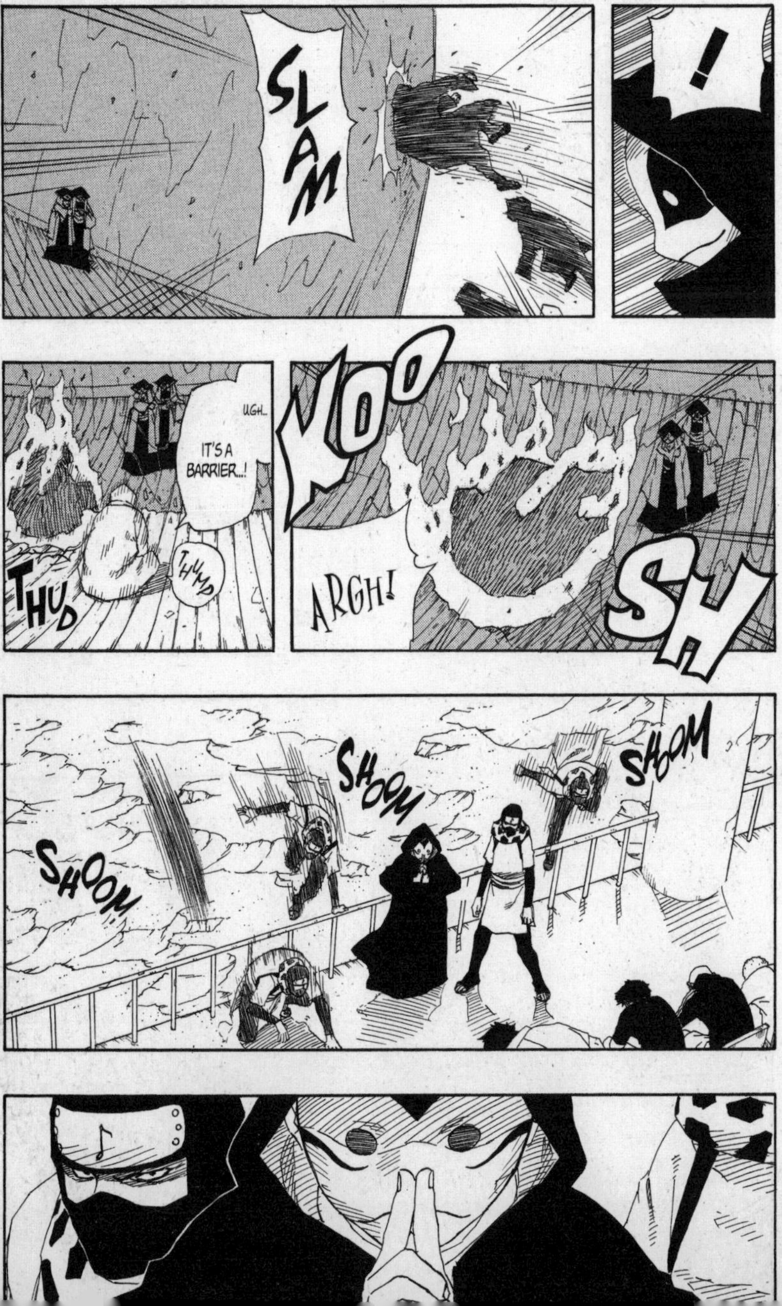
!
SLAM
WOO
SH
ARGH!
UGH...
IT'S A BARRIER...!
THUMP
THUD
SHOOM
SHOOM
SHOOM

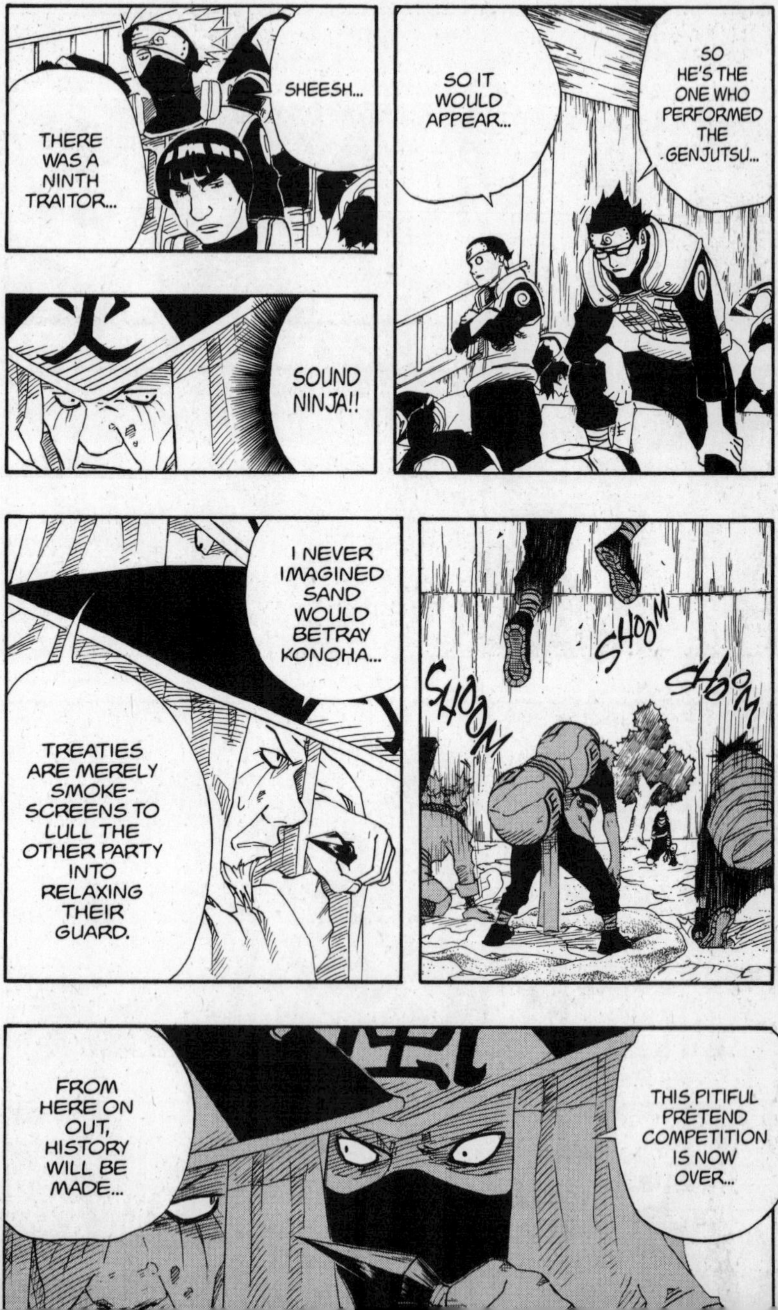

SO HE'S THE ONE WHO PERFORMED THE GENJUTSU...
SO IT WOULD APPEAR...
SHEESH...
THERE WAS A NINTH TRAITOR...
SOUND NINJA!!
SHOOM
SHOOM
SHOOM
I NEVER IMAGINED SAND WOULD BETRAY KONOHA...
TREATIES ARE MERELY SMOKE-SCREENS TO LULL THE OTHER PARTY INTO RELAXING THEIR GUARD.
THIS PITIFUL PRETEND COMPETITION IS NOW OVER...
FROM HERE ON OUT, HISTORY WILL BE MADE...

READ THIS WAY

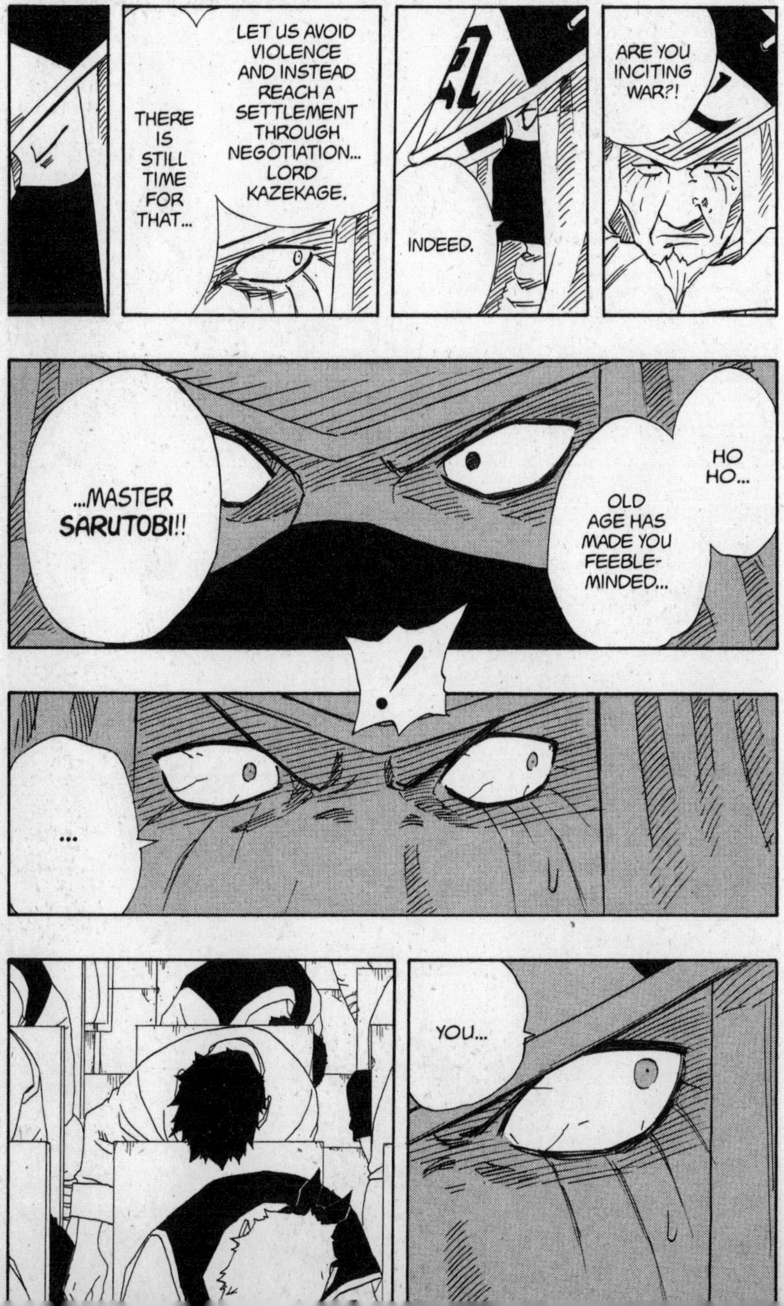
ARE YOU INCITING WAR?!
INDEED.
LET US AVOID VIOLENCE AND INSTEAD REACH A SETTLEMENT THROUGH NEGOTIATION... LORD KAZEKAGE.
THERE IS STILL TIME FOR THAT...
HO HO...
OLD AGE HAS MADE YOU FEEBLE-MINDED...
...MASTER SARUTOBI!!
!
...
YOU...

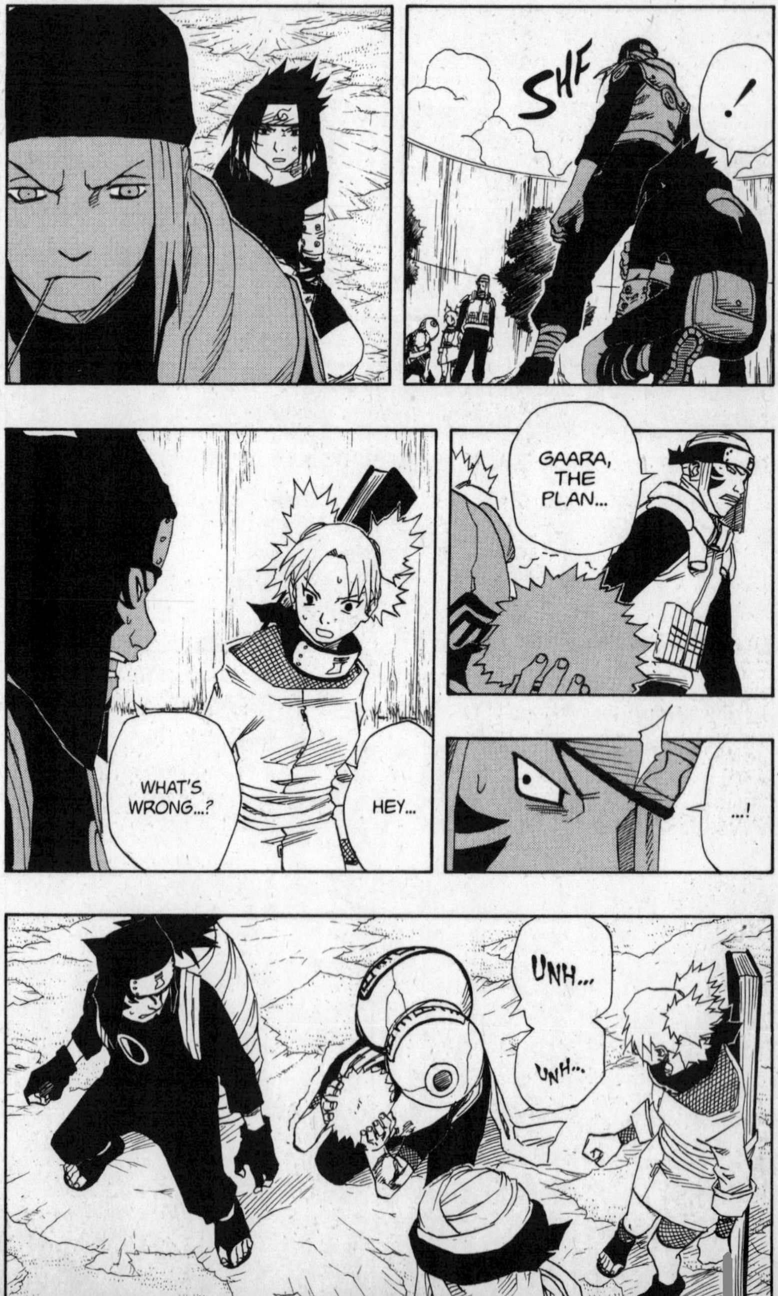
SHF
!
GAARA, THE PLAN...
...!
HEY...
WHAT'S WRONG...?
UNH...
UNH...

READ THIS WAY

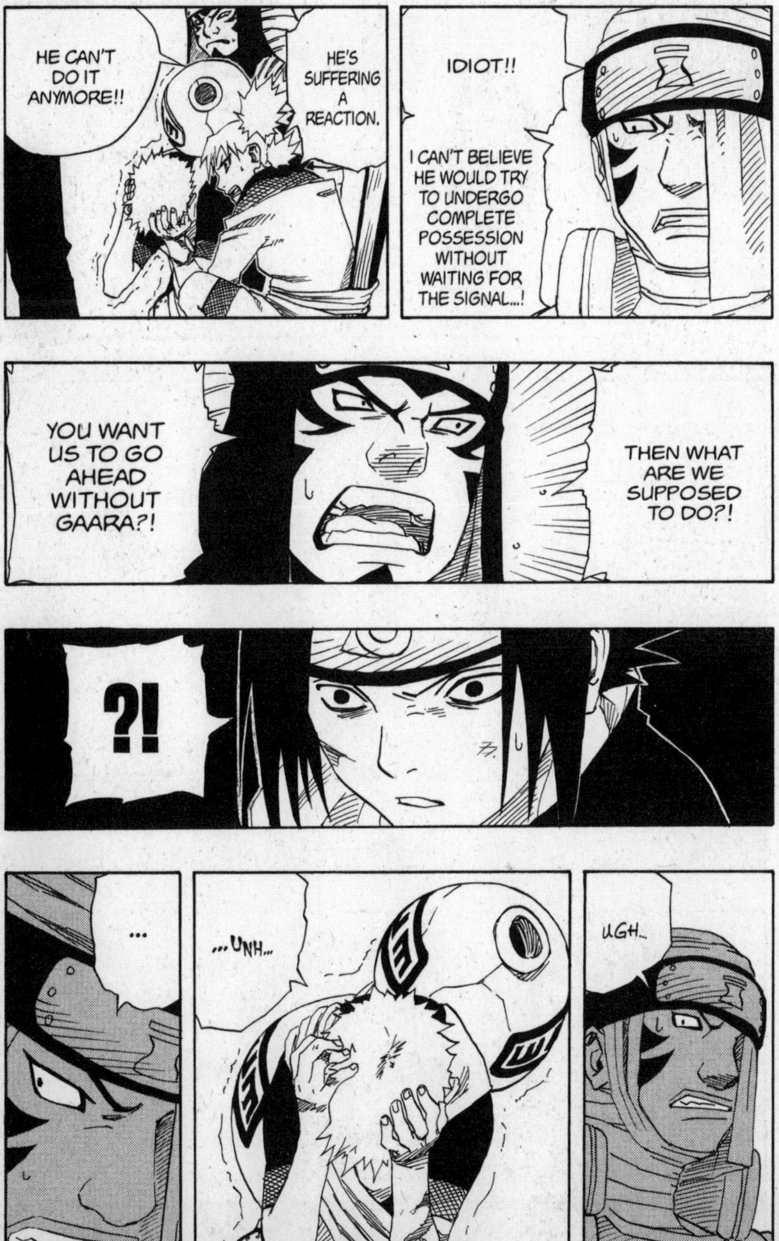
IDIOT!!
I CAN'T BELIEVE HE WOULD TRY TO UNDERGO COMPLETE POSSESSION WITHOUT WAITING FOR THE SIGNAL...!
HE'S SUFFERING A REACTION.
HE CAN'T DO IT ANYMORE!!
THEN WHAT ARE WE SUPPOSED TO DO?!
YOU WANT US TO GO AHEAD WITHOUT GAARA?!
?!
UGH...
...UNH...
...

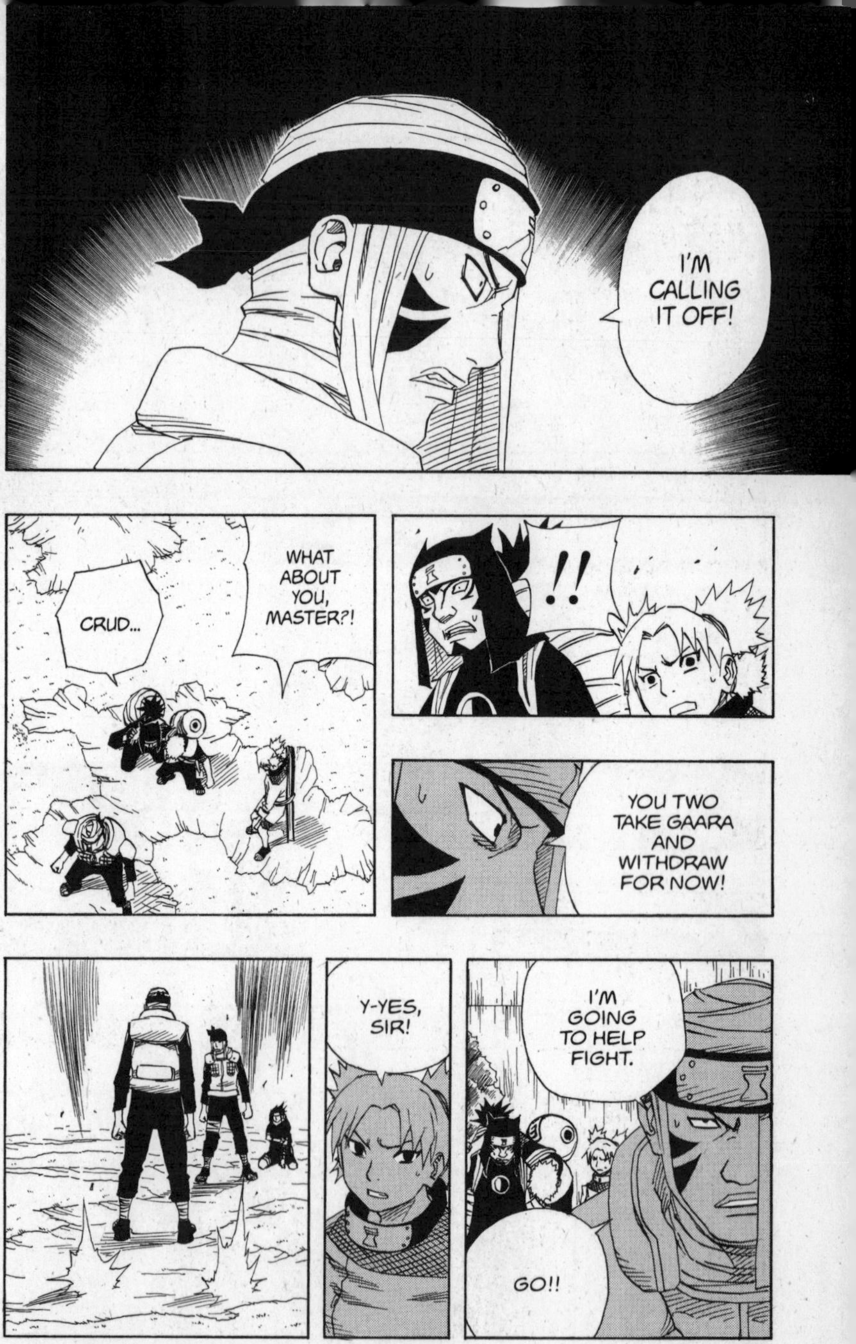

I'M CALLING IT OFF!
!!
YOU TWO TAKE GAARA AND WITHDRAW FOR NOW!
WHAT ABOUT YOU, MASTER?!
CRUD...
I'M GOING TO HELP FIGHT.
GO!!
Y-YES, SIR!

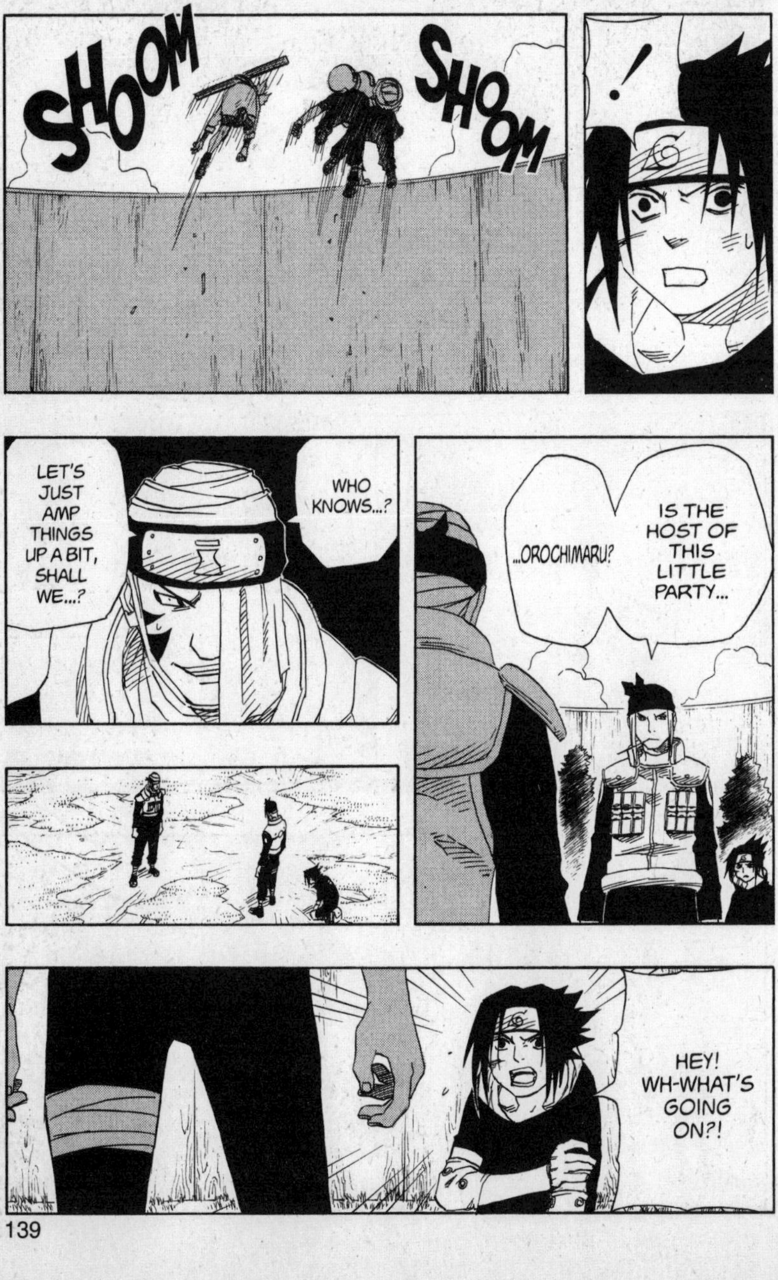
!
SHOOM
SHOOM
IS THE HOST OF THIS LITTLE PARTY...
...OROCHIMARU?
WHO KNOWS...?
LET'S JUST AMP THINGS UP A BIT, SHALL WE...?
HEY! WH-WHAT'S GOING ON?!

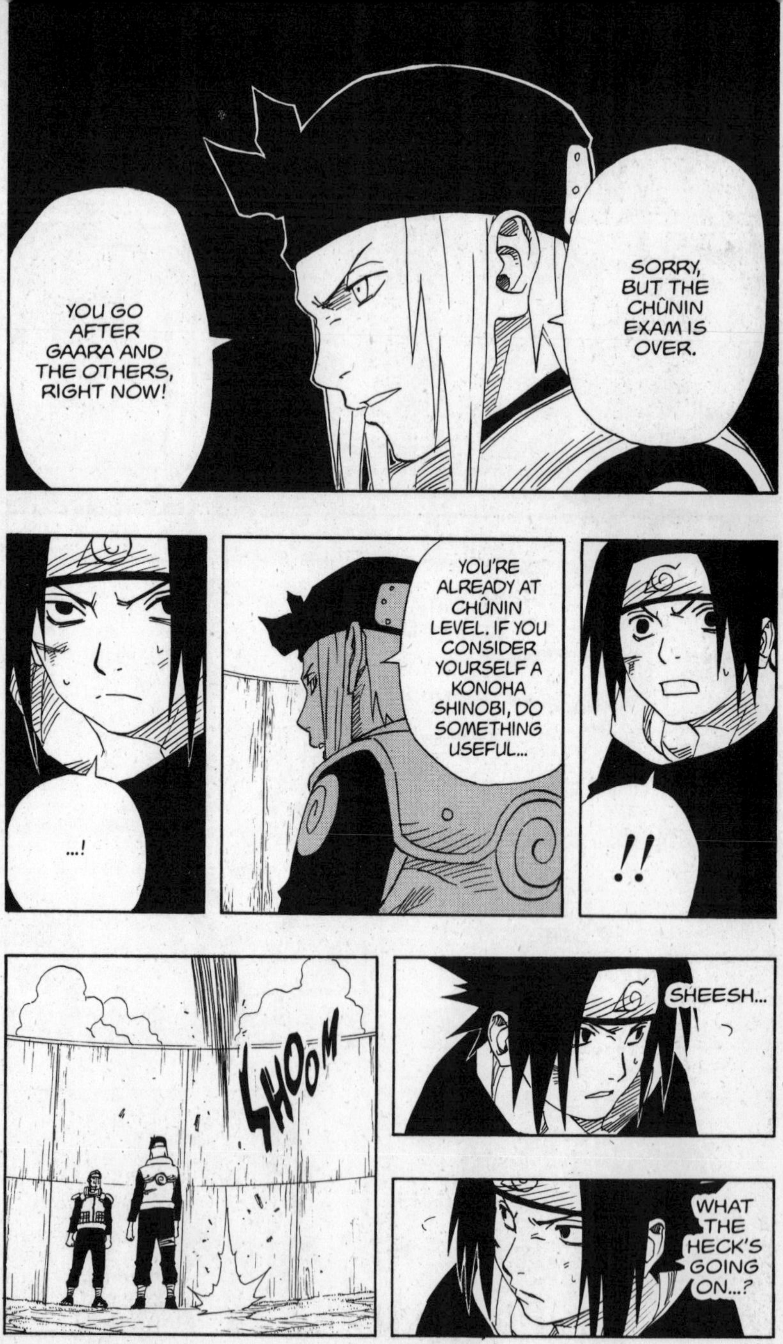
SORRY, BUT THE CHÛNIN EXAM IS OVER.
YOU GO AFTER GAARA AND THE OTHERS, RIGHT NOW!
!!
YOU'RE ALREADY AT CHÛNIN LEVEL. IF YOU CONSIDER YOURSELF A KONOHA SHINOBI, DO SOMETHING USEFUL...
...!
SHEESH...
WHAT THE HECK'S GOING ON...?
SHOOM

READ THIS WAY

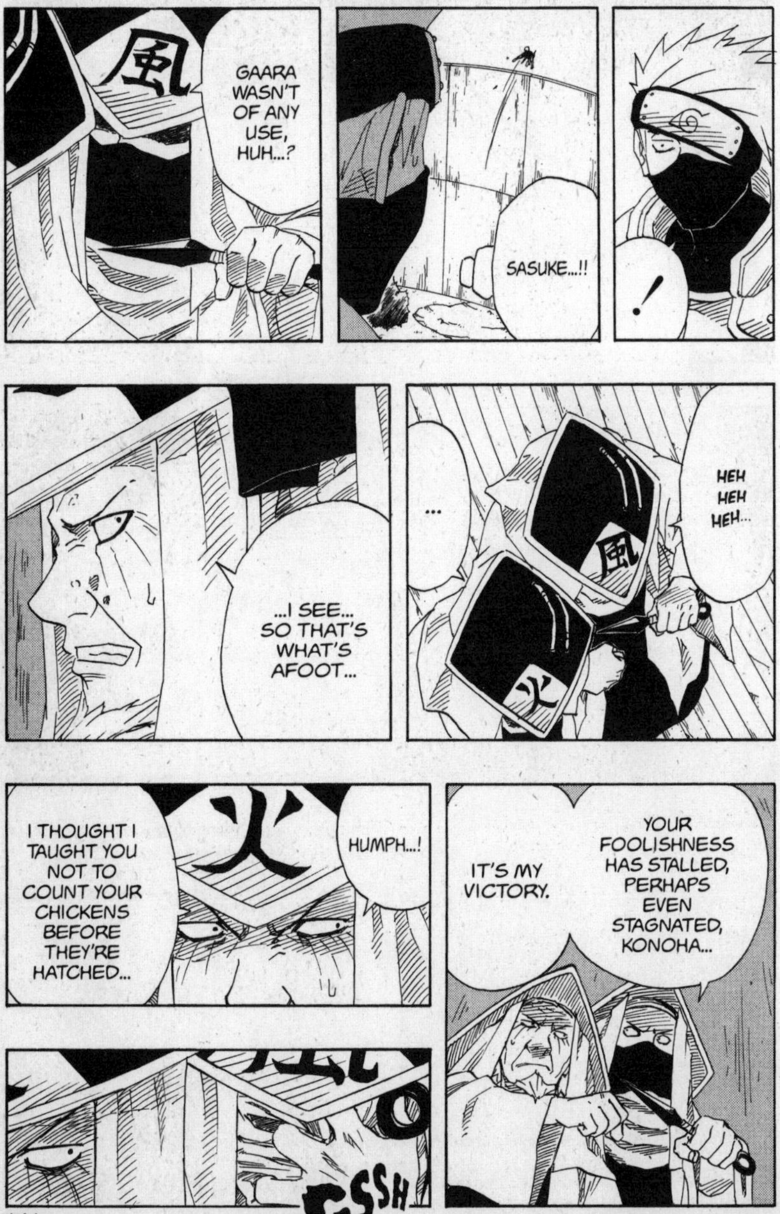
!
SASUKE...!!
GAARA WASN'T OF ANY USE, HUH...?
HEH HEH HEH...
...
...I SEE... SO THAT'S WHAT'S AFOOT...
YOUR FOOLISHNESS HAS STALLED, PERHAPS EVEN STAGNATED, KONOHA...
IT'S MY VICTORY.
HUMPH...!
I THOUGHT I TAUGHT YOU NOT TO COUNT YOUR CHICKENS BEFORE THEY'RE HATCHED...
GSSH

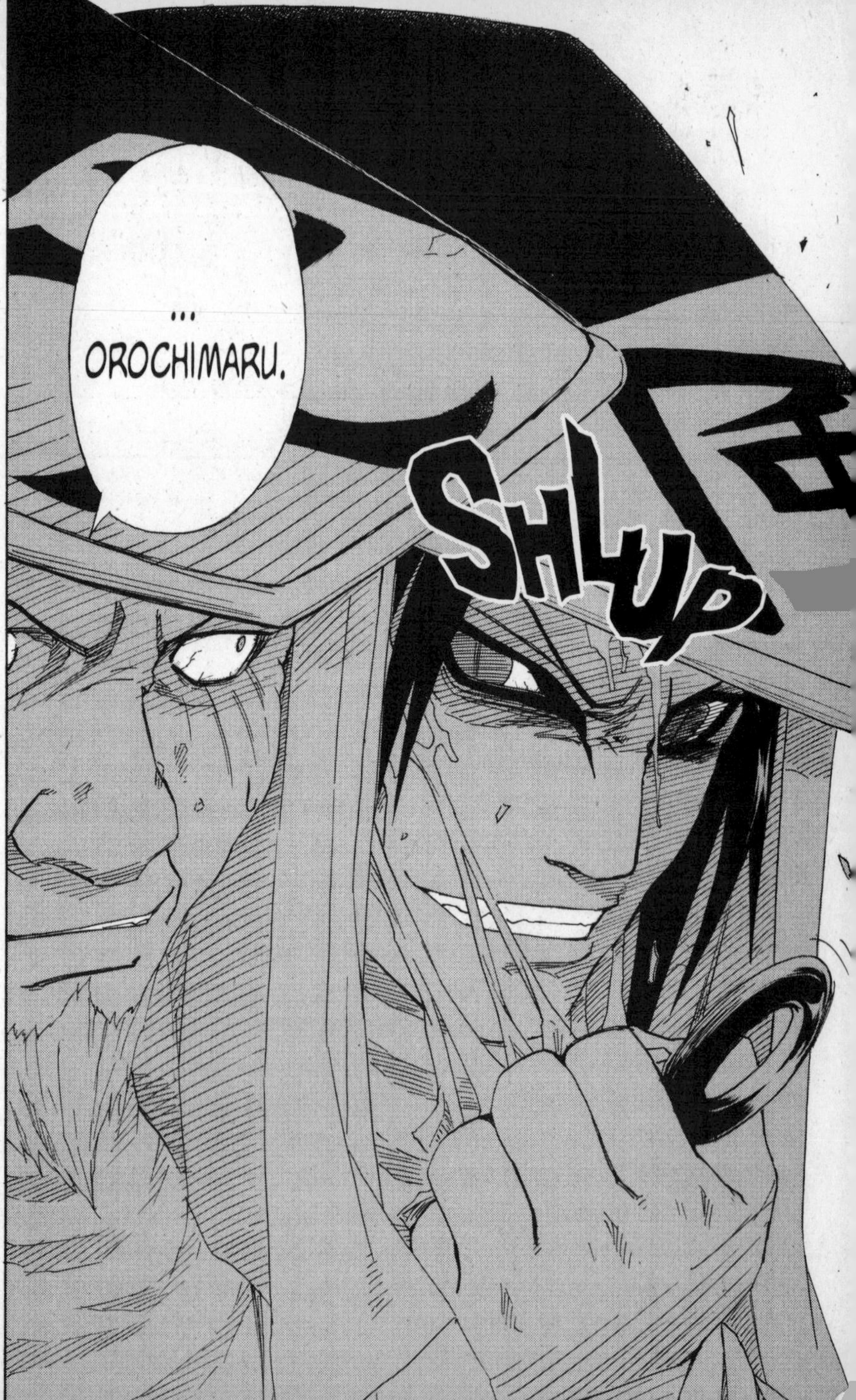
... OROCHIMARU.
SHLUP

READ THIS WAY

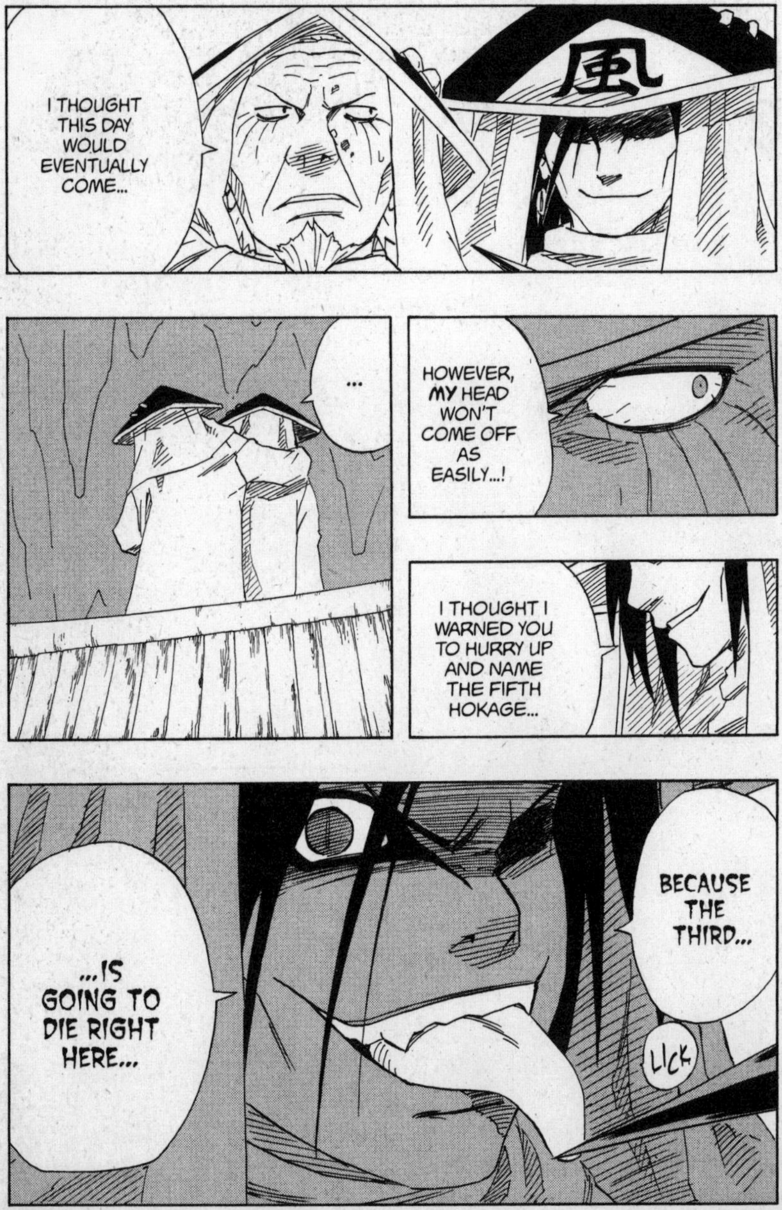

I THOUGHT THIS DAY WOULD EVENTUALLY COME...
HOWEVER, MY HEAD WON'T COME OFF AS EASILY...!
I THOUGHT I WARNED YOU TO HURRY UP AND NAME THE FIFTH HOKAGE...
...
BECAUSE THE THIRD...
LICK
...IS GOING TO DIE RIGHT HERE...

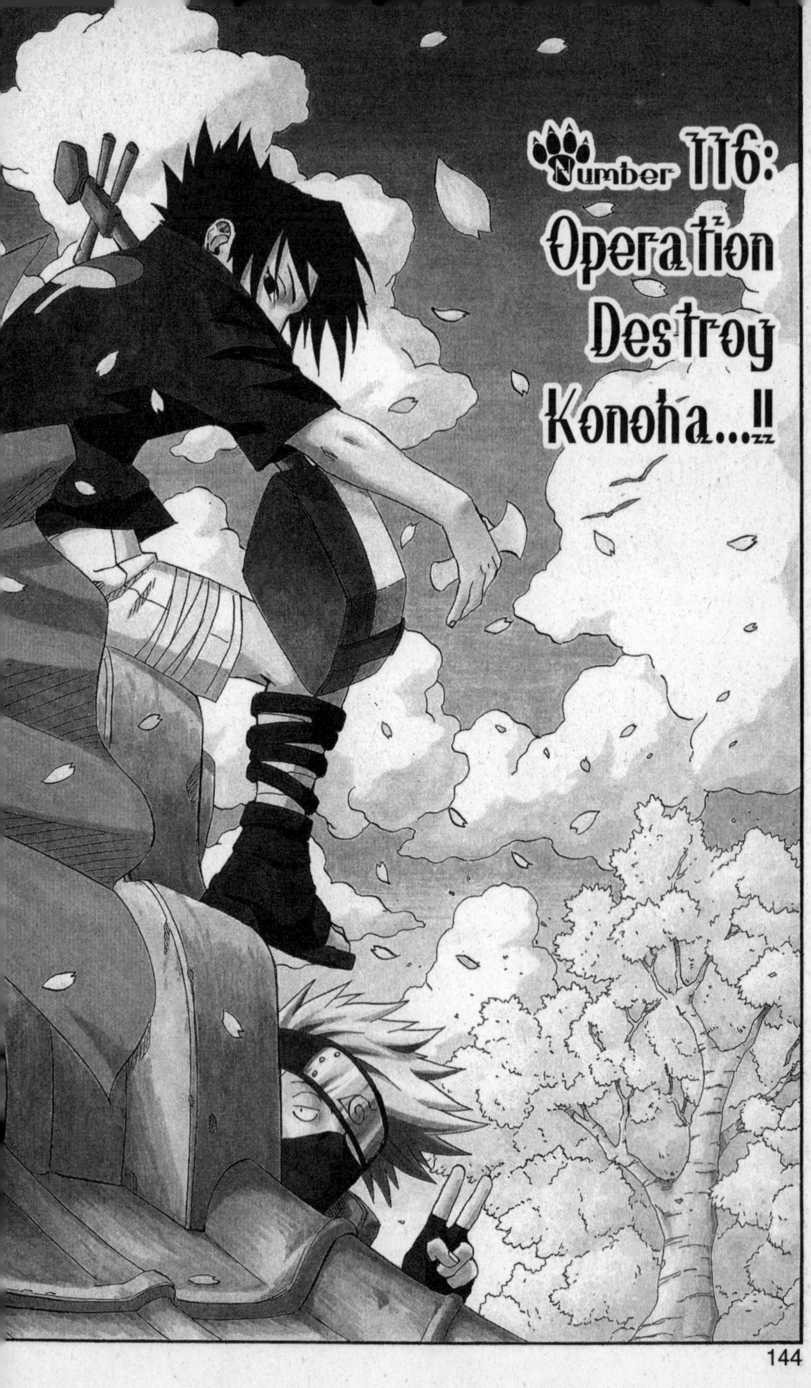
Number 116:
Operation Destroy Konoha...!!

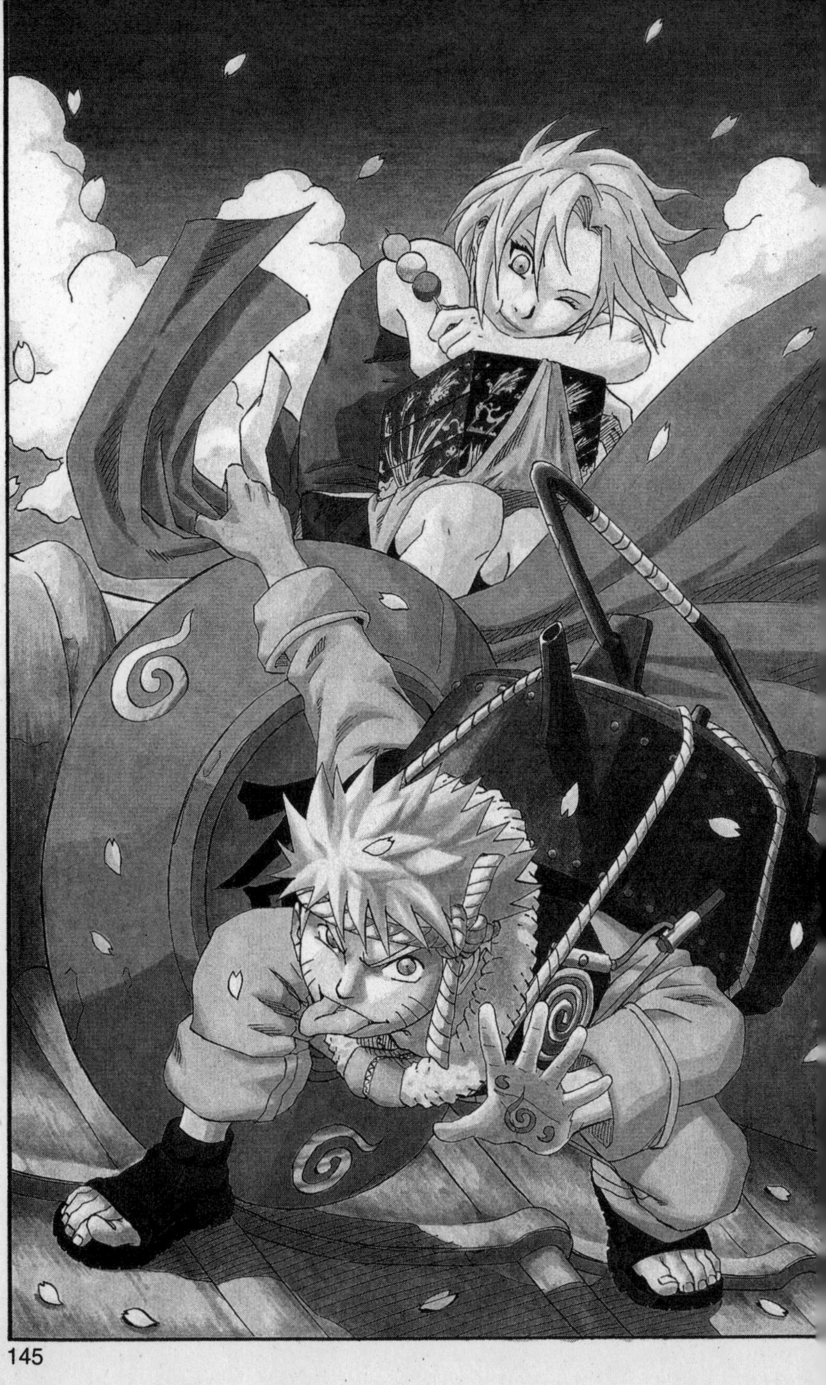

NARUTO
-ナルト-

しるこ

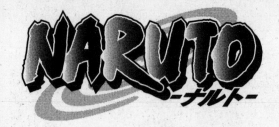

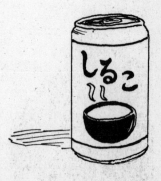

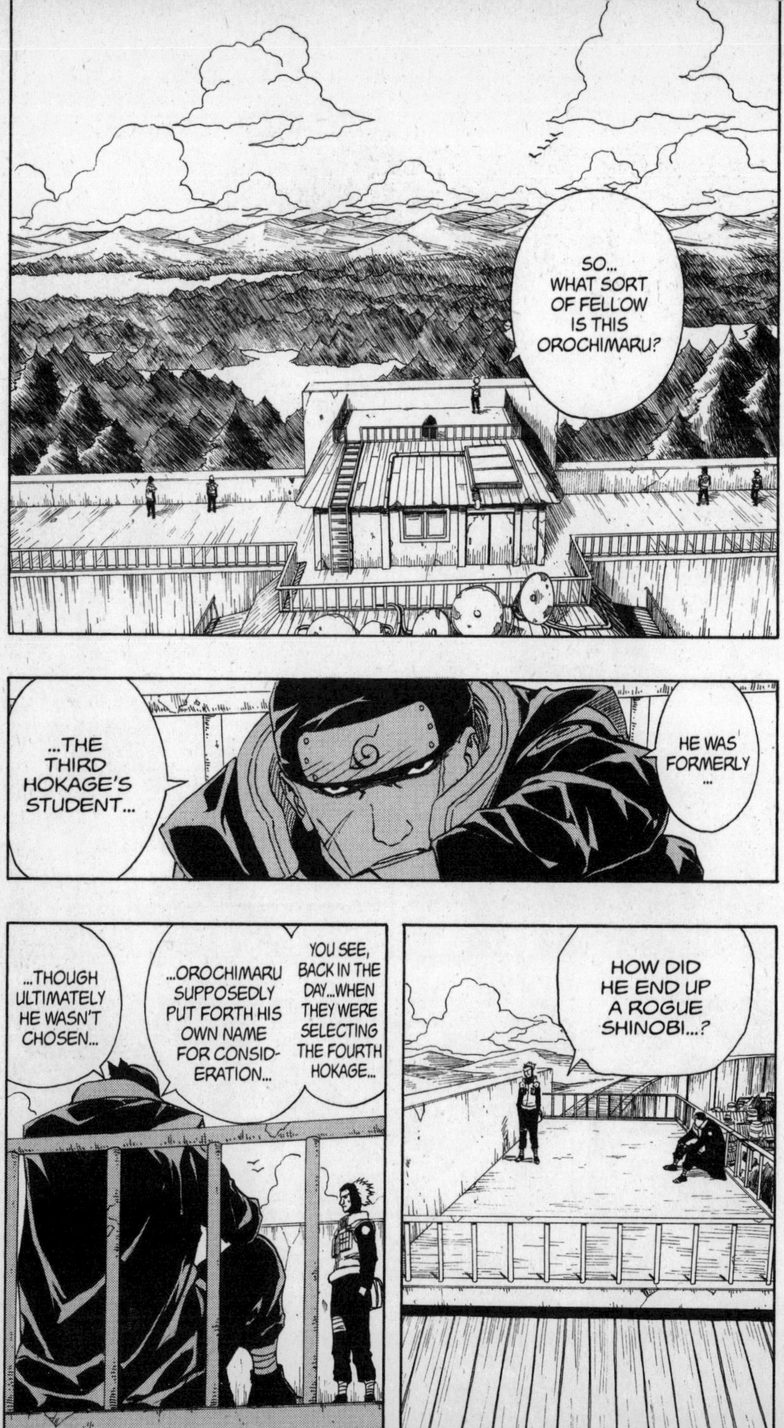
SO... WHAT SORT OF FELLOW IS THIS OROCHIMARU?
HE WAS FORMERLY ...
...THE THIRD HOKAGE'S STUDENT...
HOW DID HE END UP A ROGUE SHINOBI...?
YOU SEE, BACK IN THE DAY...WHEN THEY WERE SELECTING THE FOURTH HOKAGE...
...OROCHIMARU SUPPOSEDLY PUT FORTH HIS OWN NAME FOR CONSID- ERATION...
...THOUGH ULTIMATELY HE WASN'T CHOSEN...

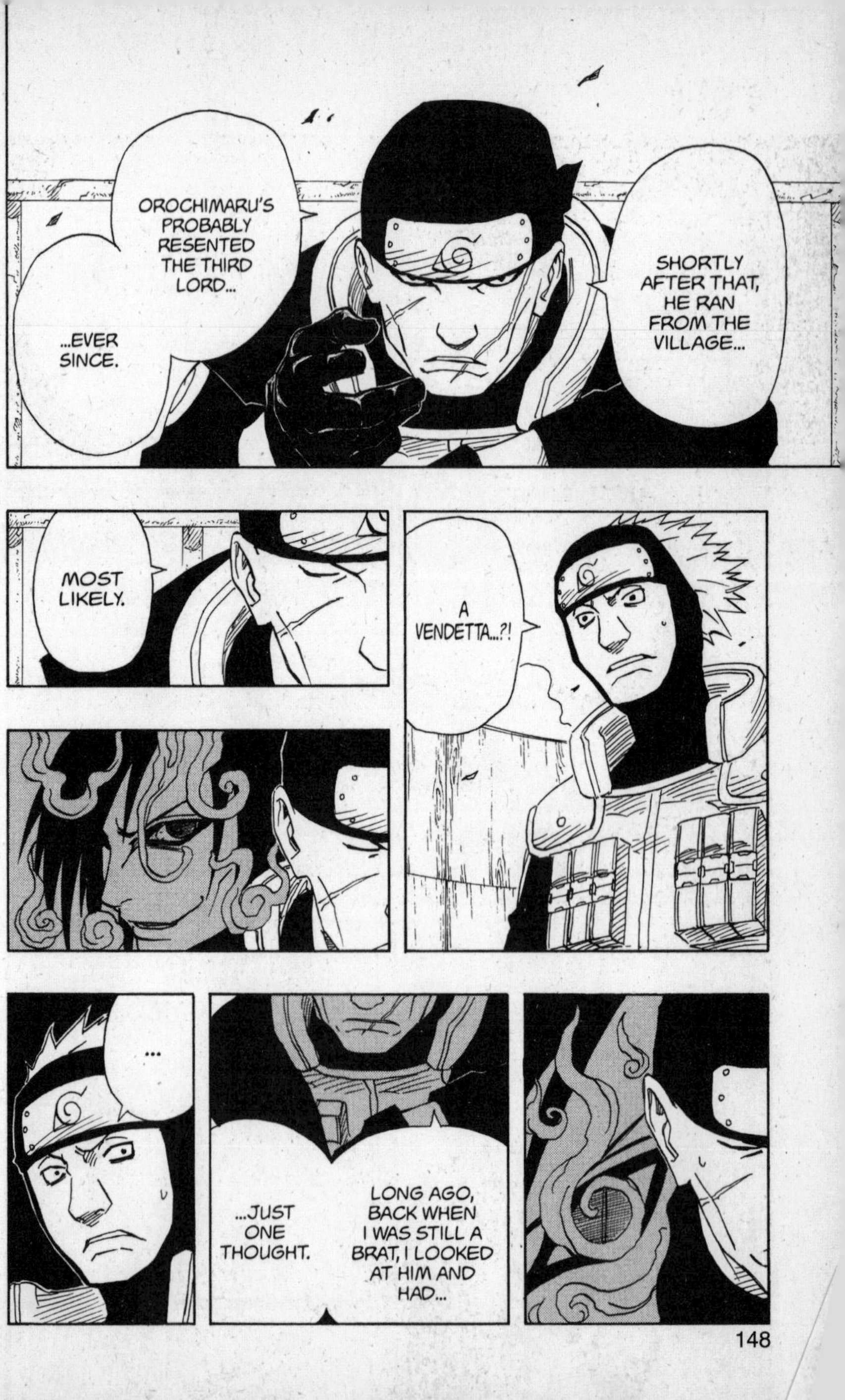

SHORTLY AFTER THAT, HE RAN FROM THE VILLAGE...
OROCHIMARU'S PROBABLY RESENTED THE THIRD LORD...
...EVER SINCE.
A VENDETTA...?!
MOST LIKELY.
LONG AGO, BACK WHEN I WAS STILL A BRAT, I LOOKED AT HIM AND HAD...
...JUST ONE THOUGHT.
...

READ THIS WAY

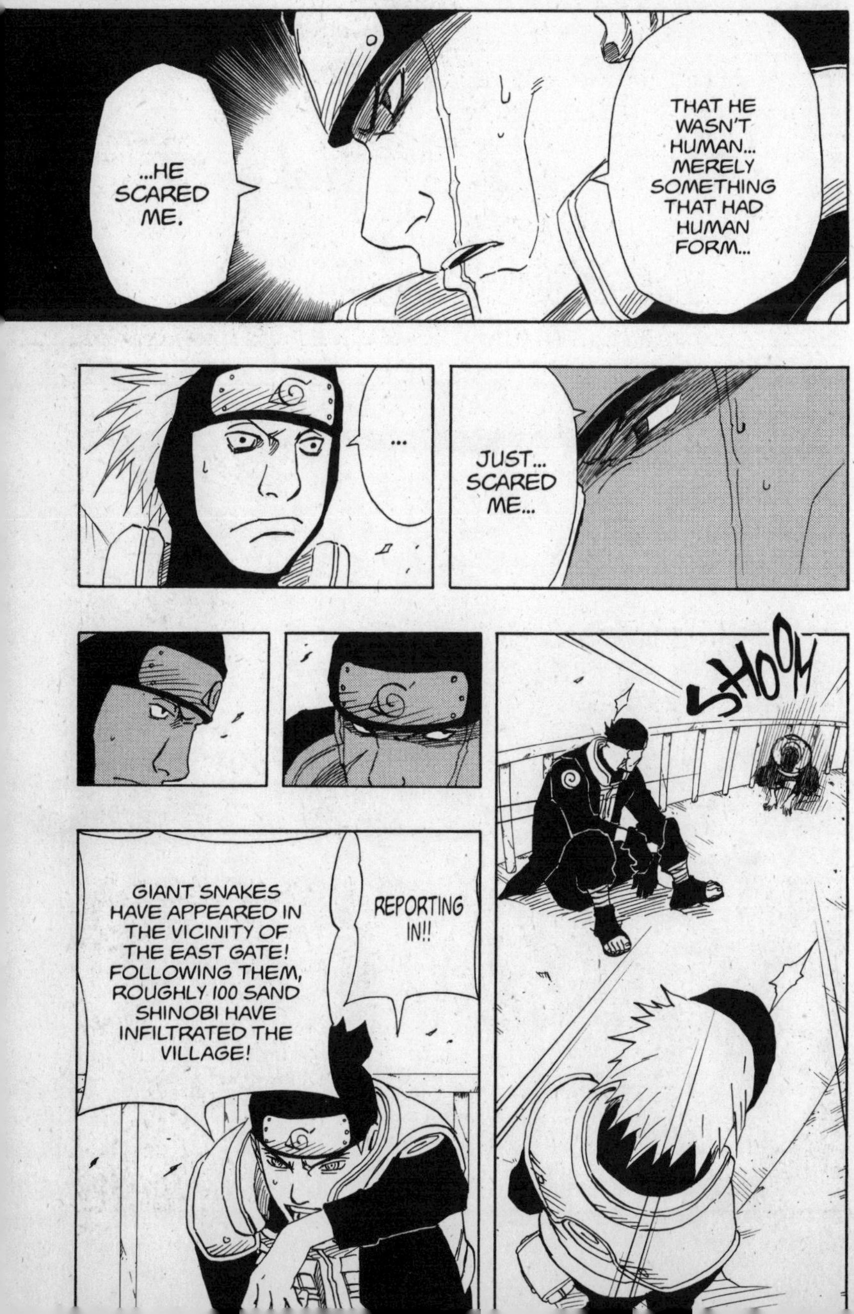

THAT HE WASN'T HUMAN... MERELY SOMETHING THAT HAD HUMAN FORM...
...HE SCARED ME.
JUST... SCARED ME...
...
SHOOM
REPORTING IN!!
GIANT SNAKES HAVE APPEARED IN THE VICINITY OF THE EAST GATE! FOLLOWING THEM, ROUGHLY 100 SAND SHINOBI HAVE INFILTRATED THE VILLAGE!

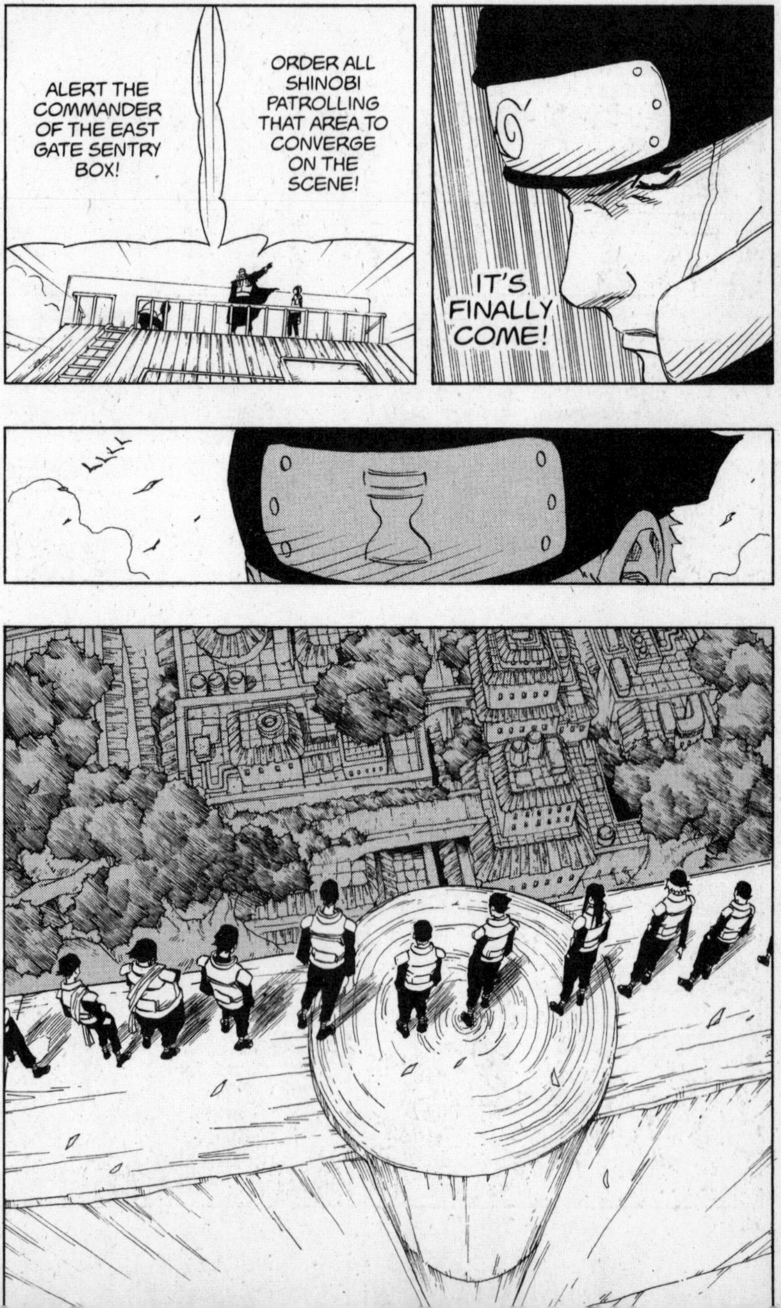
IT'S FINALLY COME!
ORDER ALL SHINOBI PATROLLING THAT AREA TO CONVERGE ON THE SCENE!
ALERT THE COMMANDER OF THE EAST GATE SENTRY BOX!

READ THIS WAY

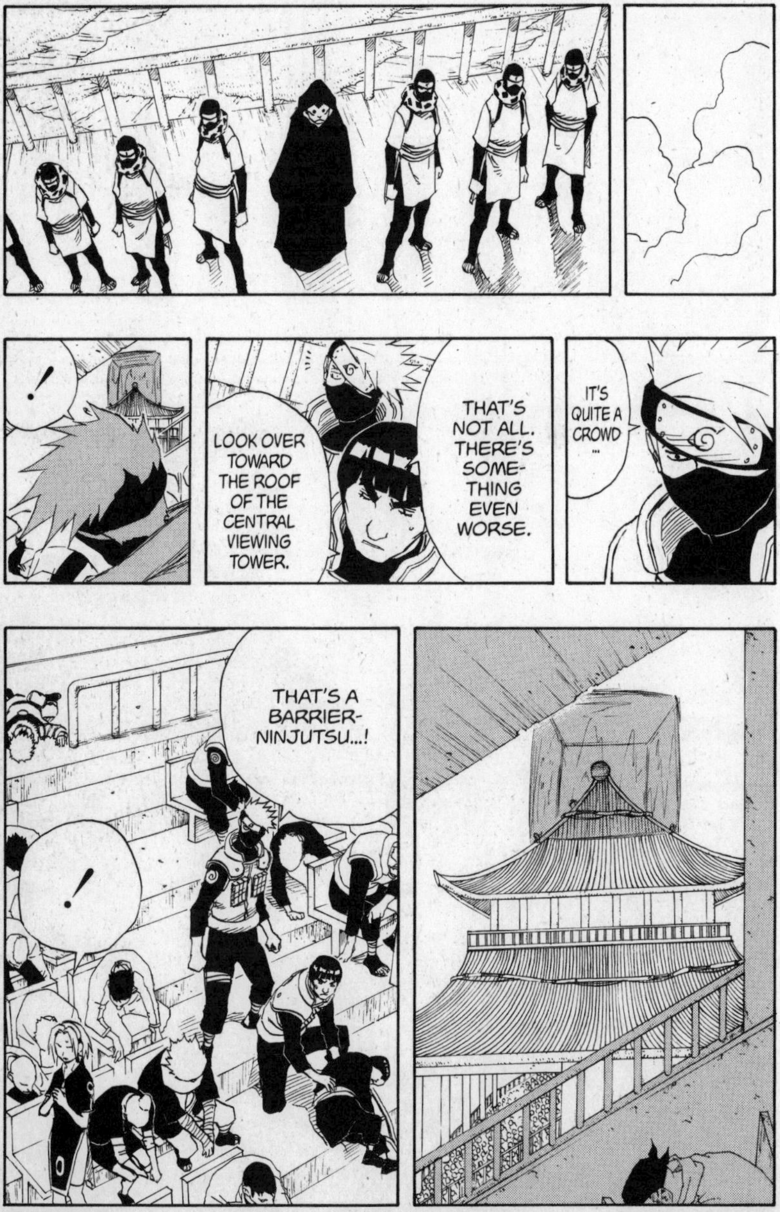
IT'S QUITE A CROWD ...
THAT'S NOT ALL. THERE'S SOME-THING EVEN WORSE.
LOOK OVER TOWARD THE ROOF OF THE CENTRAL VIEWING TOWER.
!
THAT'S A BARRIER-NINJUTSU...!
!

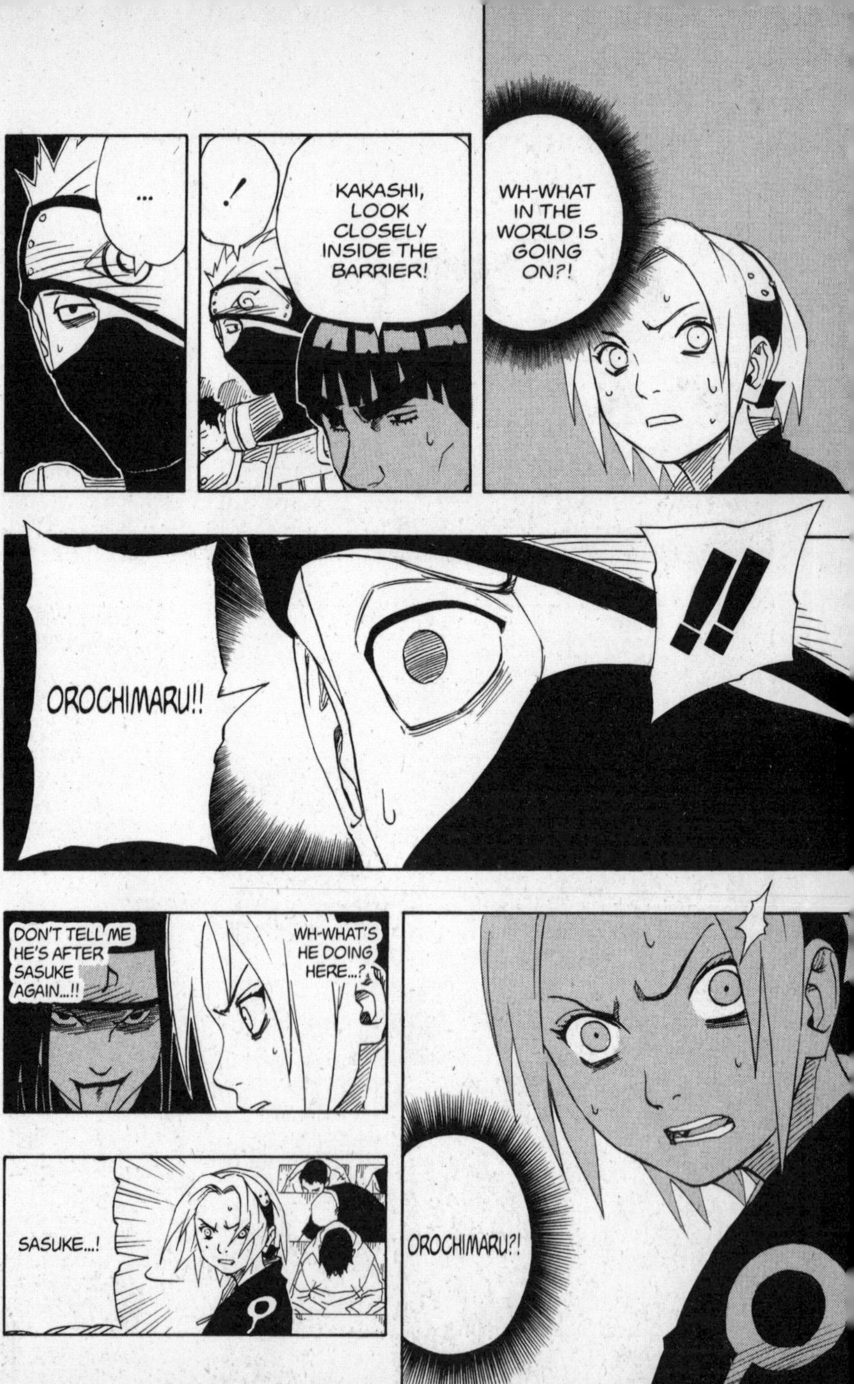
WH-WHAT IN THE WORLD IS GOING ON?!
KAKASHI, LOOK CLOSELY INSIDE THE BARRIER!
!
...
!!
OROCHIMARU!!
OROCHIMARU?!
WH-WHAT'S HE DOING HERE...?
DON'T TELL ME HE'S AFTER SASUKE AGAIN...!!
SASUKE...!

OH...

WHERE'S SASUKE...?!

HUH?

FSSH

FSSH

SHUN!

SHUNK

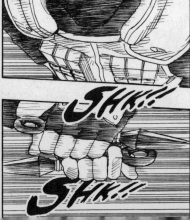

SHK!!

SHK!!

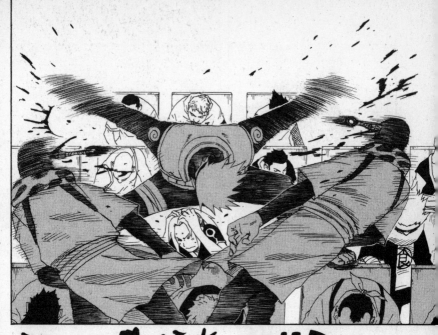

KACHINK

KACHINK

SHOOSH

THUD

THUD

...

...

PEEK

SAKURA, STAY THERE FOR A LITTLE WHILE... I'LL GO THIN OUT THE ENEMY RANKS.

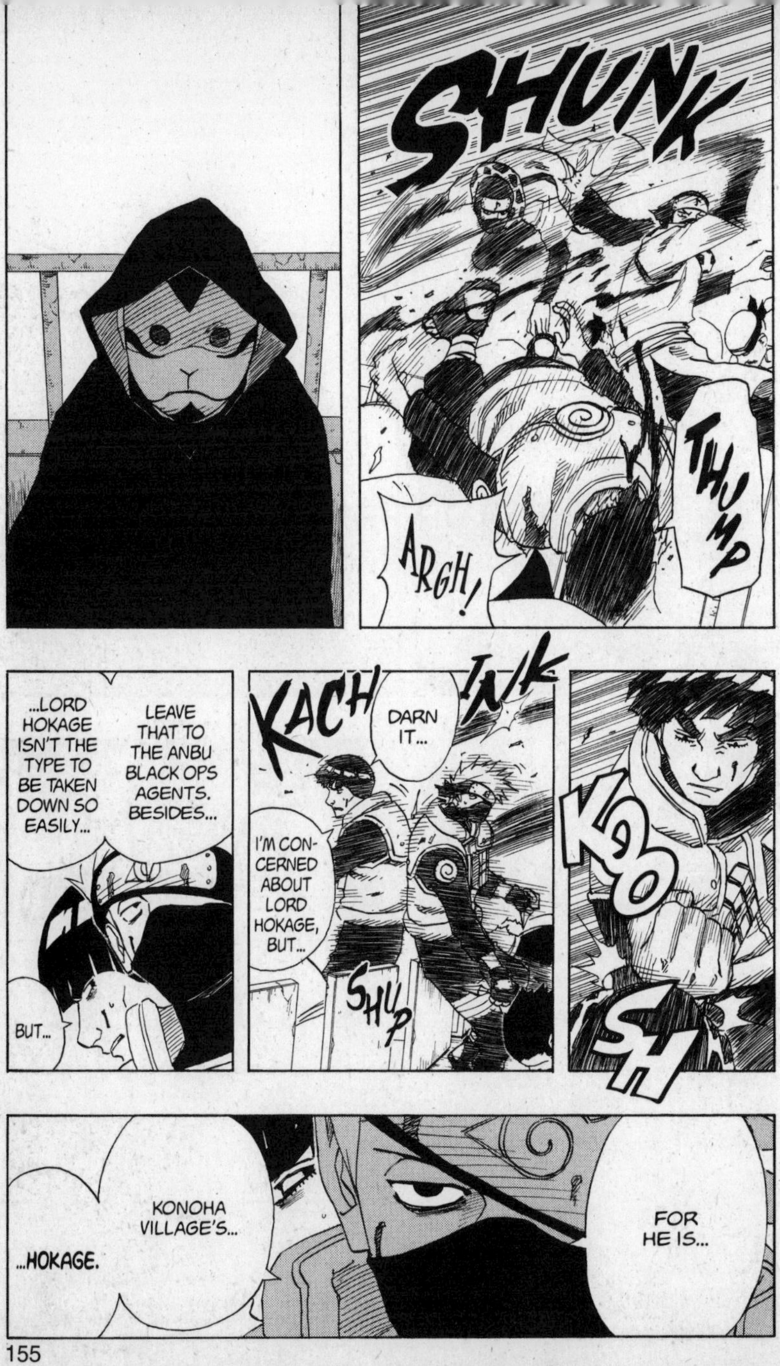
SHUNK
THUMP
ARGH!
KOO
SH
KACHINK
DARN IT...
I'M CONCERNED ABOUT LORD HOKAGE, BUT...
SHUP
LEAVE THAT TO THE ANBU BLACK OPS AGENTS. BESIDES...
...LORD HOKAGE ISN'T THE TYPE TO BE TAKEN DOWN SO EASILY...
BUT...
FOR HE IS...
KONOHA VILLAGE'S...
...HOKAGE.

ARE YOU THAT OVER-JOYED...?

OR IS IT...

PLIP

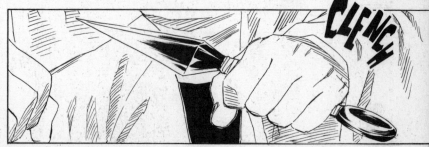

CLENCH

READ THIS WAY

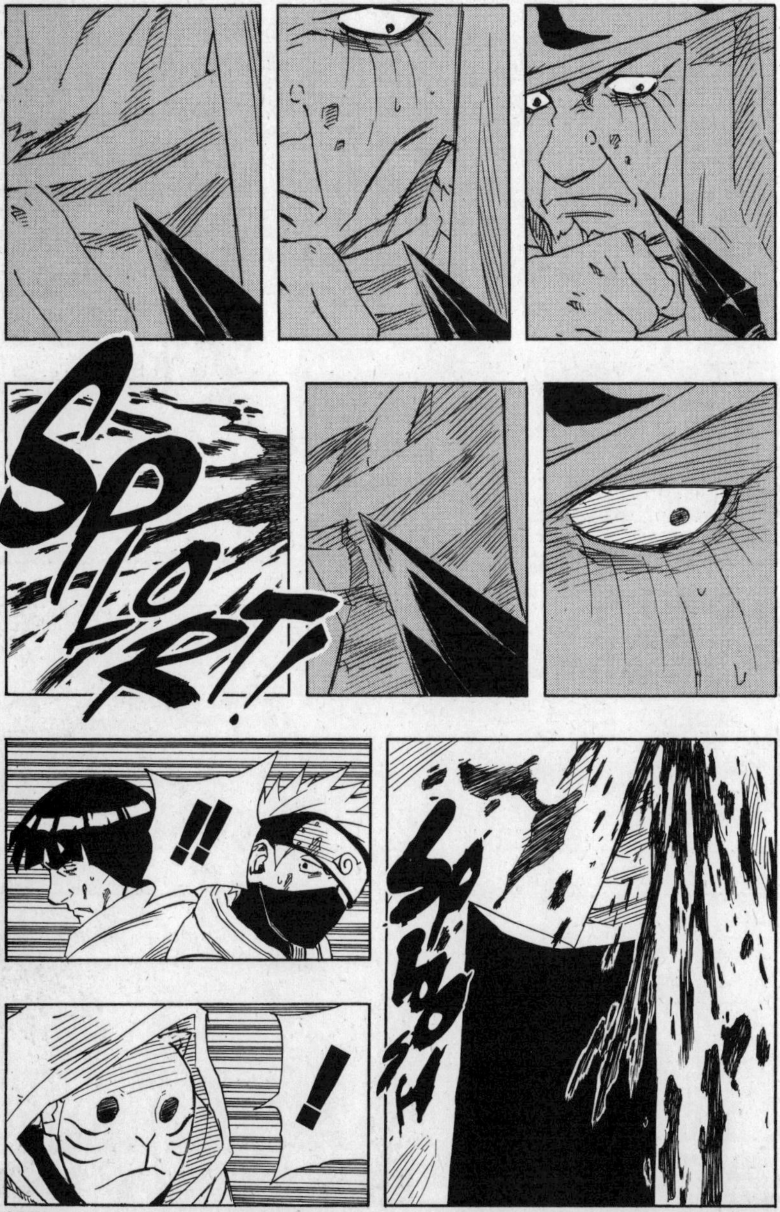
SPLORT!
SPLOOSH
!!
!

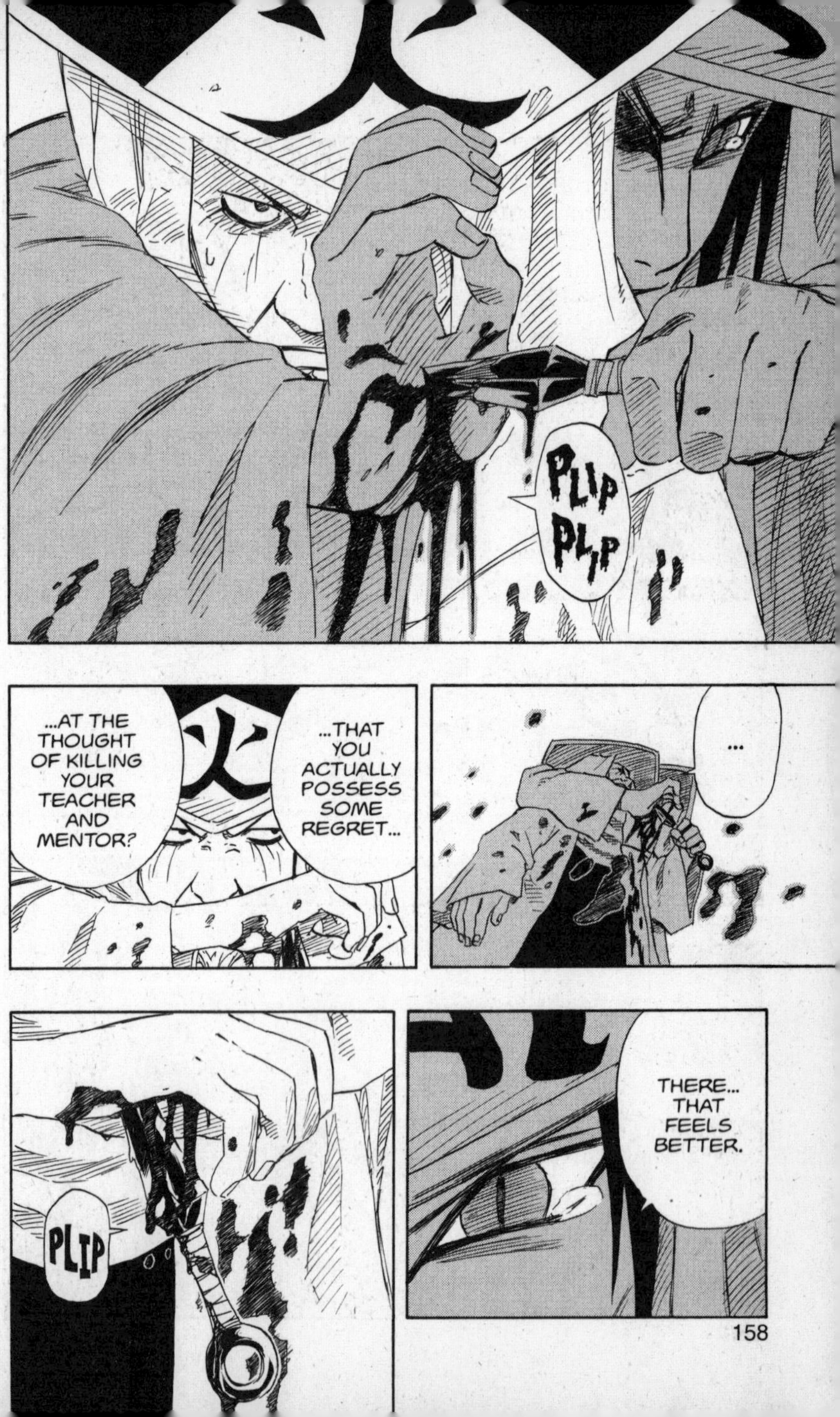
PLIP PLIP
...
...THAT YOU ACTUALLY POSSESS SOME REGRET...
...AT THE THOUGHT OF KILLING YOUR TEACHER AND MENTOR?
THERE... THAT FEELS BETTER.
PLIP

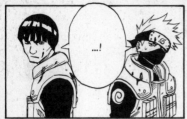

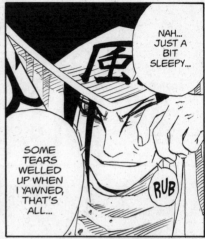

NAH... JUST A BIT SLEEPY...
RUB
SOME TEARS WELLED UP WHEN I YAWNED, THAT'S ALL...
...!
...!
EXACTLY AS I SUSPECTED...
TMP
I KNOW YOU'RE NOT A MAN TO BE MOVED BY HATRED...
YOU HAVE NEITHER MOTIVES NOR PURPOSE.
HMM... ACTUALLY, I DO HAVE PURPOSE.
WELL, TO PUT IT SIMPLY...

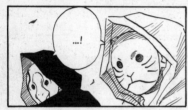

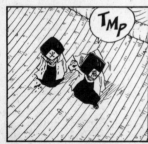

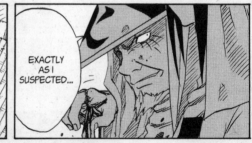

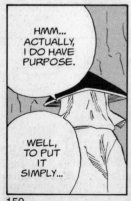

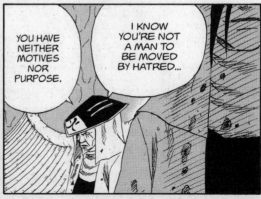

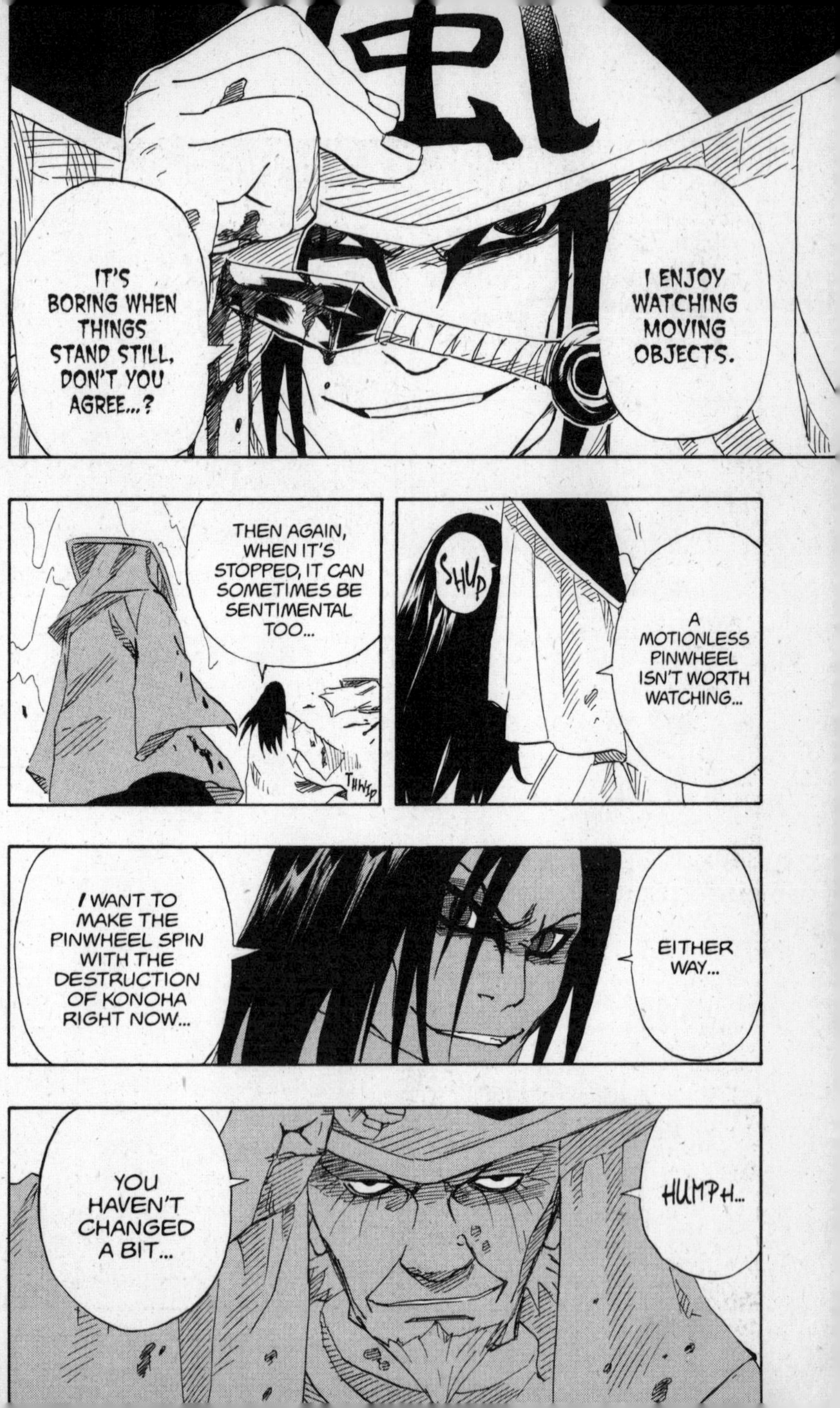
I ENJOY WATCHING MOVING OBJECTS.
IT'S BORING WHEN THINGS STAND STILL. DON'T YOU AGREE...?
SHUP
A MOTIONLESS PINWHEEL ISN'T WORTH WATCHING...
THEN AGAIN, WHEN IT'S STOPPED, IT CAN SOMETIMES BE SENTIMENTAL TOO...
THWSP
EITHER WAY...
I WANT TO MAKE THE PINWHEEL SPIN WITH THE DESTRUCTION OF KONOHA RIGHT NOW...
HUMPH...
YOU HAVEN'T CHANGED A BIT...

READ THIS WAY

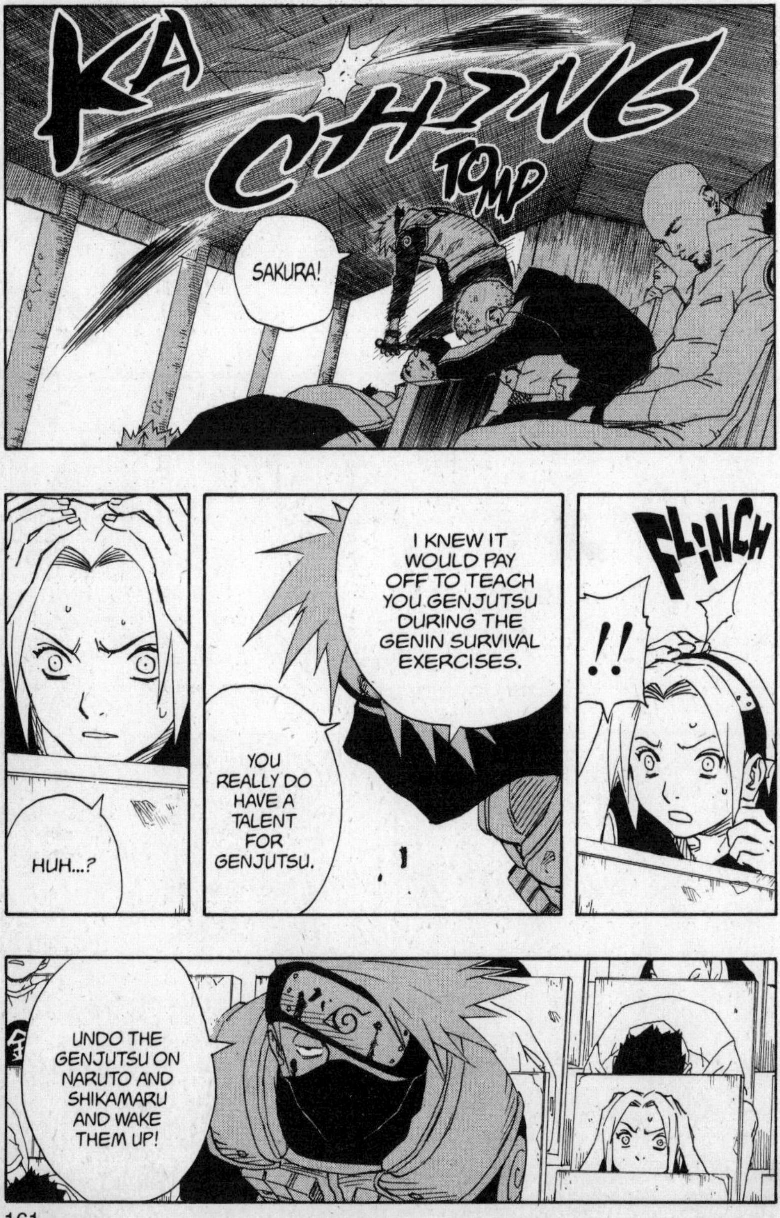
KA CHING
TOMP
SAKURA!
FLINCH
!!
I KNEW IT WOULD PAY OFF TO TEACH YOU GENJUTSU DURING THE GENIN SURVIVAL EXERCISES.
YOU REALLY DO HAVE A TALENT FOR GENJUTSU.
HUH...?
UNDO THE GENJUTSU ON NARUTO AND SHIKAMARU AND WAKE THEM UP!

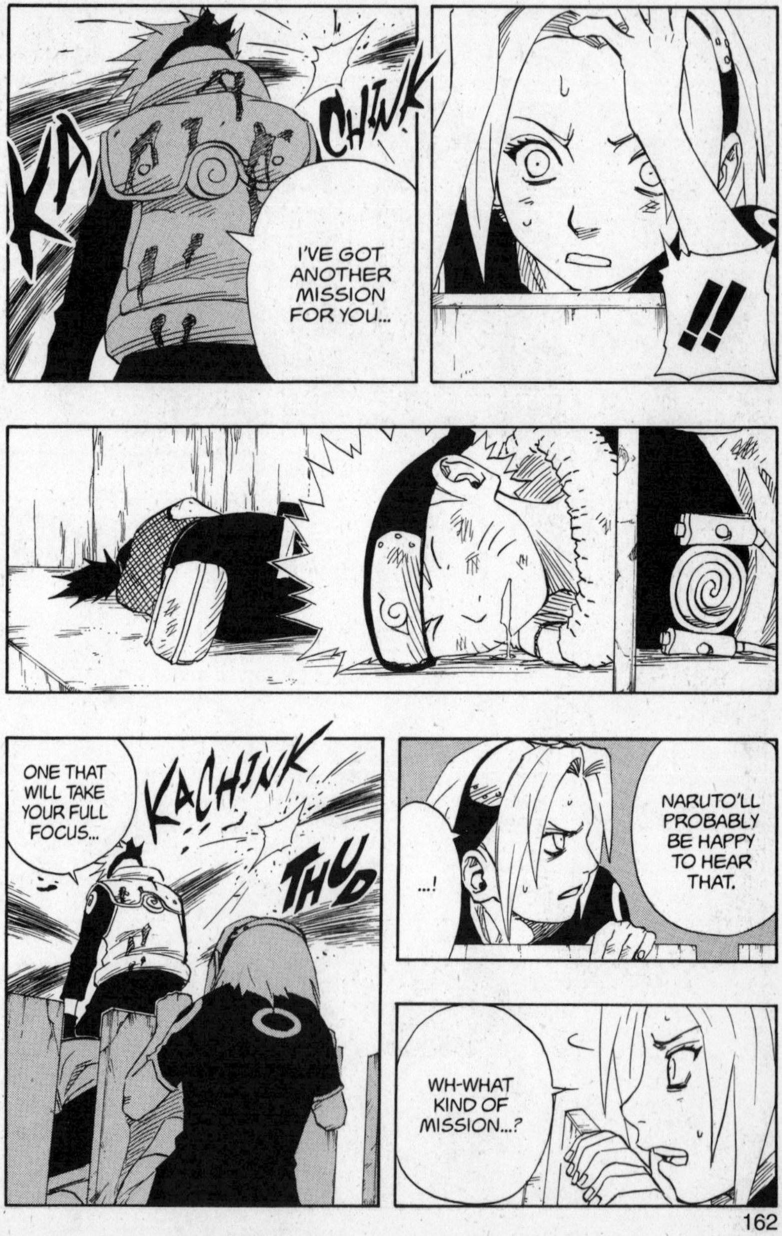
!!
KA
CHINK
I'VE GOT ANOTHER MISSION FOR YOU...
NARUTO'LL PROBABLY BE HAPPY TO HEAR THAT.
...!
WH-WHAT KIND OF MISSION...?
ONE THAT WILL TAKE YOUR FULL FOCUS...
KACHINK
THUD

READ THIS WAY

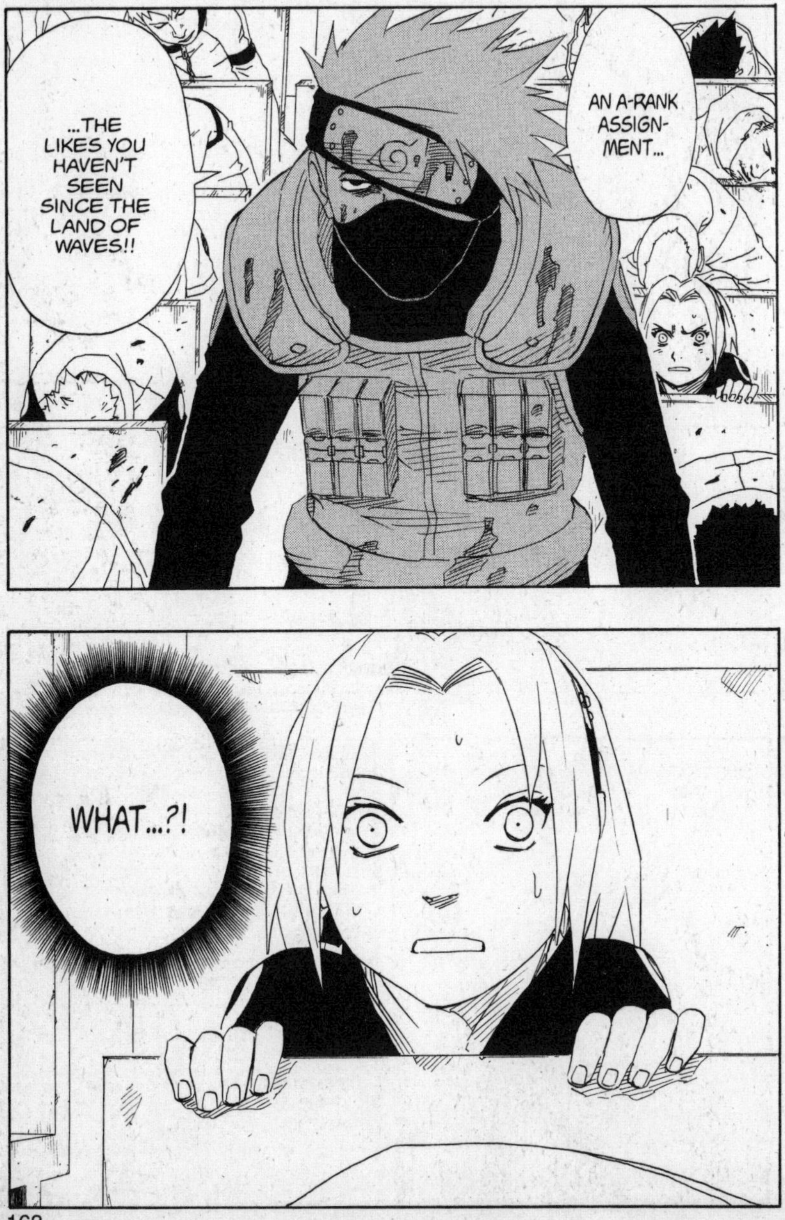
AN A-RANK ASSIGN-MENT...
...THE LIKES YOU HAVEN'T SEEN SINCE THE LAND OF WAVES!!
WHAT...?!

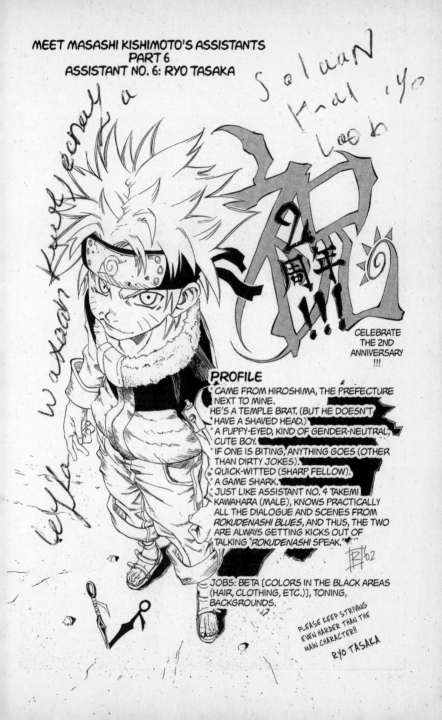

MEET MASASHI KISHIMOTO'S ASSISTANTS
PART 6
ASSISTANT NO. 6: RYO TASAKA

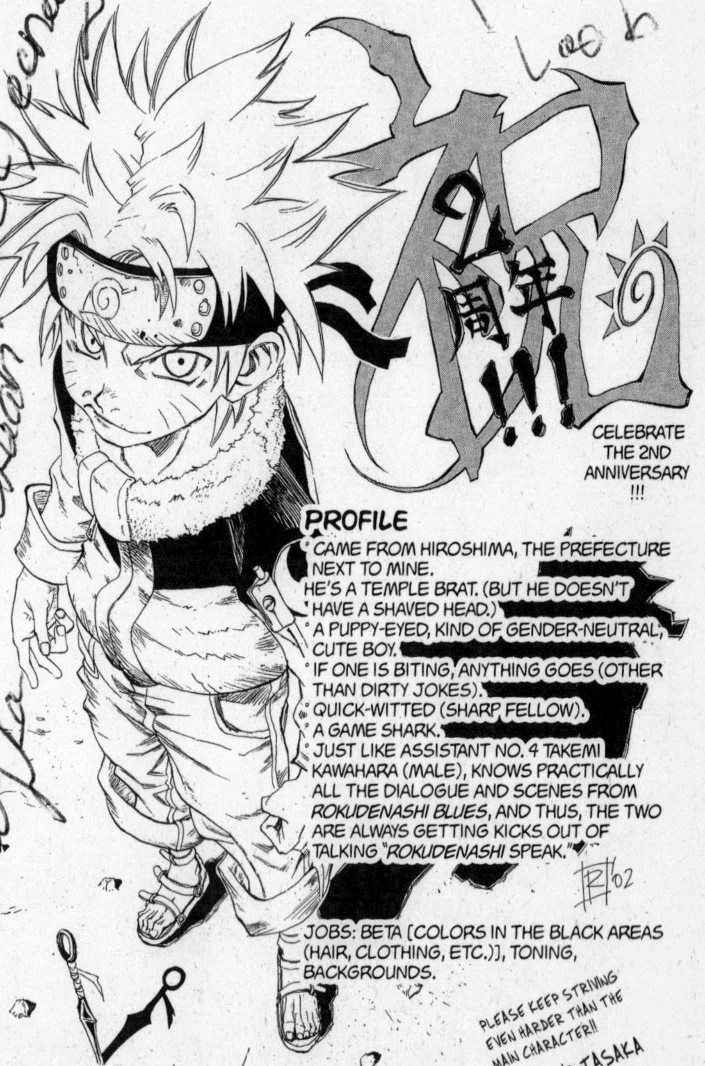
祝
2周年!!!
R '02

CELEBRATE THE 2ND ANNIVERSARY !!!

PROFILE

- CAME FROM HIROSHIMA, THE PREFECTURE NEXT TO MINE.
- HE'S A TEMPLE BRAT. (BUT HE DOESN'T HAVE A SHAVED HEAD.)
- A PUPPY-EYED, KIND OF GENDER-NEUTRAL, CUTE BOY.
- IF ONE IS BITING, ANYTHING GOES (OTHER THAN DIRTY JOKES).
- QUICK-WITTED (SHARP FELLOW).
- A GAME SHARK.
- JUST LIKE ASSISTANT NO. 4 TAKEMI KAWAHARA (MALE), KNOWS PRACTICALLY ALL THE DIALOGUE AND SCENES FROM *ROKUDENASHI BLUES*, AND THUS, THE TWO ARE ALWAYS GETTING KICKS OUT OF TALKING "*ROKUDENASHI* SPEAK."

JOBS: BETA [COLORS IN THE BLACK AREAS (HAIR, CLOTHING, ETC.)], TONING, BACKGROUNDS.

PLEASE KEEP STRIVING EVEN HARDER THAN THE MAIN CHARACTER!!

RYO TASAKA

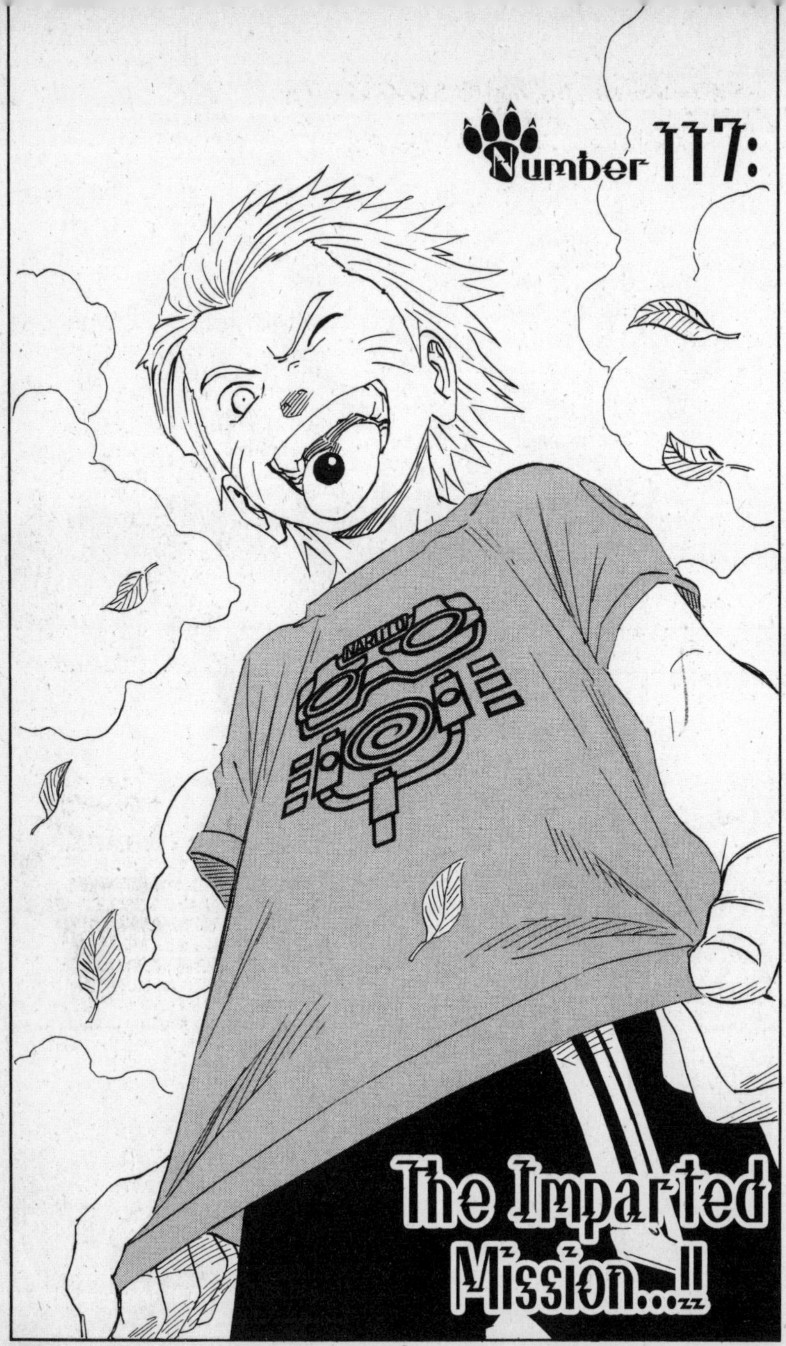
Number 117:
NARUTO
The Imparted Mission...!!

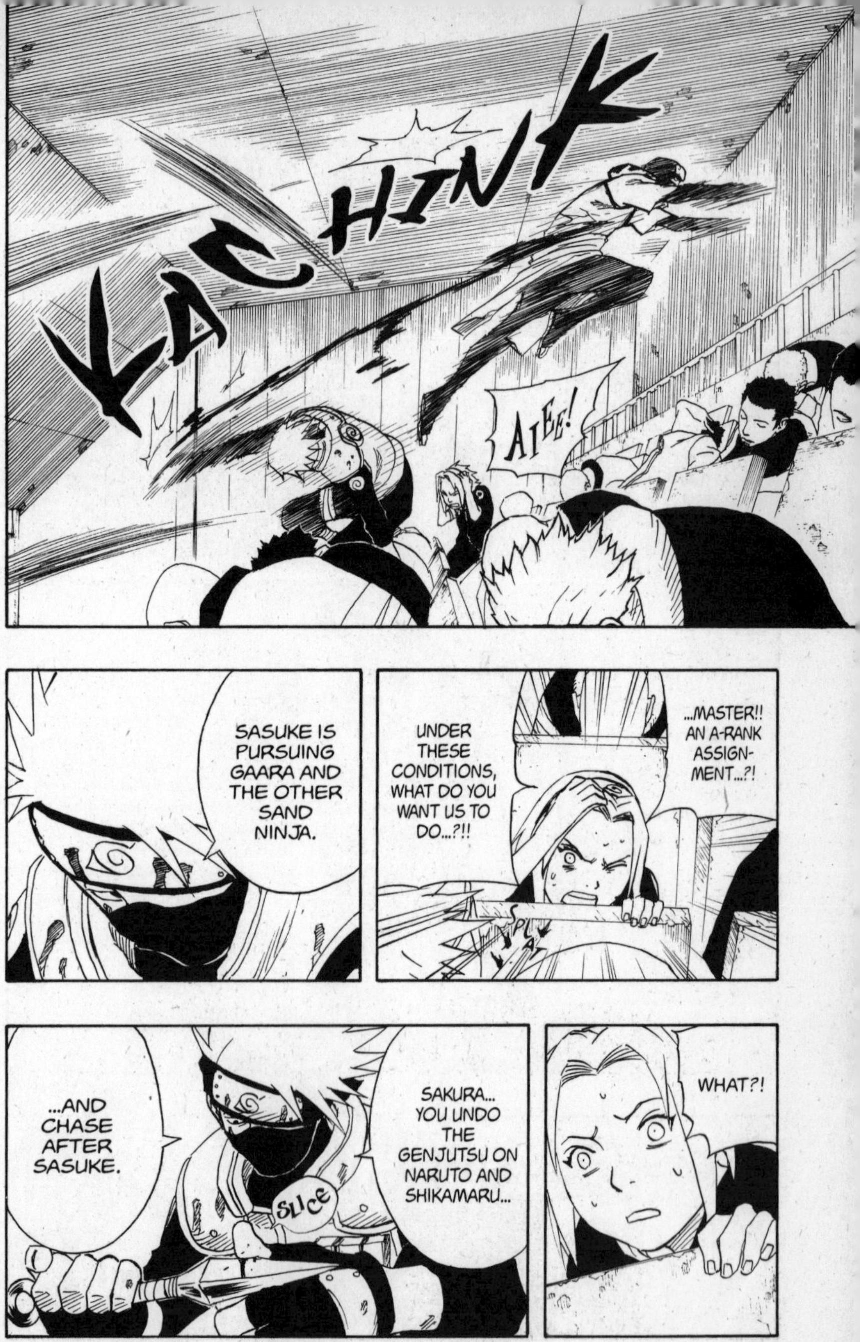
KACHINK
AIEE!
...MASTER!! AN A-RANK ASSIGNMENT...?!
UNDER THESE CONDITIONS, WHAT DO YOU WANT US TO DO...?!!
SPLAT
SASUKE IS PURSUING GAARA AND THE OTHER SAND NINJA.
WHAT?!
SAKURA... YOU UNDO THE GENJUTSU ON NARUTO AND SHIKAMARU...
SLICE
...AND CHASE AFTER SASUKE.

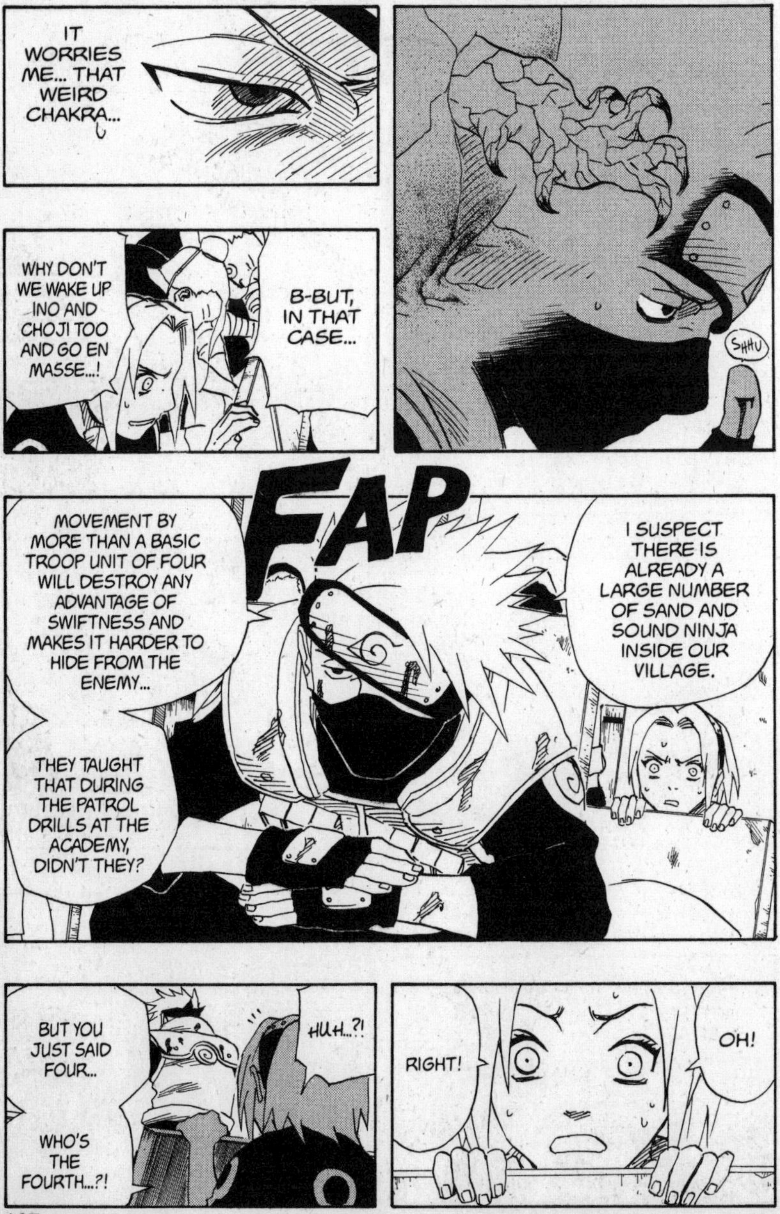
SHHU
IT WORRIES ME... THAT WEIRD CHAKRA...
B-BUT, IN THAT CASE...
WHY DON'T WE WAKE UP INO AND CHOJI TOO AND GO EN MASSE...!
FAP
I SUSPECT THERE IS ALREADY A LARGE NUMBER OF SAND AND SOUND NINJA INSIDE OUR VILLAGE.
MOVEMENT BY MORE THAN A BASIC TROOP UNIT OF FOUR WILL DESTROY ANY ADVANTAGE OF SWIFTNESS AND MAKES IT HARDER TO HIDE FROM THE ENEMY...
THEY TAUGHT THAT DURING THE PATROL DRILLS AT THE ACADEMY, DIDN'T THEY?
OH!
RIGHT!
HUH...?!
BUT YOU JUST SAID FOUR...
WHO'S THE FOURTH...?!

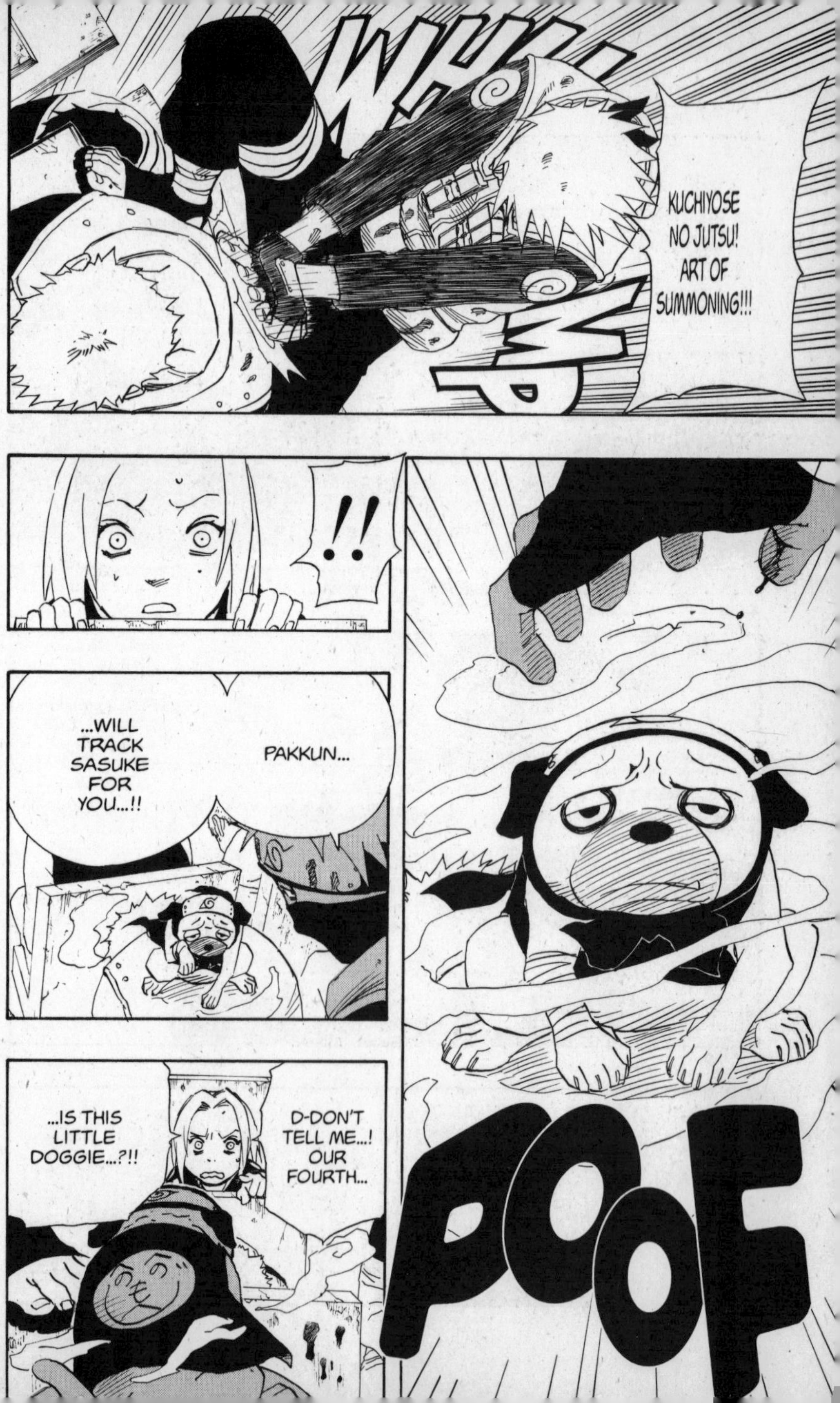
KUCHIYOSE NO JUTSU! ART OF SUMMONING!!!
POOF
!!
PAKKUN...
...WILL TRACK SASUKE FOR YOU...!!
D-DON'T TELL ME...! OUR FOURTH...
...IS THIS LITTLE DOGGIE...?!!

READ THIS WAY

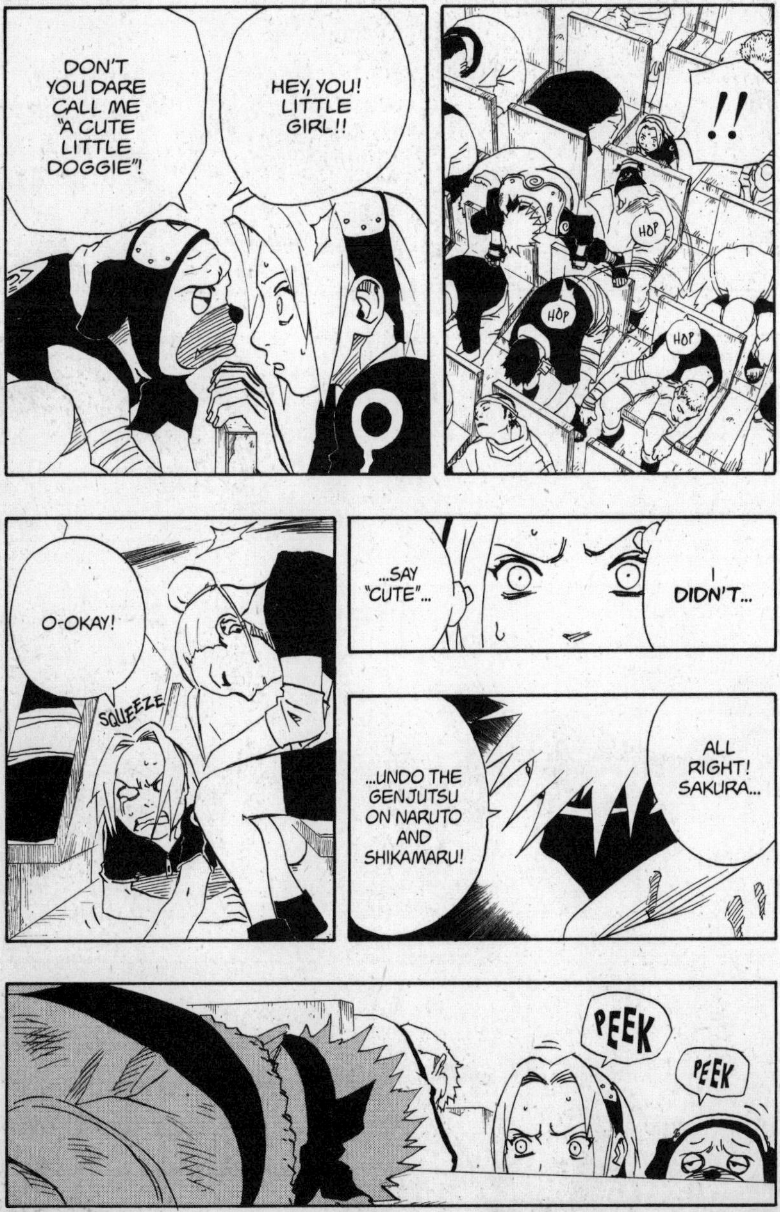

!!
HOP
HOP
HOP
HEY, YOU! LITTLE GIRL!!
DON'T YOU DARE CALL ME "A CUTE LITTLE DOGGIE"!
I DIDN'T...
...SAY "CUTE"...
ALL RIGHT! SAKURA...
...UNDO THE GENJUTSU ON NARUTO AND SHIKAMARU!
O-OKAY!
SQUEEZE
PEEK
PEEK

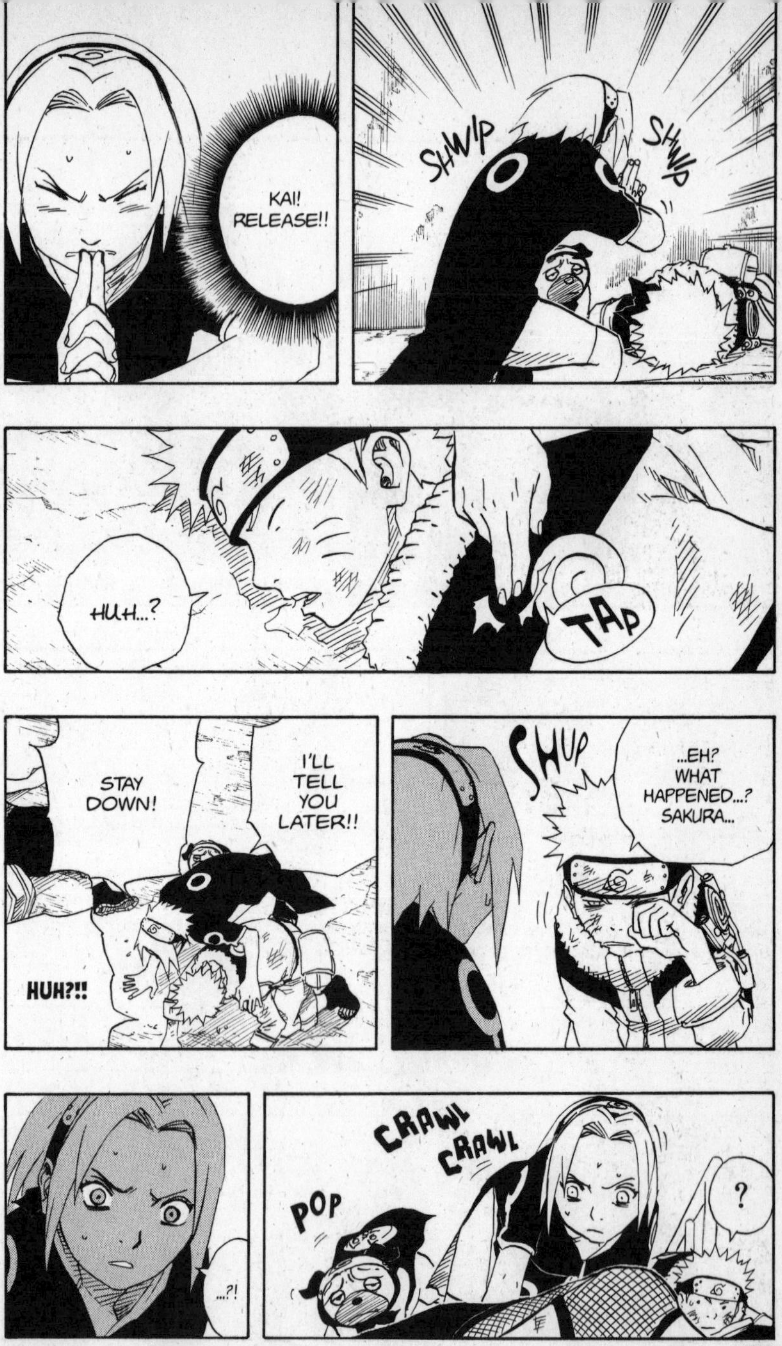
SHWIP
SHWIP
KAI! RELEASE!!
TAP
HUH...?
SHUP
...EH? WHAT HAPPENED...? SAKURA...
I'LL TELL YOU LATER!!
STAY DOWN!
HUH?!!
?
CRAWL CRAWL
POP
...?!

READ THIS WAY

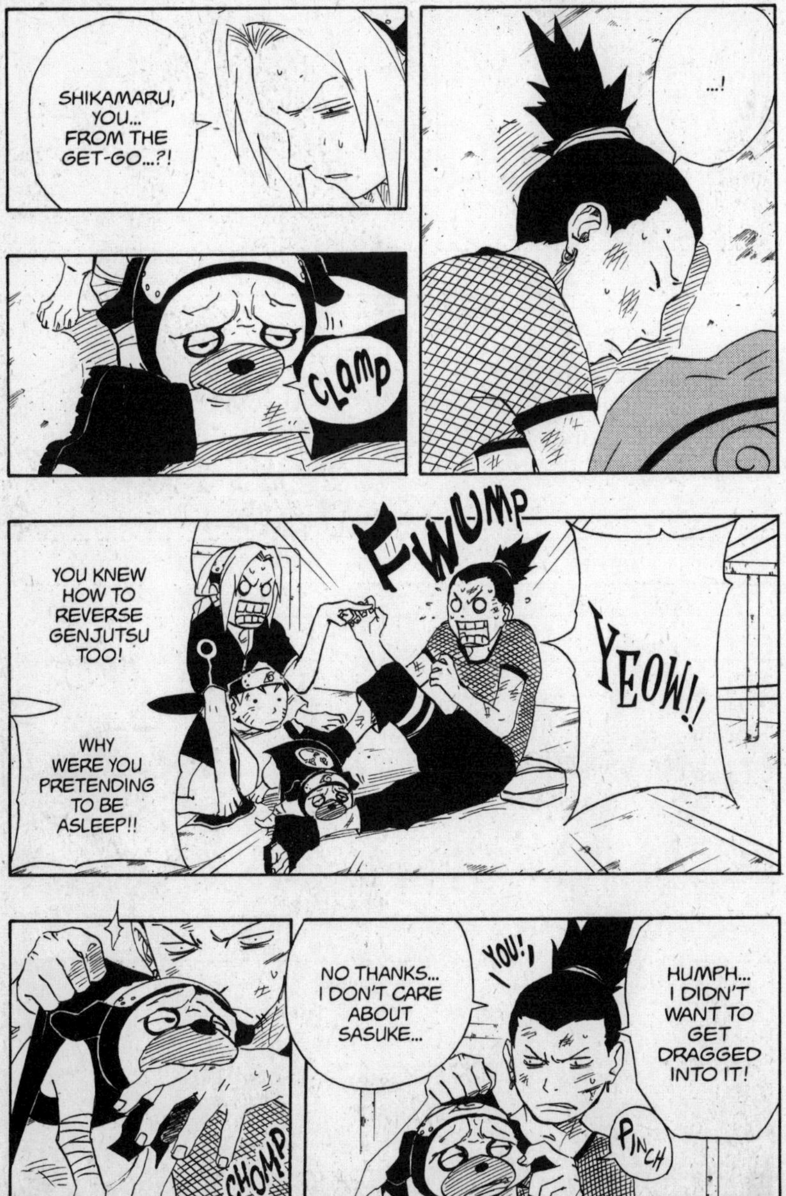

...!
SHIKAMARU, YOU... FROM THE GET-GO...?!
CLAMP
FWUMP
YEOW!!
YOU KNEW HOW TO REVERSE GENJUTSU TOO!
WHY WERE YOU PRETENDING TO BE ASLEEP!!
YOU!!
HUMPH... I DIDN'T WANT TO GET DRAGGED INTO IT!
NO THANKS... I DON'T CARE ABOUT SASUKE...
PINCH
CHOMP

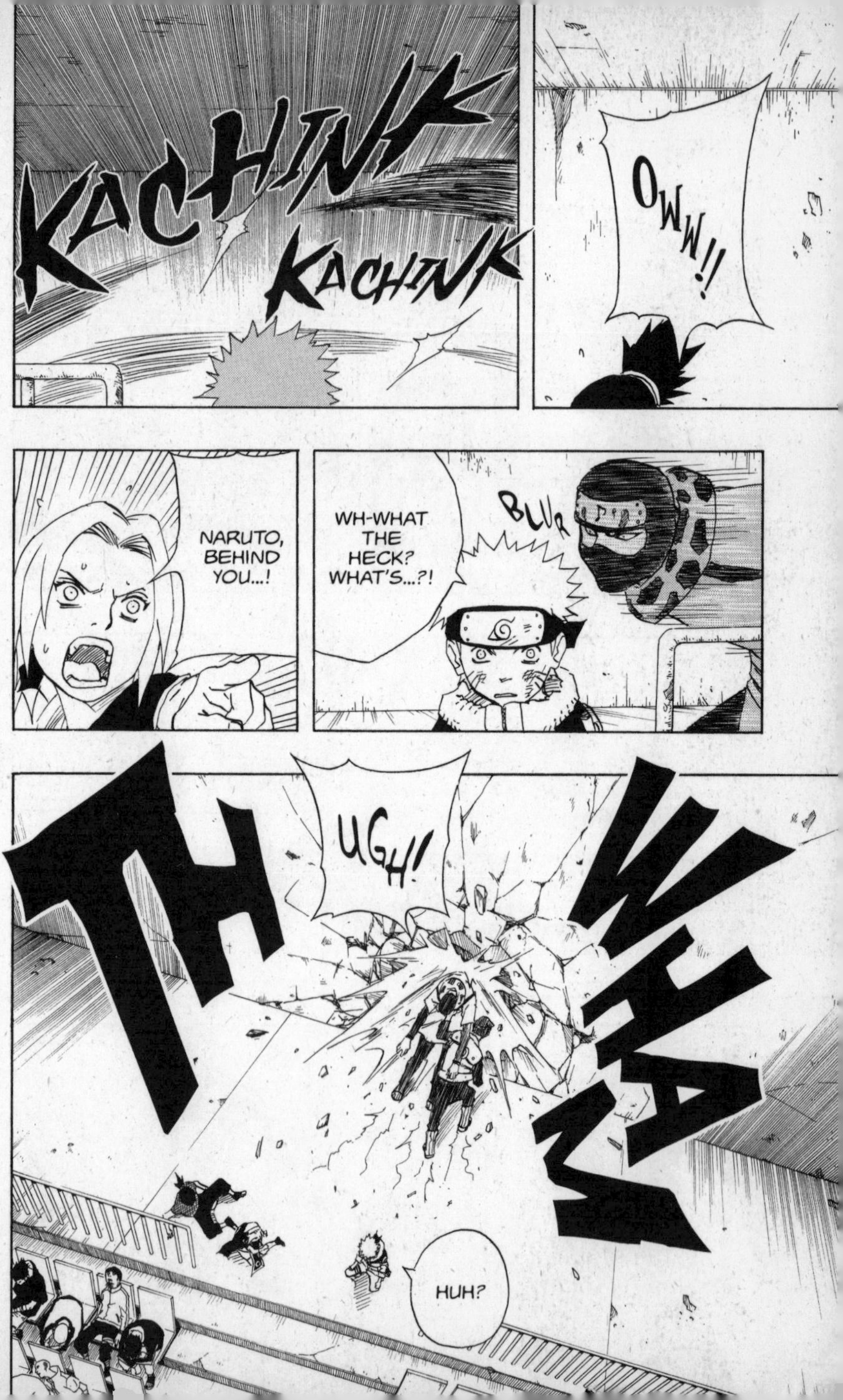
OWW!!
KACHINK
KACHINK
BLUR
WH-WHAT THE HECK? WHAT'S...?!
NARUTO, BEHIND YOU...!
UGH!
THWHAM
HUH?

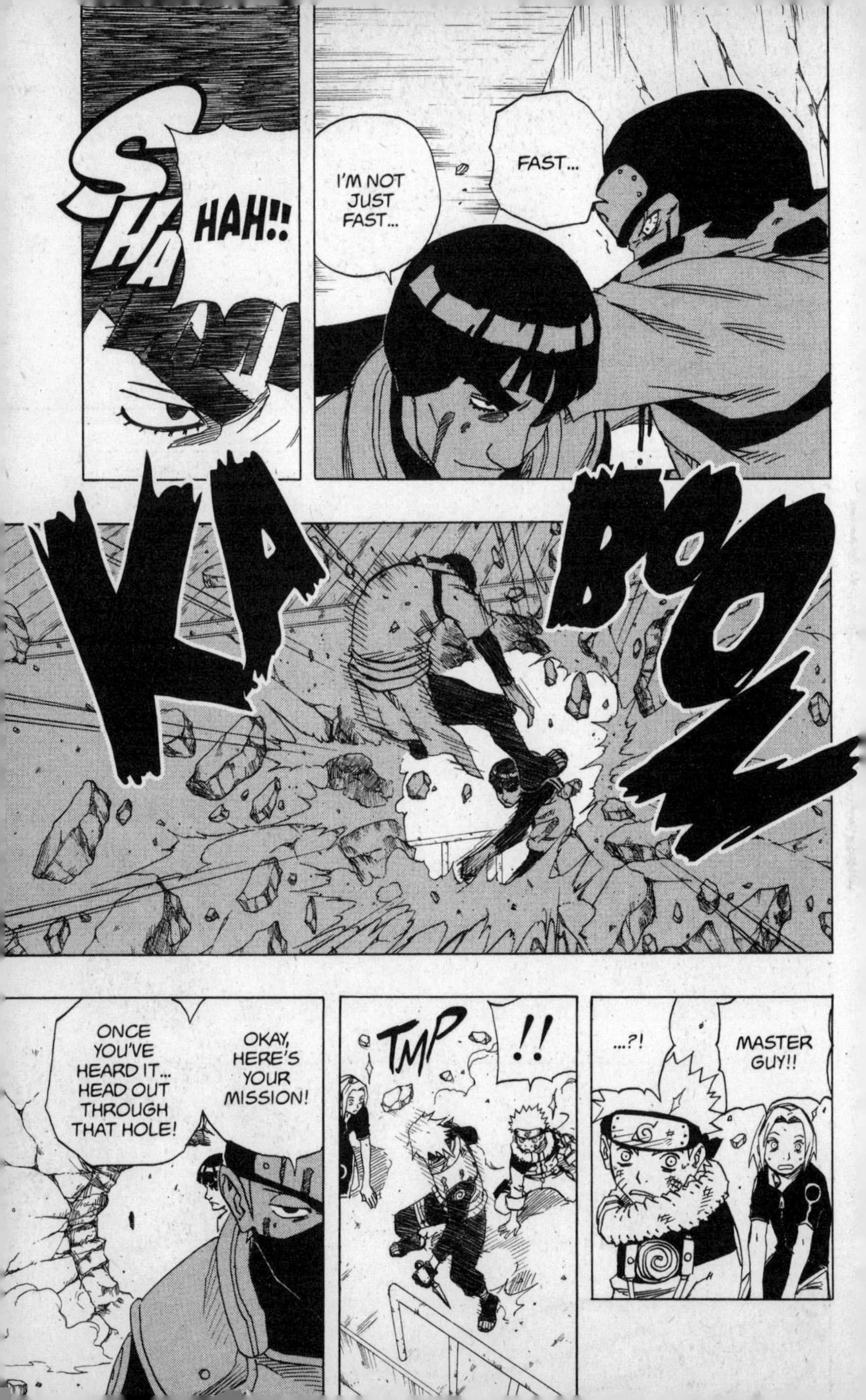
FAST...
I'M NOT JUST FAST...
SHA
HAH!!
KA
BOOM
MASTER GUY!!
...?!
!!
TMP
OKAY, HERE'S YOUR MISSION!
ONCE YOU'VE HEARD IT... HEAD OUT THROUGH THAT HOLE!

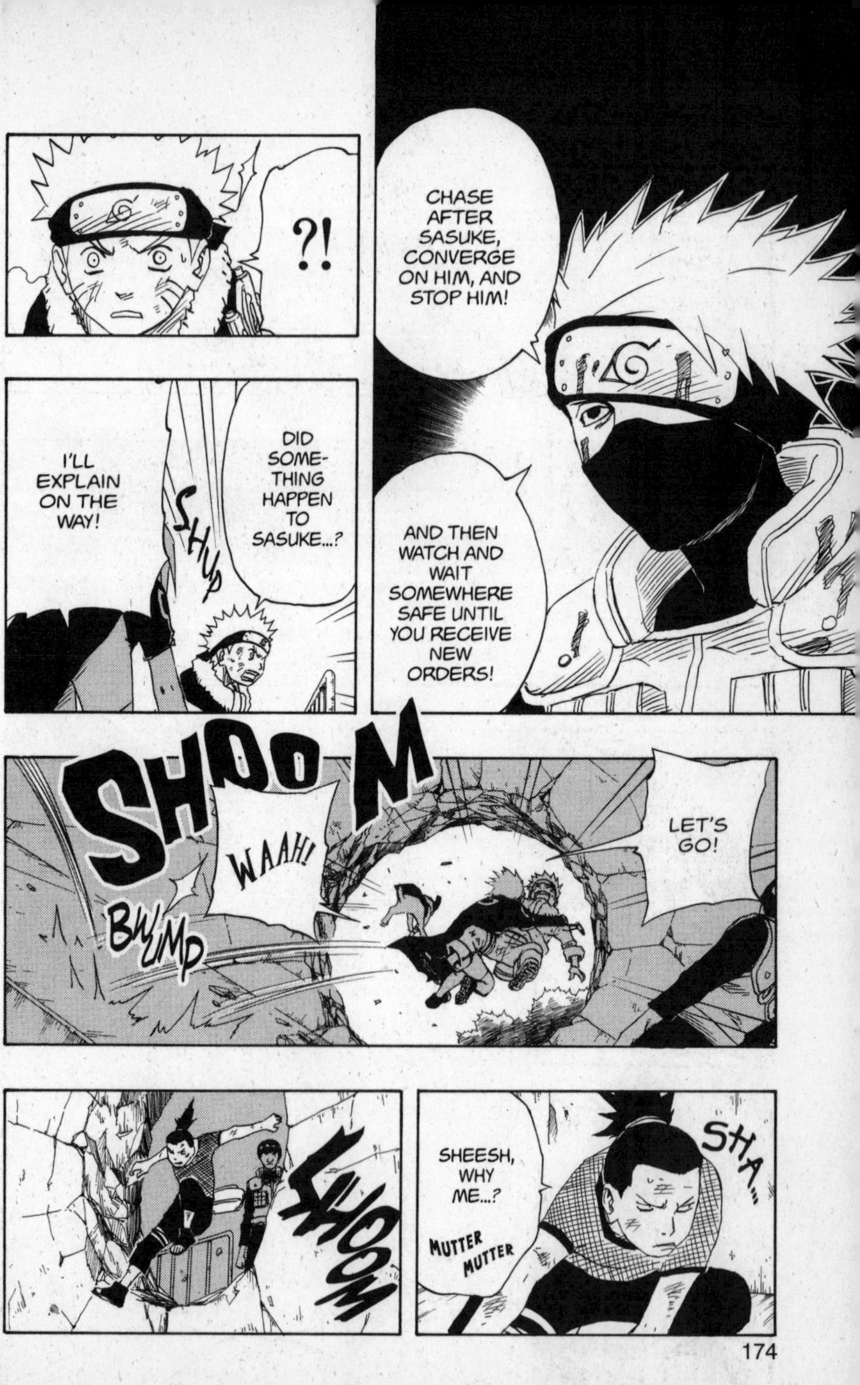
CHASE AFTER SASUKE, CONVERGE ON HIM, AND STOP HIM!
AND THEN WATCH AND WAIT SOMEWHERE SAFE UNTIL YOU RECEIVE NEW ORDERS!
?!
DID SOME-THING HAPPEN TO SASUKE...?
SHUP
I'LL EXPLAIN ON THE WAY!
LET'S GO!
SHOOM
WAAH!
BWUMP
SHA...
SHEESH, WHY ME...?
MUTTER MUTTER
WHOOM

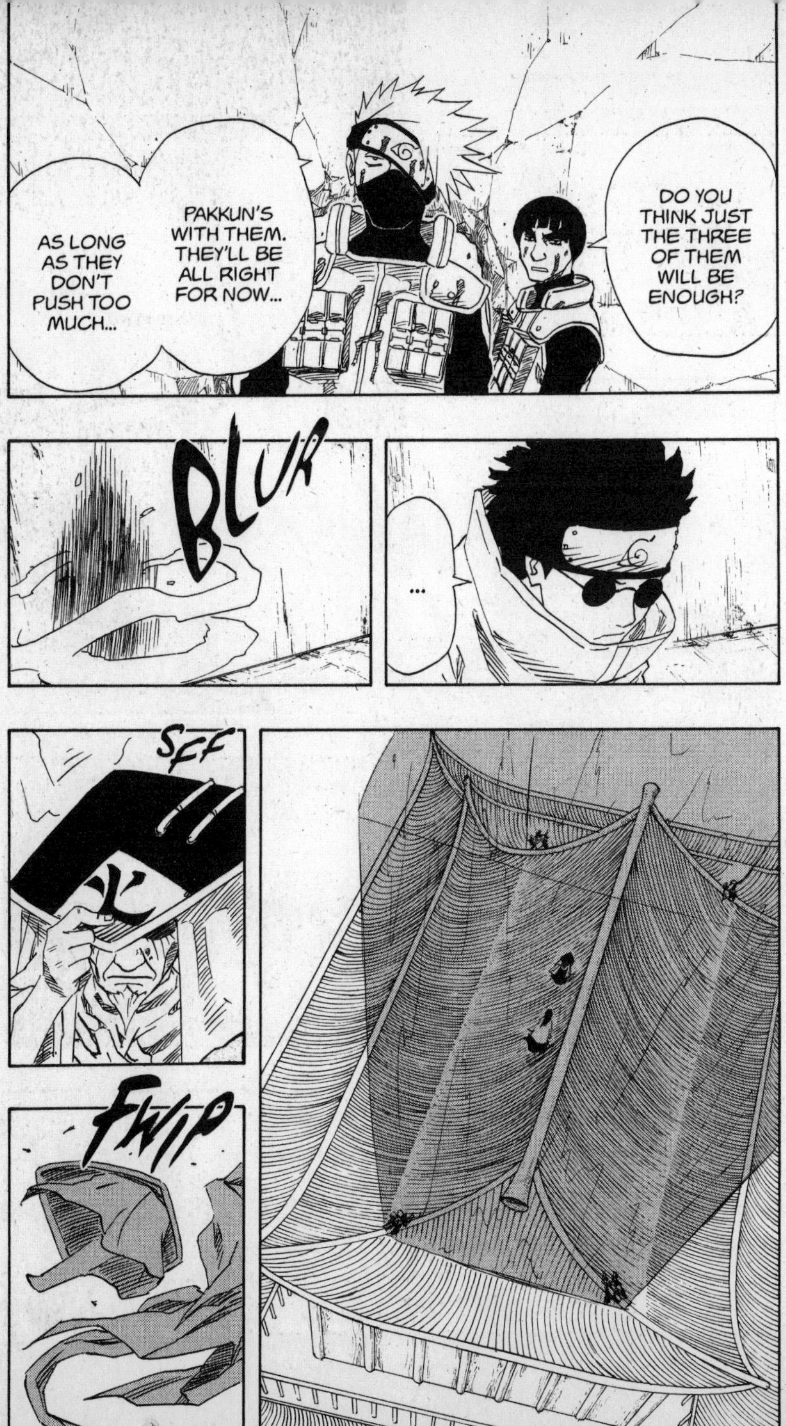
DO YOU THINK JUST THE THREE OF THEM WILL BE ENOUGH?
PAKKUN'S WITH THEM. THEY'LL BE ALL RIGHT FOR NOW...
AS LONG AS THEY DON'T PUSH TOO MUCH...
...
BLUR
SFF
FWIP

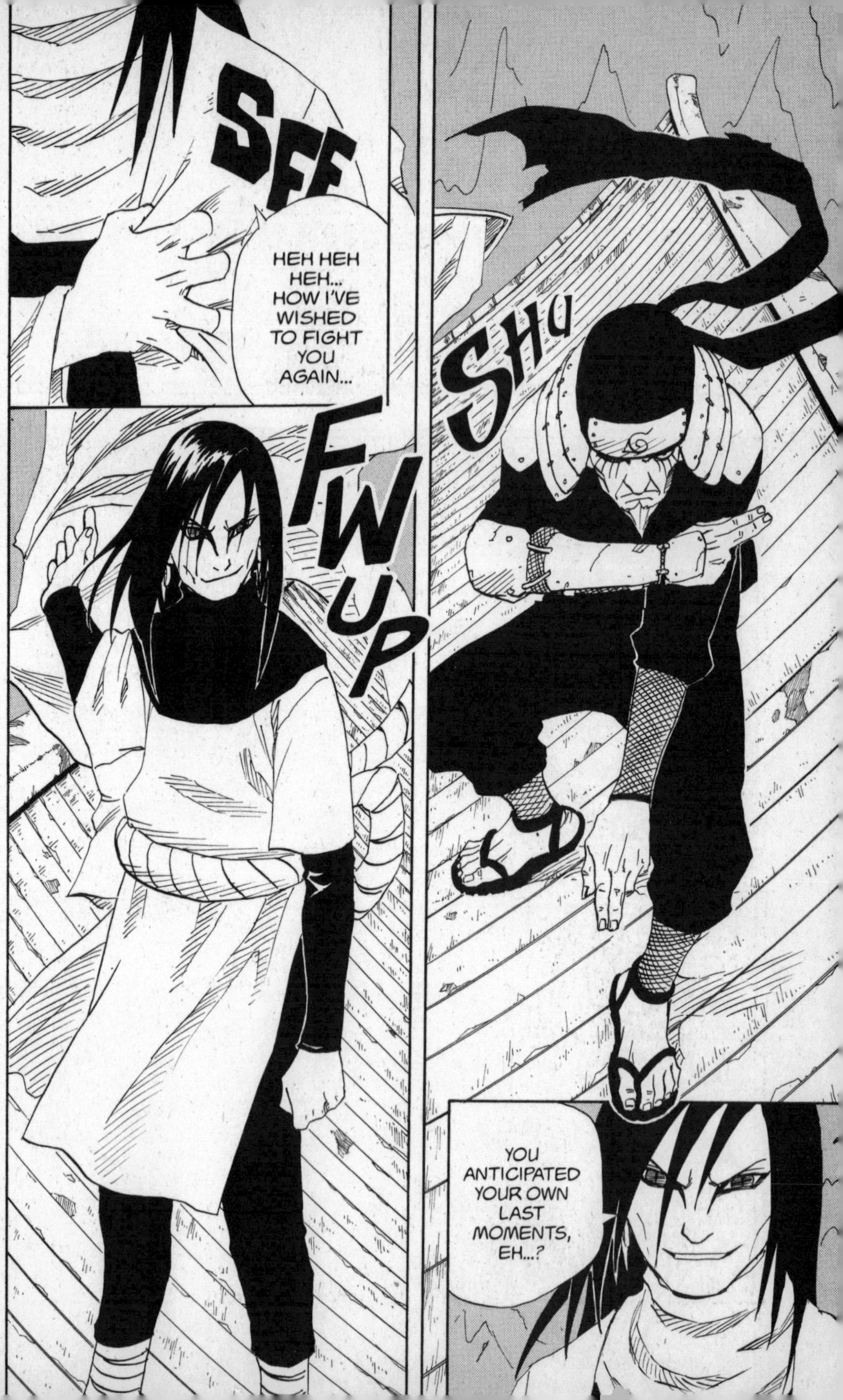
SHU
SFF
HEH HEH HEH... HOW I'VE WISHED TO FIGHT YOU AGAIN...
FWUP
YOU ANTICIPATED YOUR OWN LAST MOMENTS, EH...?

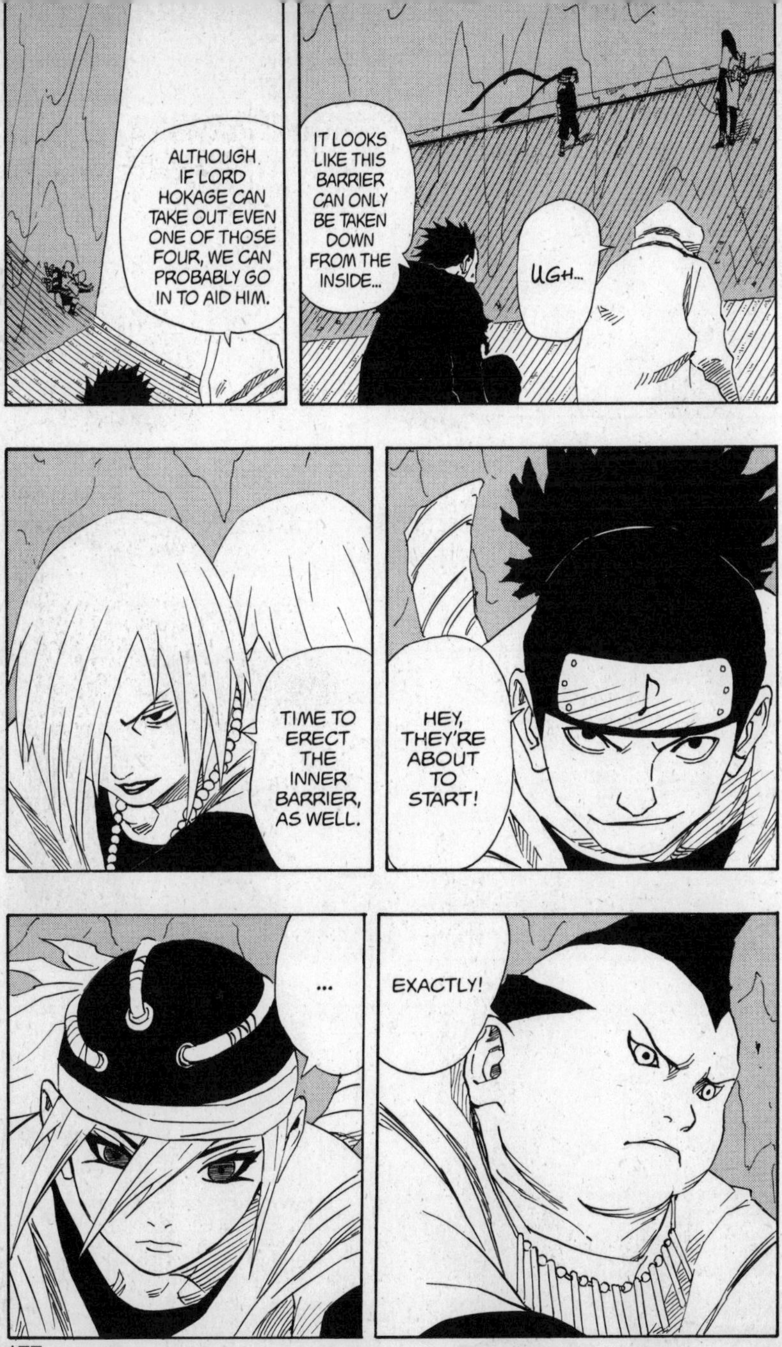
UGH...
IT LOOKS LIKE THIS BARRIER CAN ONLY BE TAKEN DOWN FROM THE INSIDE...
ALTHOUGH IF LORD HOKAGE CAN TAKE OUT EVEN ONE OF THOSE FOUR, WE CAN PROBABLY GO IN TO AID HIM.
HEY, THEY'RE ABOUT TO START!
TIME TO ERECT THE INNER BARRIER, AS WELL.
EXACTLY!
...

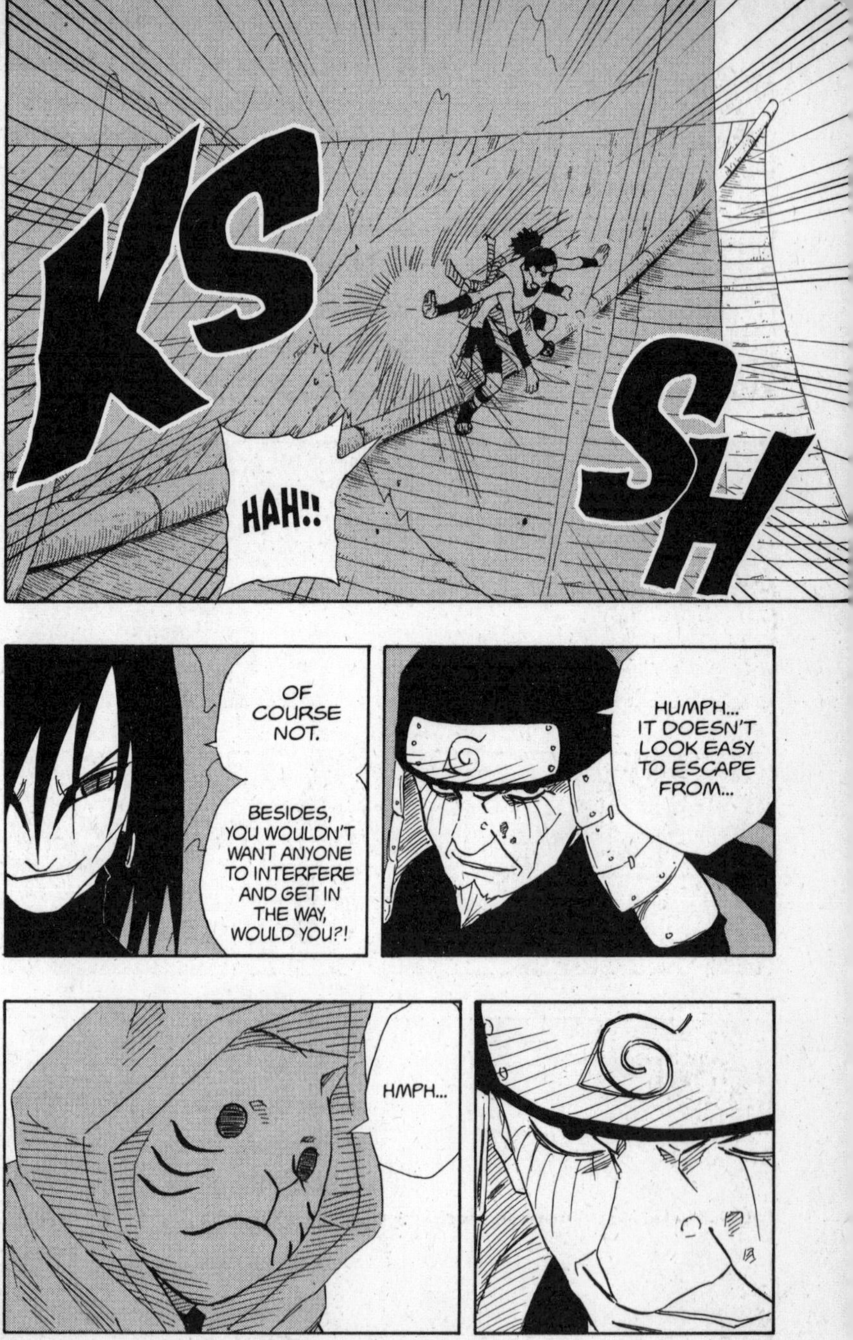
SH
KS
HAH!!
HUMPH... IT DOESN'T LOOK EASY TO ESCAPE FROM...
OF COURSE NOT.
BESIDES, YOU WOULDN'T WANT ANYONE TO INTERFERE AND GET IN THE WAY, WOULD YOU?!
HMPH...

READ THIS WAY

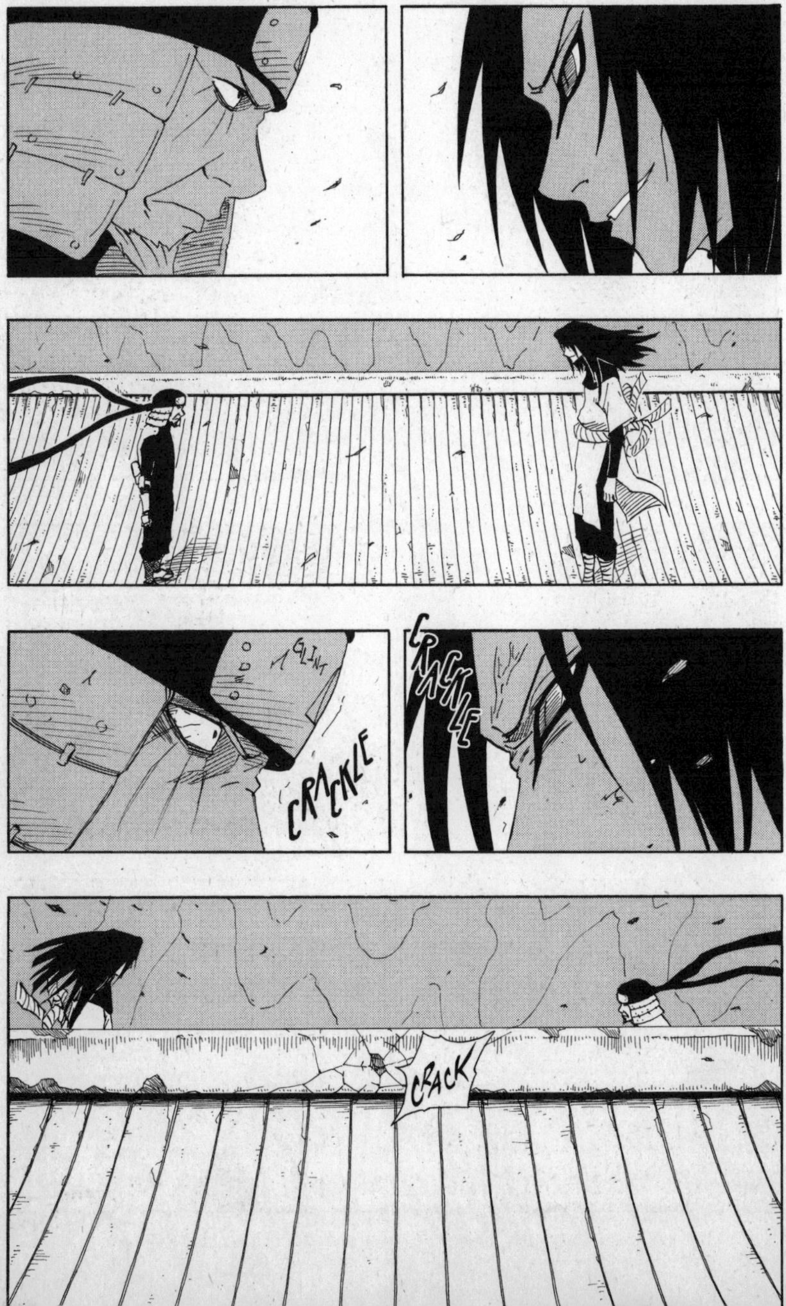
CRACKLE
GLINT
CRACKLE
CRACK

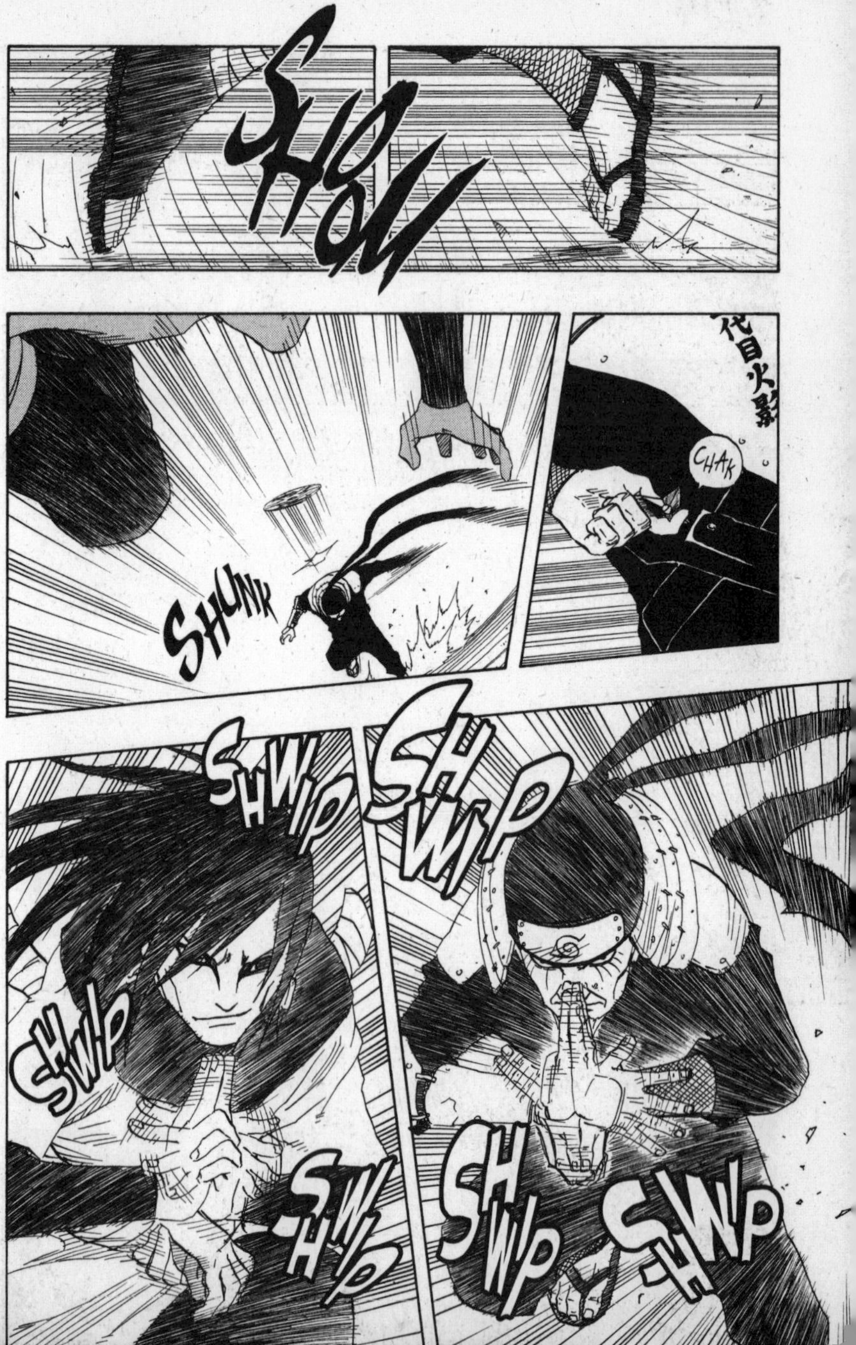
SHOW
代目火影
CHAK
SHUNK
SHWIP
SHWIP
SHWIP
SHWIP
SHWIP
SHWIP

SHURIKEN SHADOW DOPPELGANGER TECHNIQUE!

SHOWER

BRALL

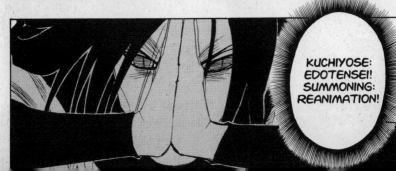

KUCHIYOSE: EDOTENSEI! SUMMONING: REANIMATION!

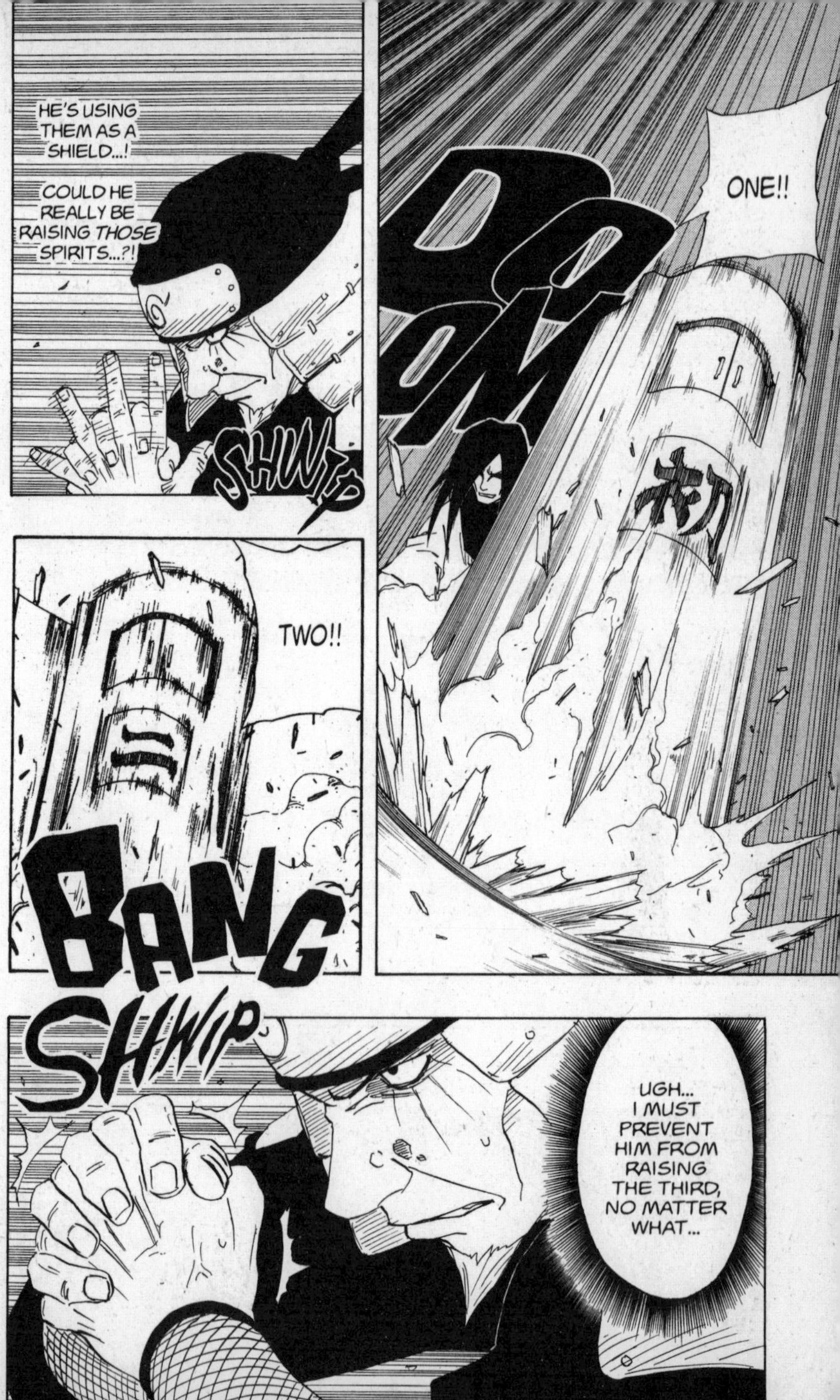
ONE!!
DOOM
初
HE'S USING THEM AS A SHIELD...!
COULD HE REALLY BE RAISING THOSE SPIRITS...?!
SHWIP
TWO!!
BANG
SHWIP
UGH... I MUST PREVENT HIM FROM RAISING THE THIRD, NO MATTER WHAT...

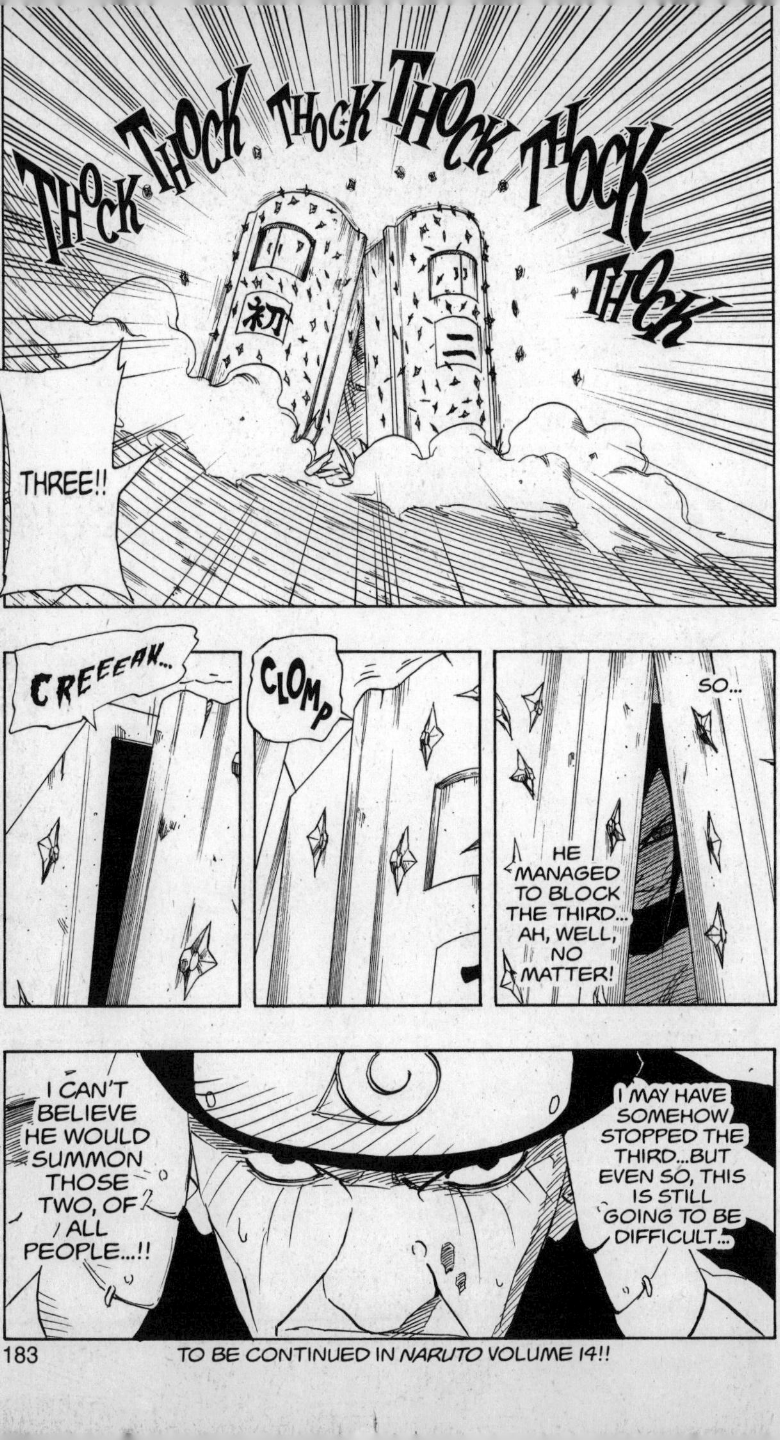
THOCK
THOCK
THOCK
THOCK
THOCK
THOCK
二
初
THREE!!
SO...
HE MANAGED TO BLOCK THE THIRD... AH, WELL, NO MATTER!
CLOMP
CREEEAK...
I MAY HAVE SOMEHOW STOPPED THE THIRD...BUT EVEN SO, THIS IS STILL GOING TO BE DIFFICULT...
I CAN'T BELIEVE HE WOULD SUMMON THOSE TWO, OF ALL PEOPLE...!!

TO BE CONTINUED IN *NARUTO* VOLUME 14!!

IN THE NEXT VOLUME...

HOKAGE VS. HOKAGE!!

Their village is under attack, and Naruto, Sakura and
Shikamaru can't stay behind to defend it. They have a top
priority mission to track down Sasuke and the Sand genin.
But with nine bloodthirsty ninja on their heels, the hunters
have quickly become the hunted! Back at the village, the
Third Hokage is still trapped in Orochimaru's impenetrable
barrier. Pushed to the breaking point, the Hokage must
decide how far he will go to save what is precious to him!

AVAILABLE NOW!

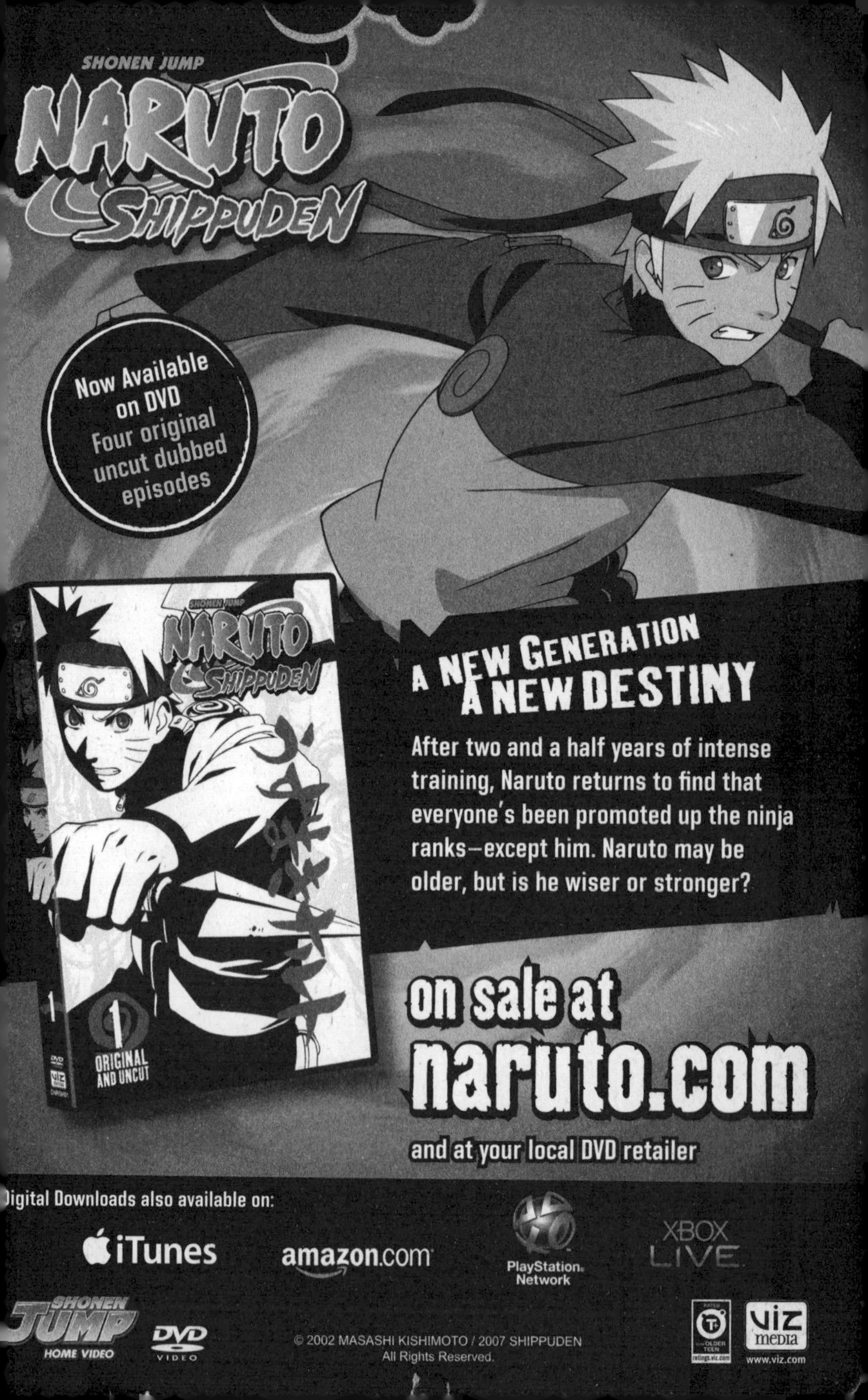
SHONEN JUMP
NARUTO SHIPPUDEN
Now Available on DVD
Four original uncut dubbed episodes
SHONEN JUMP
NARUTO SHIPPUDEN
1
ORIGINAL AND UNCUT
A NEW GENERATION
A NEW DESTINY
After two and a half years of intense training, Naruto returns to find that everyone's been promoted up the ninja ranks—except him. Naruto may be older, but is he wiser or stronger?
on sale at
naruto.com
and at your local DVD retailer
Digital Downloads also available on:
iTunes
amazon.com
PlayStation Network
XBOX LIVE
SHONEN JUMP HOME VIDEO
DVD VIDEO
© 2002 MASASHI KISHIMOTO / 2007 SHIPPUDEN
All Rights Reserved.
OLDER TEEN
ratings.viz.com
viz media
www.viz.com

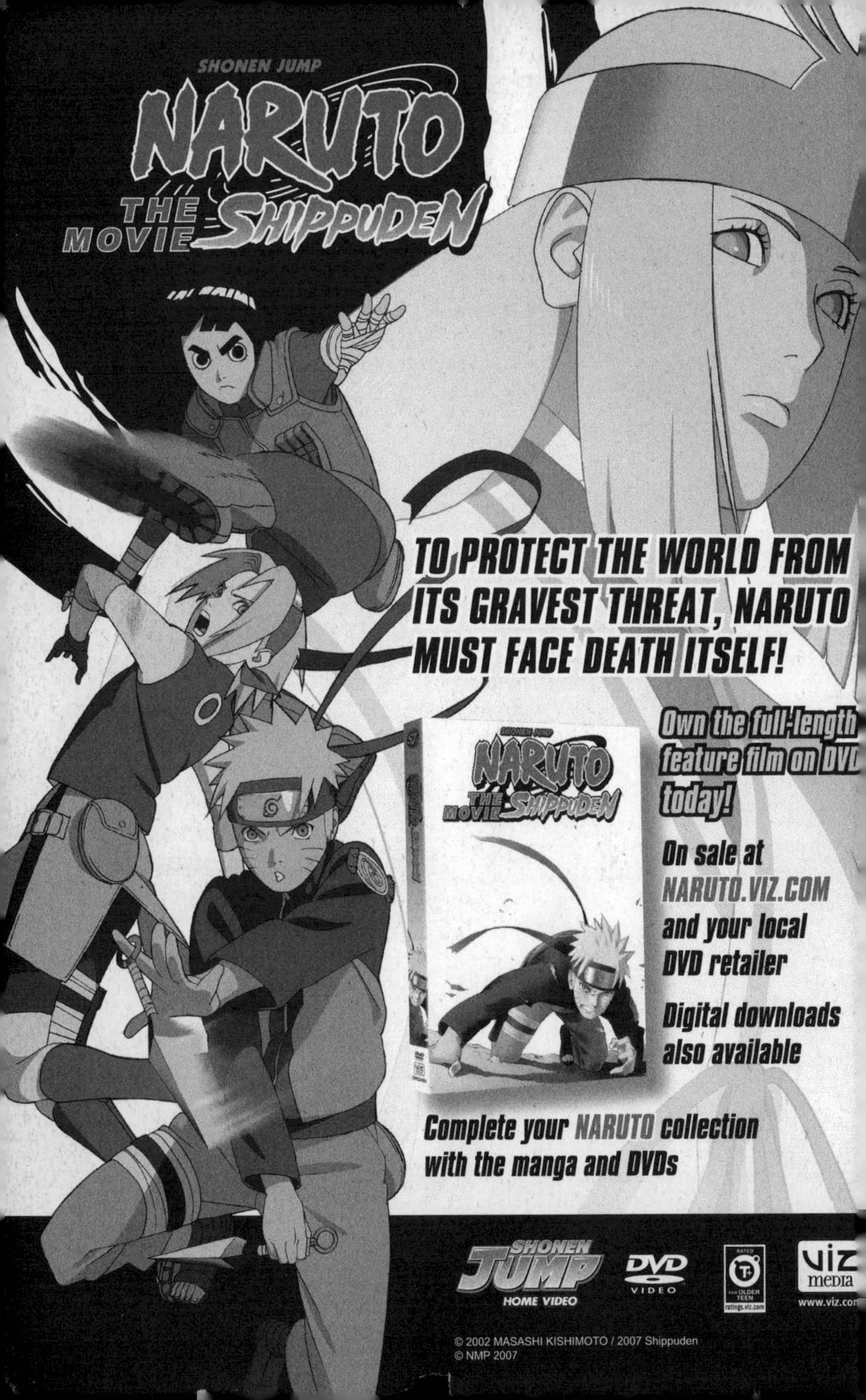
SHONEN JUMP
NARUTO THE MOVIE SHIPPUDEN
TO PROTECT THE WORLD FROM ITS GRAVEST THREAT, NARUTO MUST FACE DEATH ITSELF!
Own the full-length feature film on DVD today!
On sale at NARUTO.VIZ.COM and your local DVD retailer
Digital downloads also available
Complete your NARUTO collection with the manga and DVDs
SHONEN JUMP HOME VIDEO
DVD VIDEO
RATED T+ FOR OLDER TEEN ratings.viz.com
VIZ media
www.viz.com
© 2002 MASASHI KISHIMOTO / 2007 Shippuden
© NMP 2007

SHONEN JUMP

THE WORLD'S MOST POPULAR MANGA

BLEACH

**STORY AND ART BY
TITE KUBO**

ONE PIECE

**STORY AND ART BY
EIICHIRO ODA**

Tegami Bachi

**STORY AND ART BY
HIROYUKI ASADA**

JUMP INTO THE ACTION BY TELLING US WHAT YOU LOVE (AND WHAT YOU DON'T)

LET YOUR VOICE BE HEARD!

SHONENJUMP.VIZ.COM/MANGASURVEY

HELP US MAKE MORE OF THE WORLD'S MOST POPULAR MANGA!